Creating Web Graphics

FOR

DUMMIES®

W9-DHM-188

MONTGOMERY COLLEGE
ROCKVILLE CAMPUS LIBRARY
ROCKVILLE, MARYLAND

Creating Web Graphics FOR DUMMIES®

by Bud Smith and Peter Frazier

WILEY

Wiley Publishing, Inc.

288570

APR 7 2004

Creating Web Graphics For Dummies®

Published by
Wiley Publishing, Inc.
909 Third Avenue
New York, NY 10022
www.wiley.com

Copyright © 2003 by Wiley Publishing, Inc., Indianapolis, Indiana

Published by Wiley Publishing, Inc., Indianapolis, Indiana

Published simultaneously in Canada

No part of this publication may be reproduced, stored in a retrieval system or transmitted in any form or by any means, electronic, mechanical, photocopying, recording, scanning or otherwise, except as permitted under Sections 107 or 108 of the 1976 United States Copyright Act, without either the prior written permission of the Publisher, or authorization through payment of the appropriate per-copy fee to the Copyright Clearance Center, 222 Rosewood Drive, Danvers, MA 01923, (978) 750-8400, fax (978) 646-8700. Requests to the Publisher for permission should be addressed to the Legal Department, Wiley Publishing, Inc., 10475 Crosspoint Blvd., Indianapolis, IN 46256, (317) 572-3447, fax (317) 572-4447, e-mail: permcoordinator@wiley.com.

Trademarks: Wiley, the Wiley Publishing logo, For Dummies, the Dummies Man logo, A Reference for the Rest of Us!, The Dummies Way, Dummies Daily, The Fun and Easy Way, Dummies.com, and related trade dress are trademarks or registered trademarks of Wiley Publishing, Inc., in the United States and other countries, and may not be used without written permission. Macromedia Flash MX, Dreamweaver MX, Shockwave MX, and Freehand Copyright (c) 1994-2003. Macromedia, Inc. 600 Townsend Street, San Francisco, CA 94103 USA. All other trademarks are the property of their respective owners. Wiley Publishing, Inc., is not associated with any product or vendor mentioned in this book.

LIMIT OF LIABILITY/DISCLAIMER OF WARRANTY: WHILE THE PUBLISHER AND AUTHOR HAVE USED THEIR BEST EFFORTS IN PREPARING THIS BOOK, THEY MAKE NO REPRESENTATIONS OR WAR-RANTIES WITH RESPECT TO THE ACCURACY OR COMPLETENESS OF THE CONTENTS OF THIS BOOK AND SPECIFICALLY DISCLAIM ANY IMPLIED WARRANTIES OF MERCHANTABILITY OR FITNESS FOR A PARTICULAR PURPOSE. NO WARRANTY MAY BE CREATED OR EXTENDED BY SALES REPRESENTA-TIVES OR WRITTEN SALES MATERIALS. THE ADVICE AND STRATEGIES CONTAINED HEREIN MAY NOT BE SUITABLE FOR YOUR SITUATION. YOU SHOULD CONSULT WITH A PROFESSIONAL WHERE APPRO-PRIATE. NEITHER THE PUBLISHER NOR AUTHOR SHALL BE LIABLE FOR ANY LOSS OF PROFIT OR ANY OTHER COMMERCIAL DAMAGES, INCLUDING BUT NOT LIMITED TO SPECIAL, INCIDENTAL, CON-SEQUENTIAL, OR OTHER DAMAGES.

For general information on our other products and services or to obtain technical support, please contact our Customer Care Department within the U.S. at 800-762-2974, outside the U.S. at 317-572-3993, or fax 317-572-4002.

Wiley also publishes its books in a variety of electronic formats. Some content that appears in print may not be available in electronic books.

Library of Congress Control Number: 2002114834

ISBN: 0-7645-2595-6

Manufactured in the United States of America

10 9 8 7 6 5 4 3 2 1

 WILEY is a trademark of Wiley Publishing, Inc.

About the Authors

Peter Frazier is a partner with UI Architects, a usability-centered consulting firm. He was previously with Zanzara User Experience as senior graphic designer and usability engineer. Mr. Frazier owned and operated Confluence Communications, a Web and print design business, for 10 years. His work in graphics, design, and usability has benefited such clients as Boeing, Charles Schwab, Hewlett-Packard, Microsoft, Palm, and Sprint.

Bud Smith started in the computer industry as a data entry clerk facing a room full of punch cards and quickly became a programmer and data processing manager. Later work included technical writing, an editorial position at a computer magazine, and work in marketing and Web development for companies such as AltaVista, AOL, Apple, IBM, and Microsoft. Bud is the author of the wildly successful *Creating Web Pages For Dummies*, currently in its 6th edition, with Arthur Bebak, *Internet Marketing For Dummies*, with Frank Catalano, and many other books within and outside of the *For Dummies* series. Bud has a Bachelor of Arts degree in Information Systems Management from the University of San Francisco. He is currently a writer and consultant in London.

Dedication

This book is dedicated by the authors to those who donated, and who continue to donate, immense effort and countless hours to develop the freely-shared standards that provide the underpinnings of the Internet and the World Wide Web.

Acknowledgments

Both authors would like to thank Christine Berman, our dedicated Project Editor, and Steve Hayes, who pushed everyone who needed pushing to make this book a reality. Jake Richter, our Technical Editor, is a long-time friend of Bud's, but was nonetheless merciless — uh, we mean thorough — in going through the manuscript and pointing out needed changes.

Publisher's Acknowledgments

We're proud of this book; please send us your comments through our online registration form located at www.dummies.com/register/.

Some of the people who helped bring this book to market include the following:

Acquisitions, Editorial, and Media Development

Project Editor: Christine Berman

Acquisitions Editor: Steve Hayes

Copy Editor: Jean Rogers

Technical Editor: Jake Richter

Editorial Manager: Leah Cameron

Senior Permissions Editor: Carmen Krikorian

Media Development Specialist: Greg Stafford

Media Development Manager: Laura VanWinkle

Media Development Supervisor: Richard Graves

Editorial Assistant: Amanda Foxworth

Cartoons: Rich Tennant, www.the5thwave.com

Production

Project Coordinator: Nancee Reeves

Layout and Graphics: Seth Conley, LeAndra Johnson, Tiffany Muth, Mary Virgin

Proofreaders: TECHBOOKS Production Services

Indexer: TECHBOOKS Production Services

Publishing and Editorial for Technology Dummies

Richard Swadley, Vice President and Executive Group Publisher

Andy Cummings, Vice President and Publisher

Mary C. Corder, Editorial Director

Publishing for Consumer Dummies

Diane Graves Steele, Vice President and Publisher

Joyce Pepple, Acquisitions Director

Composition Services

Gerry Fahey, Vice President of Production Services

Debbie Stailey, Director of Composition Services

Contents at a Glance

Table of Contents

Introduction

Web graphics are a strange beast. Their low resolution inspires the disdain of print graphics experts — yet their attractiveness can make a Web page a work of art. They can be easy to create and put on the Web — but performing these so-called simple tasks has driven many thousands of very smart people to distraction.

The Web has the potential to make millions of people into publishers and to drive the quality of graphics in everyday use forward significantly. That potential is not being fully met.

It's time for a book that takes the mystery out of Web graphics. *Creating Web Graphics For Dummies* is for amateur and semi-professional Web site creators who also create their own graphics or would like to. It's also written for the pro who wants a handy source of explanations to use with those who ask seemingly simple, yet surprisingly hard-to-answer questions, such as why is this stuff so hard? How can it be made easier? The answers are here.

About This Book

This book isn't designed solely to be read straight through, from cover to cover. We'd like it if a few of you would do so, then tell us what great writers we are, but no one has to do it this way. You can — and probably should — also use this as a reference book that you dip in and out of as you run into new topics. Look in the index or the table of contents to locate the information you want, find out what you need to know, and then get back to work.

This book is also not completely comprehensive. There are so many issues relating to Web page design and graphics that trying to cover them all would result in a very broad survey. Instead of trying to tackle it all, we rely on several other *For Dummies* books to tackle other related topics:

- *Creating Web Pages For Dummies,* 6th Edition, by Bud Smith and Arthur Bebak, tells you how to create an initial Web page.

- *Web Design For Dummies,* by Lisa Lopuck, tells you how to design a Web site that gets your ideas across in an attractive overall package.

- *Web Usability For Dummies,* by Richard Mander, Ph.D. and Bud Smith, tells you how to make sure your Web site works well for the broadest possible range of users.

Many other *For Dummies* books cover topics related to Web page creation that we don't cover in this book, such as the Internet, graphics programs such as Photoshop, programming languages used with the Web, Web page editors, and more. The existence of these books has allowed us to focus our book on a few questions that, we find, drive people crazy.

This book answers those questions in depth and shows you how to actually create and compress graphics for the Web. Among other interesting things, this book shows you the following:

- What GIF and JPEG graphics formats are.

- When to use GIF versus JPEG — and whether you should consider using PNG, an alternative graphics format.

- How to take advantage of advanced GIF features such as interlacing, transparency, and animation.

- How to use JPEG in a way that respects, rather than obliterates, the quality inherent in good photos.

- How to get started using Jasc's Paint Shop Pro.

- How to get started using Adobe's Photoshop and its little brother, Photoshop Elements.

- How to use graphics to create an attractive Web page that loads quickly.

Foolish Assumptions

We assume that, as a person buying a book called *Creating Web Graphics For Dummies*, you're interested in Web graphics, but you're not yet an expert. We further assume that you actually want to create graphics, or compress existing graphics in acceptable formats, and put them on the Web. Daring of us, we know, but that's just the kind of guys we are.

We don't assume that you know much about computer technology or graphics display technology as you start reading this book. But by reading this book, you'll find out how to create and publish attractive graphics on the Web.

Conventions Used in this Book

We use several conventions in this book to make it easier for you to scan the pages for just what you need and to remember key points while you're working. Whenever we introduce a new term, we put it in italics and define it immediately after. That way you're part of the conversation and not stuck on the outside, wondering what we're talking about.

This is a sidebar head

And this is an example of how sidebar text looks. Pretty cool, huh? Try making text look like this on a Web site! (It's hard, but it can be done.) Two-column text is real popular with the authors who can't always fit all their great ideas into the main flow of the text. And now back to our regularly scheduled programming. . . .

We use many bulleted and step lists in this book. These are devices that help you quickly grasp what's important and yet also find those crucial details that can really make a difference in doing things right the first time. Step lists let you know when it's important that things be done in a specific order.

Web addresses and bits of HTML code are given in a monospaced font like this: `www.dummies.com`. We actually use the *For Dummies* Web site as an example in this book.

The command arrow is your guide through the sequence of menu choices. When you see it used in a command such as File⇨Open, it means to click the File menu and choose the Open option on that menu.

Sidebars also are set off in their own typeface, with a fancy heading all their own, and are surrounded by a shaded box; you can find a sidebar nearby in this introduction.

How This Book Is Organized

We organized our book to allow a certain progression. We start with a whirl-wind introduction to both topical and how-to information that allows you to start doing things right away, but to have enough understanding to make sure they're the right things. We don't save you complications up front if that just means you'll cause your Web users pain later.

The following sections describe the parts into which we've organized our book.

Part I: Getting Going with Web Graphics

Part I gets you oriented to the most important Web graphics terms and shows you how to create Web graphics starting right in Chapter 1. Part I explains key Web graphics options and shows you how HTML works to help you put graphics in Web pages. Not bad for a few chapters, huh?

Part II: Discovering and Using Cool Graphics Tools

You can use a nearly infinite number of tools for different parts of the task of creating Web graphics. But we focus on three tools that everyone has, or can get at least a trial version of: Windows Paint, which comes with every copy of Windows; Paint Shop Pro, once a shareware product that's moved into the big leagues; and Photoshop, which you can get as an expensive, full-featured program, or as a slightly less capable program called Photoshop Elements.

Part II explains the JPEG and GIF standards in some detail — we would have loved to explain even more, but this isn't a book just about compression standards. In Part II, we show you how to use Windows Paint, Paint Shop Pro, and Photoshop to create simple Web-ready images.

Part III: Getting Photos in Your Web Site

With digital photography you can create, manipulate, and publish the image, all digitally. If you don't have a digital camera, you can use a scanner to digitize images, or you can use a film camera and order a Photo CD with digital images when you process the film. Part III shows you how to get your digital photos and how to enhance them with Paint Shop Pro or Photoshop so that you don't have washed-out photos or people with red eyes scratching the heads of dogs with green eyes.

Part IV: Using GIF in Your Web Site

In Part IV, we show you how to use GIF properly, both for static images and for animations. Yes, inexpensive programs with free trial versions can even make GIF animations! And we show you where to look for GIF images and animations on the Web. We even get flashy and introduce Macromedia Flash, a program used to create animations for the Web.

Part V: The Part of Tens

No *For Dummies* book is complete without the Part of Tens, in which we authors get to write fun Top Ten lists to show you how to do things quickly and well. We came up with two good ones for this book. One is ten do's and don'ts for Web graphics. The only trouble with this is that some of you might read this chapter and figure you don't need the rest of the book! The other

Part of Tens chapter features ten cool online resources you can use to get graphics, download tools, and drill down on graphics topics.

The first appendix describes the contents of this book's CD-ROM, a cool treasure trove of tools for Web graphics. Use it with care — you could get so caught up in creating Web graphics that you never get around to putting them on the Web where people can see them!

The second appendix is a glossary — an extremely useful tool for making sense of those detailed discussions of obscure Web graphics points that you find online and in print.

Icons Used in This Book

Icons are little images that point you to the right (or warn you of the wrong) way to do things. *For Dummies* books are justly famous for their icons, and we hold up our end of the tradition. These icons are much like those used in many computer programs, except there are fewer of them, we use them more consistently than software developers do, and ours are simpler and more readable. Besides that, not much difference.

This icon helps you identify pointed insights that keep you on target and save you work and worry as you create and improve your Web site or work with users on the next round of changes. If scratching your ear with your elbow helps you concentrate on the right thing to do next in your Web site design, a Tip will point that out to you.

This is our favorite icon because it lets us warn you when there's stuff you don't absolutely have to read. When you see the Dummies Man pointing his finger skyward and the words "Technical Stuff," you've found something in the book that you can safely ignore — temporarily, for a while, or forever. Use the areas marked Technical Stuff for more in-depth information in areas you're especially interested in.

The Technical Stuff icon is your indicator of things you really may not need to know. Unless you really want to dive deeply into details, detour around these demarcations.

It's possible to really mess things up in your typical Web graphic with just one or two wrong keystrokes or mouse clicks. When you're a step or two from disaster, a Warning alerts you and tells you how to stay on the straight and narrow.

Sometimes we tell you so many things that we're afraid you might forget something important. Or that, in skipping through the book, you might miss a pearl of wisdom that you need to get through a tough spot. The Remember icon points out key things that we might have already mentioned, but wanted to remind you of. Think of it as a nagging, but caring, aunt.

We have a great collection of tools on the CD that comes with this book. So when we mention one of those tools in the text, we place an On the CD icon nearby to remind you that the tool we're discussing is just an easy installation away from your hard disk.

Where to Go from Here

Well, just dive in! Turn the page and start reading — or flip through the book and find something especially interesting to start with. We look forward to seeing your work on the Web.

Part I
Getting Going with Web Graphics

The 5th Wave By Rich Tennant

"Well, it's not quite done. I've animated the gurgling spit sink and the rotating Novocaine syringe, but I still have to add the high-speed whining-drill audio track."

In this part . . .

A Web page with the right graphics is a joy forever, the poet once said — or something like that. But making mistakes with Web graphics is easy when you're first starting out. In this part, we get you quickly over that stormy start and into the sunny meadows of competence.

Chapter 1

Handling Web Graphics Tasks

Graphics are the key to making the Web interesting and useful. Before the Web became popular, users employed the Internet largely to send text messages back and forth. In the early 90s, Marc Andreesen added the <IMG>, or image, tag to the first widely used Web browser, Mosaic. Suddenly, the Web came to life.

Text alone is boring, but add graphics and it becomes interesting. Think of the difference between a traditional text-only book and a magazine or newspaper. Text-only books are vitally important, of course, but newspapers and magazines catch and hold the eye. Now more and more books, such as the one you are holding in your hand, use graphics and sophisticated layouts to make them more readable and fun.

Graphics clearly make the Web fun for users, but what do they mean to people who create Web pages? Most Web page creators know how to write fairly presentable text for Web pages. However, people are taught the three R's — reading, writing, and arithmetic — and there's no G for graphics or D for design in the three R's. So, although most people can create a Web page with fairly interesting text, they might have trouble using graphics to make the page look good or to help make a point.

This book closes that gap by showing you the basics for using graphics in your Web pages and designing them so that they make a positive impression on all your Web page users — even you!

Words for the Web-Wise

You probably know quite a few Web graphics terms; in fact, you may not even realize how many of them you do know. Although widely used, many of these terms are poorly understood. So we take a moment to explain them. In doing so, we can also begin to communicate some of our philosophy about how to create great Web graphics.

A few Web words

Before you do anything on the Web, the first word you need to know is *HTML* — HyperText Markup Language. HTML is a mix of ordinary text with special commands called *tags*.

Because HTML tells computers what to do, it's referred to as *code,* even though it's not a full programming language. However, HTML is much easier to read than computer programming languages are. Here's a snippet of HTML code:

```
<H2>Fun with Clowns</H2>
Here's an example of an image within a Web page: a clown!<P>
<IMG SRC="clown.jpg">
```

Figure 1-1 shows the code snippet, along with the Web page it produces. As you can see, "Fun with Clowns" is a heading. Here's a simplified description of what all the pieces in the HTML snippet do:

- ✔ `<H2>` **tag:** Tells the Web browser to display the following text as a header.
- ✔ **"Fun with Clowns":** This text is displayed as a header because it is preceded by the `<H2>` tag.
- ✔ `</H2>`: Tells the Web browser to stop displaying text as a heading and to put the next text or graphic on a new line.
- ✔ **"Here's an example . . .":** More text. No tags affect it, so it is displayed normally.
- ✔ `<P>`: End of a paragraph. Put the next text or graphic on a new line.
- ✔ `<IMG SRC="clown.jpg">`: Display an image. The file to display is `clown.jpg`.

Don't be afraid to go over this code a few times. Compare the HTML code to the Web page it produces. After you understand how the code works, you'll know much of what you ever need to know about HTML.

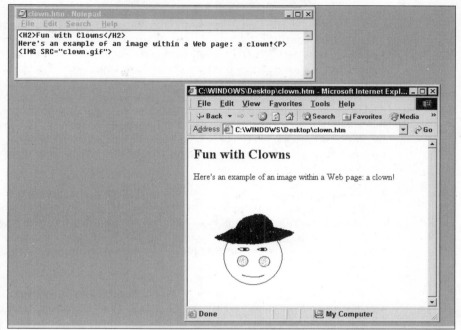

Figure 1-1:
A Web page
that's not
afraid to
clown
around.

In addition to understanding the role of HTML, you need to know what a *Web server* is. A Web server is a computer that actually stores the files that make up Web pages. When you type a Web address, such as www.dummies.com, a request goes out over the Internet for the Web server that has the name www.dummies.com. Eventually, the request reaches the Web server with that name, and the server responds by sending back an HTML page stored at the base directory, or *root,* of the Web server's file system.

Through a bit of trickery, a single Web server can contain multiple domains. Each domain is mapped to a separate subdirectory on the server. It can be a bad day for several people when one of these Hydra-headed Web servers goes down!

When you use the Web, in general here is what happens: A request from the user causes a Web server to send a particular file to the user. A Web page consists of an HTML file plus all the graphics files referred to within the HTML file. For more information on this topic, check out the sidebar "One is the loneliest number," later in this chapter.

Finally, you need to understand *download time,* the time it takes a file to be transferred from a Web server to your computer. Download time includes the time it takes your computer to request an HTML file and then request each graphics file, along with the time it takes the Web server to start transferring the files and the time it takes all the files to arrive at your computer.

As you can probably see, having a slow connection to the Web at any point greatly increases the download time for a Web page. Some users, of course, have fast connections such as a shared corporate data line, or a cable line and cable modem, or a DSL phone line and DSL modem. Others have a slow connection — a regular phone line and a 28.8 Kbps, 33.6 Kbps, or 56 Kbps modem.

A slow user connection makes download time longer, but so does a slow or busy Web server, or a slow connection between the Web server and the Internet, or congestion on a corporate user's Local Area Network (LAN), or on the Internet as a whole. Web pages can take a long time to download for many reasons.

However, the biggest limiting factor on download speed is still the user's connection. It takes about 1 second to download 3K of data over a typical modem connection, so a 30K graphic takes 10 seconds to download. That's a long time for the user to sit and wait! This book will give you many tips and techniques for achieving good-looking results while minimizing the user's waiting time.

To summarize, HTML is the code in which Web pages are written. You may already know how to use HTML. If not, *HTML 4 For Dummies,* 4th Edition, by Ed Tittel and Natanya Pitts (Wiley Publishing, Inc.) is a good place to start — or use a tool such as FrontPage or Dreamweaver to create the Web page without dealing directly with HTML.

A Web server sends HTML files and the graphics files associated with them to the user's computer. Each Web page is one HTML file plus the graphics to which the HTML file refers (except for framed pages, described in the section, "A few Web design words"). The total amount of time it takes for all the files to be sent over the Internet is the download time of the page.

Some graphic language

In our explanation of how HTML works, you may have noticed that the image of a clown's face was stored in a file called `clown.jpg`. This image is a *JPEG file,* a term you've no doubt heard before. Check out the upcoming sidebar, "Convention-al filenames," for information on naming HTML, JPEG, and GIF files.

JPEG stands for Joint Photographic Experts Group. Many years ago, a group of experts joined together to specify a way to compress photographic images so that they would take up much less space when stored in a computer file, with as little loss of quality as possible. JPEG is the answer they came up with, and it's a good one.

As you may already know, JPEG is used almost exclusively for compressing photographs. It's *lossy compression* — you actually lose information when you store an image in JPEG format. The beauty of JPEG is that you keep most of the impact of the original photograph while storing the image in a file that's much smaller than the original.

The complement to a JPEG file is a *GIF* file (GIF standing for Graphics Interchange Format). Several people invented GIF — the argument over just whom is still going on — and was popularized by the CompuServe online service about 20 years ago.

GIF is good for storing images that don't have lots of colors in them, which includes most images created from scratch on a computer. GIF files are used for storing just about any image that didn't originate as a photograph. Most of the little graphics in a Web page are GIF files.

GIF also supports three neat tricks that you won't usually find in JPEG files: interlacing, transparency, and GIF animation. *Interlacing* allows a GIF file to download in bands so that a blurry version of the image appears quickly and then sharpens as the rest of the image data downloads. *Transparency* allows you to drop the background around an image so that it appears to be embedded directly in the page, not surrounded by a rectangular window. *GIF animation* is also the easiest way to create animated images on your Web pages. You find more on all these features in Chapter 2.

Special effects such as interlacing, transparency, and animation are important, but the most important thing about HTML, GIF, and JPEG files is that they're the only file types recognized by nearly every Web browser (this differs greatly from typical PCs and Macintosh computers, which are likely to have scores of different file types). If you understand how HTML, GIF, and JPEG files work, you've already gone a long way toward understanding how Web pages function.

A few Web design words

There are libraries of books on page layout for printed pages, with specific coverage of layout for books, magazines, newspapers, and other kinds of printed material. The Web is a relative newcomer here; the art of page design for the Web is still in its infancy.

However, some good ideas are emerging, and we include them in our recommendations for how to do things. You do, however, need to know a few terms in order to participate in the discussion.

Convention-al filenames

If you just want to trust us, you can read the rest of this paragraph, follow the conventions (that is, rules) it describes, and go on: Always simplify your filenames to an 8-character filename with no uppercase letters, spaces, or special characters — just the 26 letters of the alphabet and the 10 digits, 0–9. Always end your filenames with `.htm` for HTML files, `.gif` for GIF files, or `.jpg` for JPEG files.

Some of you, however, will want to know why these rules, or conventions, should be followed. Here's a brief description.

Users are likely to employ four computer systems to transfer and store Web files, in this order of preference: PCs running Windows; Unix systems; Macintosh computers; and PCs running DOS.

Each of these computer systems has different rules for handling filenames. PCs and Macs ignore uppercase versus lowercase differences; Unix systems treat `BIGFILE.htm` and `bigfile.htm` as different files. PCs, Unix systems, and Macs all have different lists of special characters that they support, whereas PCs running DOS (or early versions of Windows) recognize only "8.3" filenames — an eight-character filename followed by a three-character extension.

The big problem is that when you send your file to be hosted on a Web server, you may not know the kind of system it will end up on. Your hosting provider may even move your Web site from, say, Windows to Unix without telling you. In addition, your file may be stored temporarily on any kind of system on its way to a long-term home on another kind of system.

Because different systems use different filename conventions, putting the wrong filename on the wrong kind of computer — even briefly, as the file is moved around — can actually cause the filename to be changed. All links to such files will instantly break. Note that navigation or the display of graphics on your Web site can stop working for reasons that are hard to determine after the fact.

The safest bet is to keep your filenames short and simple, as previously described. If you just can't stand short filenames, though — and they're harder to manage than long ones — at least follow these looser rules: Keep the main part of the filename to 30 characters or less; use three-letter, not four-letter, extensions; never use spaces; avoid special characters; and never use capital letters.

If you follow these rules, your files are much more likely to behave well as they travel through cyberspace — and to have the same filenames that you expect them to have when they finally end up in their long-term home on a server.

The first, and most important, term is page weight. *Page weight* is the total size, in kilobytes (K), of all the files in a Web page, which means the HTML file that makes up the Web page plus all the graphics referred to in the HTML file.

Figure 1-2 shows a typical Web page as it downloads. The Web page was captured partway through downloading to dramatize the fact that most users don't see the whole page at once; they see part of it and have to wait for the rest.

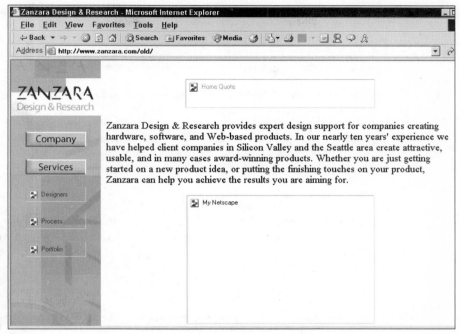

Figure 1-2:
Less page
weight
means less
waiting.

Smart Web page developers set a maximum page weight for all the pages in their sites. A typical page weight for a commercial Web site is 30K, or a 10-second download time for a typical user on a slow modem connection.

Smart Web page developers also break the page weight rule sometimes. For example, it may be a good idea to put a high-resolution photo of the hot new bicycle you're selling on your Web page, even if it's more than 30K. Fair enough — but provide a thumbnail version first so the user can get an idea of what the bike looks like before deciding whether he or she wants to click the thumbnail or a link to see a larger version of the picture and wait for the download.

Another key Web design term is tables. A *table* is an organizational tool that Web page developers use to divide a Web page into rectangular pieces. Each piece has different content.

You may have visited a badly designed Web page that didn't have a table-based format. If so, you first saw text appearing without graphics. Then, just as you started reading the text, it lurched alarmingly to one side. A graphic then started to appear where some of the text had been. With a really poorly designed page, this can happen two or three times as various graphics appear on-screen.

The good news is that a properly designed table-based page locks all the pieces into place. (You have to specify the size of table cells and images in your HTML file for this to work correctly.) Text flows into the space where it belongs, graphics appear where they should, and nothing lurches. The user can start reading even before the graphics appear. So tables are a good thing.

Frames, on the other hand, are not necessarily a good thing. Frames are like table cells on steroids. Each frame is a totally separate area in the Web page with its own separate HTML file and, potentially, its own scrollbars. Having separate scrollbars can sometimes be confusing for users. Framed pages give you a lot of options, but they tend to burden the poor user with more decisions than they may really want to make on a Web page.

Frames can be used intelligently, and we talk a bit about how in Chapter 6. For an example of a positive use of frames, see Figure 1-3, a page created by one of the authors (Bud Smith). Notice there's only one scrollbar — the fact that the page was created with frames is almost invisible to the user. In most cases, that's the way to do it.

Frame 1

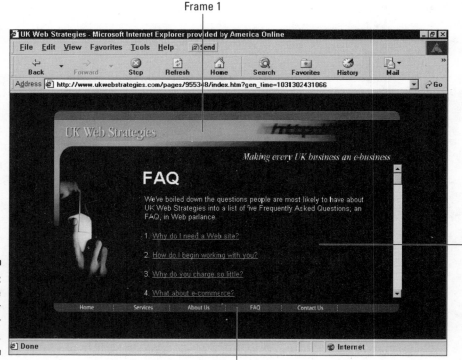

Frame 2

Frame 3

Figure 1-3:
Frames are best neither seen nor heard.

Keep in mind that page weight is an important part of managing how long users will have to wait for your Web pages to download. Tables and frames are important page layout tools to make your pages look and work better — tables are almost always good, whereas frames can be used effectively or ineffectively.

 To see all the files in a Web page, save the Web page using a recent version of Internet Explorer. The HTML file will be saved as a document, and all the images in the Web page will be saved in a folder with the same name as the document. Look in the folder to see all the graphics files associated with the Web page. Right-click any file or folder to see just how large it is in kilobytes. Divide the total of all the file sizes by 3, and you'll see how many seconds it takes a typical modem user to receive the entire Web page.

Using Paint for Web Graphics

You can create lots of useful images using a free program that comes with every Windows PC: the Paint program. Using newer versions of Paint, you can even save graphics in GIF or JPEG format. The quality of the results won't be very good, but Paint is a great tool to have handy when you're using a random PC in someone else's office, or at an Internet café, or in a hotel business area.

Paint is also great when you're just trying out ideas or are in too big a hurry to boot up a more capable program, and it saves files in Windows bitmap format (the filename ends with .bmp). Bitmap format uses *lossless compression* — it doesn't compress your file, so you can edit it and save it again and again without losing image quality.

Although bitmap format preserves image quality, when you resave a file in a GIF or JPEG format, you may lose some image quality (this is a possibility with GIF and a certainty with JPEG). Also, Paint does a lousy job of saving files, so you may want to reopen your original file in a better program later and save a superior GIF or JPEG version. Always keep a bitmap original of your Paint graphics so you can start with a pristine version before saving the final version to GIF or JPEG for display on the Web.

In this section, we give you step-by-step instructions on how to use Microsoft Paint to select a portion of a screen shot. Along the way, we provide several tips and tricks that you'll find useful no matter what image-editing program you're using.

You may have some experience with Paint or other graphics programs already, or you may be new to this kind of program. In either case, walk through these steps. You'll almost certainly discover something new.

Follow these steps to capture a screen shot using Paint:

1. **Open the Windows Paint program by choosing Start⇨Programs⇨ Accessories⇨Paint.**

   The Paint program may be in a different folder on your system — look around until you find it, and then open it.

2. **Open an interesting file on-screen.**

   You can open a graphics file, a word-processing document, or a spread-sheet. You can fire up a Web browser and go to a Web page you like. Or just leave the Paint program in the foreground.

   You can use any content you want for this exercise, because you don't end by putting something on the Web. However, always be careful when you capture content that may be protected by copyright. Don't publish such content on the Web without permission.

3. **Press the PrtScrn, or Print Screen, key.**

   It may have a slightly different name on your keyboard, such as PrtSc, but the key should still be recognizable. We refer to it as the PrtScrn key for consistency in this book.

   Pressing PrtScrn makes a copy of the current screen contents — in bitmap format — and puts the image in the Windows Clipboard.

4. **Bring the Paint program to the foreground, if it isn't already.**

   A blank drawing area appears in Paint.

5. **Choose Edit⇨Paste (Ctrl+V).**

   The screen image is pasted into the Paint drawing area. It will be larger than the window size of the Paint program.

   Now choose part of the image to make into a GIF file.

6. **Reinitialize the selection rectangle by clicking the Eraser icon and then the rectangular Select icon (the dashed-box icon in the upper-right corner).**

   When you first paste an image into Paint, the selection rectangle is drawn around the entire pasted image. To select part of the image, rather than the whole thing, you have to deselect the entire image by clicking somewhere else. But, because the screen image fills the entire Paint window, the best place to click is in the tools area.

7. **Scroll to an interesting area of the screen, and using the selection rectangle, click and drag to select the area you'll use for your graphic. Select an area about 250 x 250 pixels in size.**

   Figure 1-4 shows how the screen looks during this process.

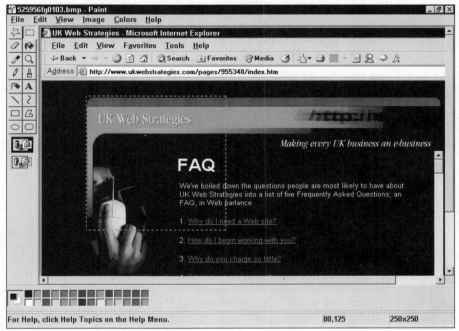

Figure 1-4:
Using Paint
to select
part of a
screenshot.

8. **Copy the selection to the clipboard by choosing Edit⇨Copy or by pressing Ctrl+C.**

9. **Clear the current image by choosing File⇨New or pressing Ctrl+N.**

   A dialog box appears to ask, "Save changes to untitled?" You've already copied the only piece of the captured screen image that you want, so click No.

10. **Press N or click the No button to bypass saving the file and close the dialog box.**

    The drawing area is cleared.

11. **Make the drawing area smaller by grabbing the lower-right corner of it and dragging it up and to the left — leave an inch or so in the upper-left corner of the screen.**

    When you do this and then paste the selection, the drawing area will automatically expand to fit the selection.

12. **Paste the selection into the drawing area by choosing Edit⇨Paste or by pressing Ctrl+V.**

    The selection will appear in the drawing area.

13. **Save your file (in bitmap format) by choosing File⇨Save or pressing Ctrl+S.**

    Because the document has not previously been saved, the Save As dialog box appears.

14. **Use the dialog box to navigate to the folder of your choice on your hard disk or to the desktop. Then press Alt+S or click Save to save the file and close the dialog box.**

    Your file is saved in bitmap format.

Creating GIF and JPEG Files

GIF files are really cool. You can do all sorts of neat things with them. However, for now, we're just going to explain the basics on how GIF works, how to create a GIF file, and how to use a GIF file in a Web page.

As we mentioned previously, GIF stands for Graphics Interchange Format. It has been around for a long time and supports neat tricks such as interlacing, transparency, and GIF animation.

The GIF format is very limited — and very efficient. No GIF graphic can have more than 256 different colors in it. This means that GIF graphics can be very small files, can be created easily, and can be displayed quickly.

Photographs, however, tend to have hundreds or thousands of different colors in order to accommodate subtle shadings found in natural images. So GIF is not usually a good choice for photographic images.

GIF is perfect, though, for most of the graphics that people create on computers, because most of us lack the patience or talent to use anything like 256 colors in the graphics we create. All the bullets, dingbats, business graphics, American and other flags, and cartoonish-looking images you see on the Web are stored and transferred as GIF files (or should be!).

JPEG, on the other hand, is perfect for photographs. Photos use hundreds or thousands of different colors to accommodate subtle shades. When you or I look at a photograph, we see a few colors — brown hair, a red sweater, a green lawn. But the photograph actually uses hundreds or thousands of shadings of hair color, or of the folds of a sweater, or of the rise and fall of a grassy hill to communicate depth and other subtle features of the image.

The JPEG file format uses some fairly tricky technology to assign color patterns to groups of pixels in a photograph. These patterns can be stored much more compactly than individual pixel colors. JPEG also allows you to control

What about the Mac (and Unix)?

This book focuses on the Windows versions of various programs such as the free Microsoft Paint utility, Paint Shop Pro, and Photoshop Elements. This is for two reasons. The first reason is, of course, that many more people use a PC than a Macintosh. Focusing on PC users makes it much easier for us to give simple, straightforward steps for solving common graphics problems.

The other reason is more subtle: Most Macintosh users already know how to perform basic graphic tasks. The Macintosh is very popular among graphics pros. Relatively few Mac users are novices when it comes to graphics in general, or Web graphics in particular.

One of us (Peter Frazier) is a graphics pro who uses a Mac whenever possible; the other (Bud Smith) worked at Apple for five years and still uses a Mac on occasion. Both of us are aware of Mac-specific concerns. But we're also aware that providing instructions for multiple platforms makes it harder for everyone to follow what should be simple steps.

Also, we're both aware that creative people who use a Mac or Unix for most of their work need a Windows PC with Web access for testing their output before it goes up on the Web. So, if you have a Windows PC available, please consider using it to run the programs mentioned in this book.

If you are a Mac user who's a graphics novice and lack even occasional PC access, please use available Macintosh programs — the Mac Notepad, the excellent BBEdit text editor, Claris Draw and Paint, and others — to duplicate the steps given here. Similarly, if you're a Unix user, utilize programs available to you to create plain text files and simple graphics. Or get access to a Windows PC to run the programs mentioned in this book, as well as to test your graphics and Web pages before putting them up on the Web. We aren't able to provide specific steps for Macintosh or Unix in this book, but we hope that, if you use these platforms, you'll be able to use your system or a borrowed Windows PC to follow along with the main concepts of the book.

how much the various shades in a photograph are averaged out into each other. You can have a crisp, high-resolution image that's stored in a fairly large file, or a bumpier, blotchier image that's quite small in file size.

In this section, we describe how to create a GIF file using a captured image. Then we show you how to create a JPEG file as well. Afterward, we demonstrate how to combine the GIF and JPEG files in a Web page.

Saving a Paint file in GIF format

In the section, "Using Paint for Web Graphics," earlier in this chapter, we show you how to capture a screen image and bring it into Paint. You can also open an existing bitmap image or a GIF or JPEG file in Paint.

One is the loneliest number

It's hard for most people to understand why graphics files take up so much space, especially compared to text. Here's a brief explanation of the answer.

A text file is made up of 26 characters — the letters of the alphabet — plus digits, capital letters, and punctuation in various combinations. A single text character or punctuation mark accounts for many, many pixels on the screen, generally at least 5 pixels across by 9 pixels high for a single character, plus many pixels of white space around each character.

A graphics file is much more complex. Every pixel has its own color. In a GIF file, a single pixel can be one of 256 colors. In other graphics formats, each pixel can be any of thousands of colors.

Here's the first tricky part. A computer stores information in bits — each bit is either a 0 or a 1. Eight bits are combined into one byte. With 8 bits available, each set to 0 or 1, a byte can contain up to 256 separate possible values.

Text characters are stored one character per byte. So a single byte holds a character that takes up about 45 pixels on the screen. But graphics images need many more bytes. A GIF image requires one byte for every pixel — 45 times more bytes per pixel than a typical text character. Other graphics formats use two, three, or four bytes per pixel — and require that much more storage than a GIF image.

A Web page full of text requires only about 2,000 bytes (2K) when stored. A Web page filled by a GIF image will require about 240K — or one-fourth of a megabyte (MB) — when stored. An image that uses more colors will be 2, 3, or 4 times as large — up to 1MB in size.

Here's the second tricky part. A typical phone modem can download about 3 kilobytes per second. That's more than a full page of text in 1 second. But the same phone modem would require nearly 2 minutes to download a full-page GIF image and 4, 6, or 8 minutes to download a full-page graphic in some other format.

Even worse, for technical reasons, the Internet is much better at transmitting lots of small files than it is at sending a few big ones. Small files are requested and sent quickly; if one is held up, others are easily transferred around it. Big files tend to cause bottlenecks all along the line, slowing transmission further. In many cases, big files don't download correctly the first time and need to be retried one or more times before they finally make it to the user.

This is why Web pages need to be text-heavy; they would take far too long to send as all-graphics or graphics-heavy pages. If you become frustrated by all the work it takes to downsize and compress your graphic images, just think how frustrated users would be if they had to wait two minutes or more every time they clicked a link to a Web page.

When you open a file in Paint, you can save it as a GIF file. Follow these steps:

1. **If you have not already done so, start Microsoft Paint by choosing Start⇨Programs⇨Accessories⇨Paint.**

2. **Press Ctrl+O or choose File⇨Open to open an existing graphics file.**

Use a file created with a screen capture, as described in the "Using Paint for Web Graphics" section, or open an existing graphics file on your hard drive.

You can use Start⇨Search⇨For Files or Folders to bring up the Search dialog box. Search for bitmap (.bmp), GIF (.gif) or JPEG (.jpg) files. Open the file you choose in Paint.

3. **To begin saving the file in GIF format, choose File⇨Save As.**

   The Save As dialog box appears.

4. **From the Save as Type drop-down list, select Graphics Interchange Format (*.gif), as shown in Figure 1-5.**

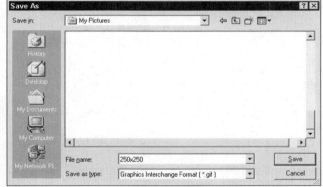

Figure 1-5:
The GIF that keeps on giving.

The * represents the filename you'll enter. .gif represents the extension that Windows will add to the filename to identify it as a GIF file.

Windows often hides the filename extension when you're looking at or selecting files. However, Windows uses an extension to identify the file type, what icon to use to display the location of the file in a folder, and so on. Understanding all this information can be important when, for example, you want to save a file you create in a text editor (normally a .txt file) as an HTML file (which ends in .htm). Simply saving the file with a name ending in .htm forces Windows to save it with that file extension, ensuring that it will be recognized as an HTML file.

5. **Enter the filename in the File Name text box.**

6. **Press Alt+S or click the Save button to save the file.**

   A dialog box appears with the following message: "Saving into this format may cause some loss of color information. Do you want to continue?" You continue, even if you may lose information in doing so, because you've already saved the file in a lossless format.

When you see a dialog box of this type in the future, always make sure that you have saved the file in a lossless format, such as Windows bitmap format or native Paint Shop Pro or Photoshop format, before proceeding.

7. **Press the Y key or click Yes to save the file.**

   The file is saved. You'll probably notice that the image in the drawing area changes colors. This change in color is caused by Paint's conversion of the file to the GIF format. When converting the file to GIF, other programs use techniques that are less likely to cause dramatic shifts in color.

8. **If you want to go on to the next section and save the same image as a JPEG file, leave Paint open for now. Otherwise, close Paint by pressing Alt+F4 or by choosing File⇨Exit to exit the program.**

Saving a Paint file in JPEG format

The preceding section shows you how to save a file in GIF format. This section shows you how to save a file in JPEG format. In Paint, the process of saving in GIF or JPEG is nearly identical. Other programs give you many more options for saving a file as GIF versus JPEG; we look into those in Chapter 3.

Follow these steps to save a file from Paint into JPEG format:

1. **If you have not already done so, start Microsoft Paint by choosing Start⇨Programs⇨Accessories⇨Paint.**

2. **Press Ctrl+O or choose File⇨Open to open an existing graphics file.**

   Use a file created with a screen capture, as described in the "Using Paint for Web Graphics" section, or open an existing graphics file on your hard disk.

   You can use Start⇨Search⇨For Files or Folders to bring up the Search dialog box. Search for bitmap (.bmp), GIF (.gif) or JPEG (.jpg) files. Open the file you select in Paint.

3. **Choose File⇨Save As to begin the process of saving the file in JPEG format.**

   The Save As dialog box appears.

4. **From the Save as Type drop-down list, select JPEG File Interchange Format (*.jpg, *.jpeg).**

   The * represents the filename you enter. .jpg represents the extension that Windows adds to the filename to identify it as a JPEG file. Windows and Paint also treat a file as a JPEG file if it ends with the extension .jpeg. However, we recommend that you use the shorter .jpg extension.

The process of saving a file as a JPEG image in Paint is much simpler than in other programs. Normally, you have to choose a level of compression for the image, which determines both the quality of the image's appearance and the size of the file needed to store the image. The higher the image quality, the larger the file. Paint automatically uses a moderate level of compression.

5. **Enter the filename in the File Name text box.**

6. **Press Alt+S or click the Save button to save the file.**

Unlike the process of saving a file as a GIF, you don't get a warning telling you that you'll lose information when saving the file as a JPEG. This is odd, because there are circumstances in which you may not lose information when saving to GIF, but you always lose information when saving from a lossless format to JPEG.

When you see a dialog box of this type in the future, always make sure that you have saved the file in a lossless format, such as bitmap format or native Paint Shop Pro or Photoshop format, before proceeding.

7. **Press the Y key or click Yes to save the file.**

The file is saved. You'll probably notice that the image in the drawing area gets a bit fuzzier. This change is caused by Paint's conversion of the file to the JPEG format. Other programs give you control over the degree of compression to use when creating the JPEG file.

Programs also differ in the quality of their JPEG compression and the size of the resulting files at various compression levels. Experimentation is the only way to be certain of usable results.

8. **Close Paint by pressing Alt+F4 or choosing File⇨Exit to exit the program.**

Chapter 2

Creating a Graphical Web Page

*1*f you're creating graphics for the Web, they will, of course, eventually end up on a Web page. In some circumstances, you have little control over the appearance of the actual Web page. If you're creating graphics to be used by others in their designs or a graphic that plugs into a spot on a fixed template, you won't have much input on how the Web page looks beyond the boundaries of the graphic you're creating.

Usually, though, creating graphics and creating the Web page they go on is an interactive process. If you need to know more about Web page creation, check out *Creating Web Pages For Dummies,* 6th Edition, by Bud Smith and Arthur Bebak (Wiley Publishing, Inc.). You can use that book as a companion to this one if you want to learn both sides of the process at once.

This book focuses on the graphics piece, which so many people don't understand but want to utilize. In this chapter, we show you how to create a Web page while focusing on the page's design and the appearance and usability of the graphics in it.

Even if you aren't a Web page creator as a rule, exploring the basics will enable you to know the limitations involved and help you do a better job on the graphics side as well.

This chapter shows you how to create a graphical Web page by working directly in HTML, the genetic code of the Web.

Graphics and HTML

We highly suggest using a tool to create Web pages, especially Web pages that use graphics. Creating a Web page involves a million details, and a tool such as Microsoft FrontPage or Macromedia Dreamweaver handles most of the details and helps you manage the rest.

However, it's also good to know something about HTML. At times, you may need to create a quick Web page to test an idea, but you don't have your favorite Web authoring tool available. Perhaps you need to fix a problem or specify a feature that your Web authoring tool doesn't allow you to access directly. In other words, sometimes there's no substitute for rolling up your sleeves and working directly in HTML.

How HTML works

As we mention in Chapter 1, HTML stands for HyperText Markup Language. HTML is a simple set of commands placed within text that tells a Web browser what to do at a certain point within a Web page. Each command is placed within angle brackets; for example, the bold command is <B>.

Some HTML commands come in beginning and ending pairs. Here's the HTML code to display a sentence with a word in bold:

```
HTML is <B>really</B> important to the Web.
```

And here's how the sentence would be displayed in a Web page:

```
HTML is really important to the Web.
```

The beginning bold tag, <B>, tells the Web browser to display the text in bold-face after this tag. The </B> tag tells the Web browser to stop displaying the text in boldface after this tag.

Because HTML commands are placed in the middle of strings of text, they don't really control where things go on a page. The Web browser just displays some text, sees an HTML command to display an image, displays the image, and then keeps going.

You can use HTML to tell the Web browser certain things, such as to put the image on the left edge, in the center of the page, or on the right edge. But you can't tell it precisely where to place the image. The Web browser just responds to the few commands it understands, at the time it sees them.

A new standard called *Cascading Style Sheets* (CSS) enables you to control layouts in the top-down, pixel-accurate manner that print designers commonly use. However, CSS is not yet fully standardized between browsers and browser versions, nor is it built into enough users' browsers to be something you can count on. So, for now, you may have to live without CSS.

Graphics and HTML tags

The most important HTML tag for graphics is the <IMG>, or image, tag. When a Web browser encounters an <IMG> tag, it immediately stops what it's doing and prepares to put an image on the screen.

If you work directly in HTML, you'll need to know that the <IMG> tag, unlike most HTML tags, has no ending tag. Most HTML tags come in pairs, such as the <B> and </B> tags to start and stop bolding. All the information needed to display an image is contained in the <IMG> tag — it doesn't have a direct effect on any text (except that the image pushes text out of the way!).

The <IMG> tag has several optional subcommands, called *attributes*. These attributes tell the Web browser several important things, such as where to go to get the image, the width and height of the image, and so on. We cover the details of these attributes in Chapter 6.

You use the <IMG> tag for both GIF and JPEG images. To the Web browser, GIF and JPEG images are almost exactly the same. The only difference occurs when you display an image on-screen. At that point, the browser uses different programming code to display a GIF image than to display a JPEG image.

You can use images in a couple of other ways. You can specify that an image be used as the background for a Web page. The image is then repeated across the background. We show you how to do this in the section, "Creating a background graphic," later in this chapter.

Layout and HTML tags

In the early days of the Web, the only option you had for viewing a layout and its relationship to HTML and graphics was horizontal placement of an image: on the left edge of the page, on the right edge, or smack in the middle.

You could also specify whether the text appearing next to an image was aligned with the top of the image, the bottom of the image, or the center of the image. The strict limitations on the tags that were available produced some very odd-looking pages.

The change came when Web page designers discovered a new use for the <TABLE> tag: They began to use it for laying out entire Web pages. (The <TABLE> tag was originally created for putting data tables in the middle of a

Web page. However, such tables are relatively rare in Web pages these days.) Web designers began to use the <TABLE> tag for laying out entire Web pages.

Then designers had a way to control just where different text and graphical elements ended up on a page. A number of basic table-based layouts were quickly developed and widely used. Web designers have never looked back.

You can also use images as the background of a cell in a table, just as you can use an image for the background of a Web page. However, this is rarely done, because the effect is usually jarring and often works differently in different Web browsers and browser versions.

We go into detail about how to use tables for page layout in Chapter 6. For now, just know that tables exist and that they allow you to have some control of the overall look of a page.

Using background images

A tiled background image is a potentially valuable Web page feature that is misused in many Web pages.

A *tiled background image* is an image that is repeated again and again to form the background of a Web page. This makes great sense from the computing point of view. A small image that can be downloaded quickly is stretched, by repetition, to make up the background for the entire Web page. The image can be chosen or designed so that it creates a very pleasant effect.

The problem is aesthetics. An image used as the base for a background needs to be very light in color; otherwise, it may interfere with readability of the text. Also, ideally, the image should be designed so that the repetition is seamless. It shouldn't be obvious that a single image is being repeated. Instead, it should appear as though there's a single, subtle background pattern.

Usually, however, a bright, colorful image with a strong central word such as SPORTSFAN is used as a tiled background image. The effect is predictable: It's very hard to read the text on the Web page, because of the lack of contrast and because the word SPORTSFAN distracts you from the smaller words on the body of the page. A user is likely to quickly leave such a Web site.

However, tiled background images are an important part of your bag of tricks as a Web page author and graphics maven. You just have to be clever about their use.

In this chapter, we show you how to quickly create an appropriate GIF image and use it as a background in your very own Web page. Then we show you how to add a JPEG image to the same page.

It's always a good idea to look for examples of good design on the Web, and background images are no exception. The San Francisco Giants baseball team has its Web site at www.sfgiants.com. On the site, the team uses a tiled background image in dark brown with the word "Giants," but they always put text and graphics on a lighter-colored background to provide good contrast. Check out the site to see how they took a Giant step toward good Web design.

Creating a Web Page with Graphics

In this section, we show you how to use HTML to create a simple Web page that incorporates a GIF image as a tiled background, includes some text, and has a JPEG image as an illustration. The result will be really ugly — but it serves as a successful start to managing graphics on the Web.

Creating a background graphic

A proper background graphic should be light in color and should contrast strongly with text. In addition, if the graphic is tiled, it should tile well — ideally, the border between one copy of the graphic and another shouldn't be obvious.

There's a tricky way to line up tiled graphics. The easy way is to not draw right up to the boundaries of the image, so that it's not too obvious where one copy of the image starts and the next copy ends. The clever way is to draw lines and curves so that a piece of a line that reaches the edge of one tile continues on the adjoining edge of the next tile.

Even a graphics novice can create a graphic that meets these criteria using a simple tool like Paint. If you want to experiment, open Paint and start trying to create a background graphic with these attributes:

- Light color
- Small file size (which usually means small in overall size, as well)
- Interesting when repeated through tiling

Save the image as a GIF file and use it in the next section as your background image in the Web page you create there.

You may prefer to follow step-by-step instructions for your first background graphic. Taking you through these steps will also give us the opportunity to provide tips that will help you when you do your own graphics for use as tiled backgrounds. Follow these steps to create a background graphic:

1. **Open Paint by choosing Start⇨Programs⇨Accessories⇨Paint.**

2. **Resize the image area by choosing Image⇨Attributes or by pressing Ctrl+E. Enter 100 pixels as the width and 100 pixels as the height.**

You can also resize the image area by clicking the selection rectangle (the icon in the upper-right corner of the drawing tools) to select it and then clicking the image area. Handles will appear that you can grab and drag to resize the image area.

3. **Save the image as a GIF file by choosing File⇨Save or by pressing Ctrl+S.**

The Save As dialog box appears. Select Graphics Interchange Format (*.GIF) from the Save as Type drop-down list. Then enter a filename and save the file.

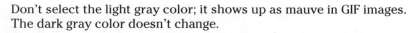

By saving the image as a GIF file now, all colors you use will appear in the drawing window in the same shade as they will appear in the final file. If you wait to save to GIF, colors will shift on you when you do save the file as GIF.

4. **To draw a suitably light-colored image, click once on the dark gray color box in the lower-left of the Paint program window.**

This sets the color to dark gray.

Don't select the light gray color; it shows up as mauve in GIF images. The dark gray color doesn't change.

5. **Click the Airbrush icon in the toolbar to select the airbrush tool.**

A few patterns appear below the toolbar.

6. **To control the image better, select the smallest of the airbrush patterns.**

7. **Zoom in on the image so you can control it better. Choose View⇨ Zoom⇨Large Size or press Ctrl+PgDn to zoom in, enlarging the view.**

8. **Draw the image. Move the cursor quickly for less spray — a more broken-up pattern — and slowly for a dense pattern.**

To make the image tile better, try to end horizontal lines at the same height as you start them, and end vertical lines the same horizontal distance from the edge as you start them. You can also create diagonal lines that "match up" for tiling purposes. Figure 2-1 shows an example of a suitable image. Experiment on your own!

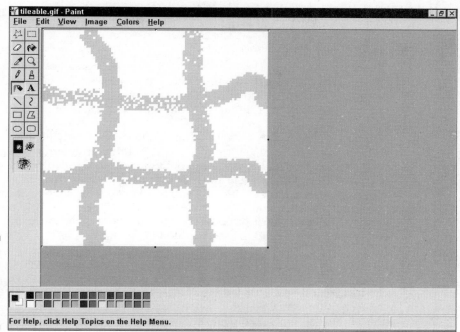

Figure 2-1:
An example
of a tiled
background
image.

Choose Edit➪Undo or press Ctrl+Z to undo your most recent drawing action, such as drawing a line. Choose Edit➪Repeat or press Ctrl+Y to redo an action. You can undo or redo up to three actions.

9. **Save the image.**

10. **Close Paint if you want to. However, you may want to leave it open so you can interactively experiment with your background image in the next section.**

You can use the image `tileme.gif` from the CD-ROM as a tiled background image if you'd like. We don't want to detract from your own efforts, but `tileme.gif` is a good file to use for experimentation if you don't want to use the file you created.

Creating a simple Web page

Being able to create a Web page seemed to be the road to riches for a while, when many Internet companies were valued at billions of dollars. Now it's like any other skill — the most talented practitioners make a good living at it, while a whole bunch of people know how to do it well enough to get the job done.

Creating simple Web pages is really, well, simple. You can do it yourself, using the Notepad program that comes with any Windows PC. Once you learn how to do this, you can quickly test various graphics ideas that come to you without having a copy of FrontPage, Dreamweaver, or a similar program handy.

Notepad is a text editor — a program that can create only plain text files, without word-processing formats such as **bolding** or underlining appearing in the program. This makes it a good tool for creating HTML files, which are plain text files. If you do use a word-processing program to create or edit a Web page, you might accidentally add formats to your document that won't be supported when you view the document as a Web page. Although it can certainly be done, most pros spend at least part of their time using a text editor such as Notepad to create or edit HTML files.

You'll find it really advantageous to be able to create and test simple Web pages on your own machine. Many of the problems that afflict live Web sites can be avoided by a little judicious local testing before the site goes up on the Web. But many Web professionals don't know how to do this testing, or don't bother if they do know how. Their sites suffer as a result.

Follow these steps to create a simple Web page with a tiled background:

1. **Start the Notepad program by choosing Start⇨Programs⇨ Accessories⇨Notepad.**

2. **Type the following lines into Notepad:**

```
<HTML>
<HEAD>
<TITLE>Test Web page with background</TITLE>
</HEAD>
<BODY BACKGROUND="TILEABLE.GIF">
This is my test page with TILEABLE.GIF as my background
        image.
</BODY>
</HTML>
```

The <HTML> and </HTML> tags specify that this is an HTML file. <HEAD> and </HEAD> tags denote the HTML file's *header* area, which is made up of *meta-information* — information that doesn't directly affect what gets displayed in the Web page itself. The text between the <TITLE> and </TITLE> tags is displayed on the title bar of the browser window, not in the Web page. The <BODY> and </BODY> tags surround the description of what actually gets displayed in the Web page.

Some search engines use the *title* — the text between the <TITLE> and </TITLE> tags — to decide what keywords should be used to find a specific Web page. And users depend on the title to tell them what a Web page is about. Sometimes the best text for the search engines is not the best text for helping orient the user, leading to conflicts for Web page designers.

3. **Save your file in the same folder as the GIF file you want to use as a background image, or to any folder you want. Use a name such as** TESTPAGE.HTM.

If you don't explicitly include the extension .htm in the name of your Web page, you won't be able to open it in your Web browser, even if the file includes HTML code.

4. **If the GIF file you want to use as a background image isn't already in the same folder as the HTML file, move it there. If it's not already named** tileme.gif, **rename it** tileme.gif.

Your HTML file and your background image, in GIF format, should now be in the same folder. The HTML file should name the GIF file as its background image. Check this carefully, or your new Web page won't work correctly.

5. **Open a Web browser such as Internet Explorer.**

Even if you prefer to use another browser such as Netscape Navigator or Opera, or if you use a Macintosh or Unix machine, you should always test your Web pages on a PC running the most current non-beta version of Internet Explorer before publishing them. If you are doing only the graphics piece, you should look at the graphics in Internet Explorer on a PC before handing them off to the people creating and publishing the Web page.

6. **Choose File⇨Open or press Ctrl+O to select the file you want to open. Navigate to your test HTML file and open it.**

The file will open as a Web page. It should have the graphic you specified as its background image. The result will look something like Figure 2-2.

If this didn't work, check that the HTML file ends in .htm or .html, that the <BODY> command names the specified GIF file as its background image, and that the GIF file has the correct name. If it still doesn't work, repeat these steps carefully, and you will probably be successful. If it still doesn't work, you may need to get help from someone familiar with HTML.

7. **If you want to try editing and viewing the graphic, open the graphic in Paint and modify it. Save the changes. Then click the Refresh button in your Web browser to reload the Web page with the new graphic. Check that they do indeed appear on the page.**

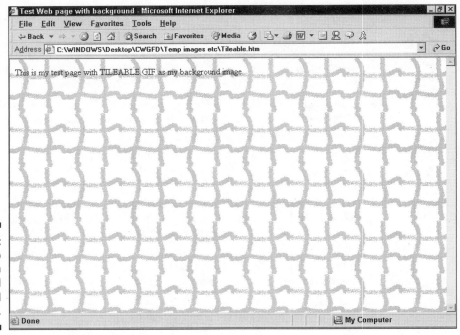

Figure 2-2:
A new Web page with a tiled background image.

This kind of interactive updating is how much Web graphics work is done and initially tested.

It's very easy to forget to save the file or to click Refresh in your Web browser. If your changes don't appear, save the file and click Refresh, and they probably will appear.

8. **Also, you might want to try changing the Web page and then viewing the change. Introduce a typo into the text that you have open in Notepad. Save the change. Then click the Refresh button on your Web page to load the changes. Check that they do indeed appear.**

As with updates to your graphics, it's easy to forget to save your HTML file or to forget to click Refresh in the browser. If your changes aren't showing up, save the file, then click the Refresh button, and you'll probably see the change appear.

Adding a JPEG image to a Web page

Here's where you add a JPEG image to your Web page. In doing so, you'll begin to get some idea of just how easy it is to add an image to your page — and just how little control you have of where it shows up, unless you create a table-based layout.

Follow these steps to add a JPEG image to your Web page:

1. **Identify a JPEG image you want to use. It should be roughly 100 x 100 pixels or smaller in size. (If you don't have anything handy that you like, you can use** 70x100.jpg**, which you can find on the CD-ROM at the back of this book.) Put the image in the folder in which you will have your Web page.**

2. **Rename the image** testjpeg.jpg.

3. **Start the Notepad program by choosing Start⇨Programs⇨ Accessories⇨Notepad.**

4. **Type the following lines into Notepad:**

```
<HTML>
<HEAD>
<TITLE>Test Web page with JPEG</TITLE>
</HEAD>
<BODY>
<IMG SRC="testjpeg.jpg">
This is my test page with testjpeg.jpg as my JPEG image.
</BODY>
</HTML>
```

The <HEAD> and </HEAD> tags and the <BODY> and </BODY> tags each surround one of the two main areas of the Web page definition, as explained in the set of steps in the preceding section.

5. **Save your file in the same folder as the JPEG file that you'll be displaying. Use a name such as** imgtest.htm.

If you don't explicitly include the extension .htm or .html in the name of your Web page, you won't be able to open it in your Web browser, even if the file includes HTML code.

6. **If the JPEG file you want to use as the image to be displayed isn't already in the same folder as the HTML file, move it there. If it's not already named** testjpeg.jpg, **rename it** testjpeg.jpg.

Your HTML file and your JPEG image should now be in the same folder. The HTML file should name the JPEG file as the image to be displayed. Check this carefully, or your new Web page won't work correctly.

7. **Open a Web browser such as Internet Explorer.**

Always test your Web pages in Internet Explorer, even if you don't use it, because most users run Internet Explorer.

8. **Choose File⇨Open or press Ctrl+O to choose a file to open. Navigate to your test HTML file and open it.**

The file will open as a Web page. It should have the graphic you specified displayed as an image. The result will look something like Figure 2-3. Congratulations!

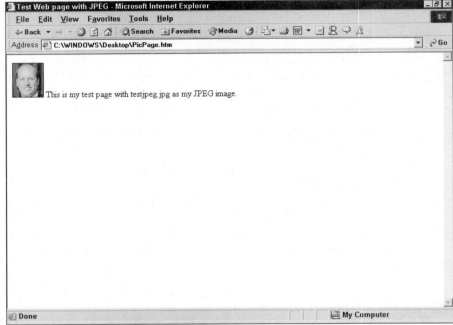

Figure 2-3:
You've done
it! A JPEG
image (of
Bud Smith)
in a Web
page.

If this didn't work, check to be sure that the HTML file ends in .htm or .html; that the <IMG> command names the specified JPEG file as the image; that you've saved the latest changes in the file; and that the JPEG file has the correct name.

9. **If you want to, try changing the Web page and then viewing the change. Change the text of the Web page that you have open in Notepad. Save the change. Then click the Refresh button on your Web page to load the changes. Check that they do indeed appear.**

Using Images in Web Pages

You may never type a line of HTML code — but you'll be affected by the features and limitations of HTML as long as you're working with graphics on the Web.

In this section, we show you all the major options for using images in a Web page as dictated by the features of the <IMG> tag. As we've mentioned throughout this chapter, the <IMG> tag is the HTML tag that brings images into your Web page.

The <IMG> tag has only eight major *attributes* — additional options within the tag that you use to tell images how to work. Four of the attributes always need to be used, three more have to be taken into account if the image is surrounded by text, and one is only for a specific use of images.

Four crucial image attributes

The four crucial image attributes in HTML are as follows: SRC, the source file that the image is stored in; ALT, the text that appears if the image isn't viewed for some reason; HEIGHT, the height of the graphic, in pixels; and WIDTH, the width of the graphic, also in pixels.

Going to the SRC

SRC is the most important attribute of the <IMG> tag. The <IMG> tag should really be referred to as the <IMG SRC=""> tag, because you never see the <IMG> tag without the SRC attribute. SRC specifies what file the image is to come from. Without SRC, there's no image to display, and no point to the <IMG> tag at all.

The exact workings of the SRC attribute cause a lot of trouble because the SRC attribute can specify a file literally from anywhere — a file on the local hard disk, a file on another computer on the same network, or a file anywhere on the Internet. It's very tricky to specify this location correctly — and it's trickier still to get the location right when the file is going to be moved around.

Web pages are nearly always created on someone's local machine, but unless your local machine is also a Web server, that isn't the end of it. Your Web page has to be transferred to a Web server before it's truly, well, a Web page. And that's where the trouble comes in.

The SRC attribute of your image file needs to be described in a way that holds up when the whole ball of wax is moved to a Web server. Also, the transfer of all the files must be done in a way that doesn't mess up the relative relationship of the files.

The following relationships are only three among the many relationships that the location of the graphics file can have to the location of the Web page calling it:

✔ **Same folder:** Please, please, please put your image files in the same folder as your Web page whenever you can. That way, links from the Web page to graphics files are simple, and when things get moved around, your HTML file and its image files are highly likely to stay together. If you do this, the SRC attribute holds the filename of the image: <IMG SRC="myjpeg.jpg">.

- ✔ **Subfolder:** It's very tempting to put your HTML file in a folder and your graphics files in their own folder one level below the HTML file in the folder hierarchy. This seems very clean — the HTML file sits by itself, and all the graphics files are with other graphics files. However, the links into the subfolder will be longer than necessary, and changing the name or location of the subfolder instantly breaks all your links. Here's an example of such a link: `<IMG SRC="graphics/myjpeg.jpg">`.

- ✔ **On the Web:** You may want to point to graphics already on the Web. This is encouraged in some cases — for example, when you use third-party services on your Web site — and is considered a copyright violation in other cases. So be careful, but this is probably an option you'll need to know how to use. It's coded like this: `<IMG SRC="http://www.dummies.com/testimg.jpg">`. (Note that this is a mythical filename.)

How Internet Explorer manages these relationships when you save a Web page to your hard disk is interesting. Internet Explorer puts the HTML file wherever you tell it to, then creates a folder with the same name, and puts the folder alongside the HTML file. It then goes into the HTML file and changes all the graphics links in it so that they point to the new graphics folder. Pretty cool, and not a bad model for how you might manage your graphics links if you ignore our advice to keep everything in one folder.

Getting the HEIGHT and WIDTH right

You can directly specify the height and width of your image in the `<IMG>` tag. In a sense, this does no good at all. Once your image is downloaded, the Web browser is able to figure out how tall and wide it is. The browser can then rearrange the Web page around the image perfectly well.

The trouble is the element of time. The `HEIGHT` and `WIDTH` attributes save your users both time and aggravation. They save time by allowing all the text in your Web page to download without waiting for the graphic to appear. The Web browser sees the `<IMG>` tag, notes that the `HEIGHT` and `WIDTH` attributes are present, sets aside the appropriate amount of space, and continues to download the text.

Without the `HEIGHT` and `WIDTH` attributes, your Web browser stops, stupefied, at the `<IMG>` tag. It halts all other activity and waits for the downloaded image to be transferred. Only when enough of the image has been downloaded for the browser to figure out its height and width does anything else happen. The poor user is stuck waiting for all this to occur.

See the next section for specifics about the process of downloading a Web page and how it relates to graphics.

There is also a large element of aggravation if these attributes aren't used. If you're using a table-based layout, as is done in most well-designed Web pages these days, the table cells can all be downloaded separately. So far, so good. But if there are no HEIGHT and WIDTH attributes for an image, the table setup may shift disconcertingly during downloading as the browser figures out the actual size of graphics as they appear. It can be really frustrating to start reading the text of a Web page, only to have it lurch alarmingly around as graphics appear and the table is shifted to fit.

The <IMG> tag is not the only culprit in shifting around by content in table-based layouts. The specific way the table is designed is also a culprit. See Chapter 15 for details.

Living in an ALTernate universe

The ALT attribute is for alternative text. Its primary purpose is to provide a textual alternative to the graphic for people who surf the Web with graphics turned off, or who use a text-only browser, or who use assistive software that reads Web pages out loud. As such, the ALT attribute is meant to contain a brief text description of the graphic so that people who can't see the graphic can at least have some idea what it contains.

Nowadays, the ALT text is displayed when a user moves the mouse over a graphic. This is a valuable feature, but it means that ALT text is serving the purpose of amplifying a graphic the user is seeing rather than substituting for a graphic the user is not seeing. For the original approach, a good ALT text description of an image of a Shaker wooden chair is, "A Shaker wooden chair." With the new purpose taken into account, the temptation is to write ALT text like this: "Now 25% off!" You can see the problem — people who can't see the chair are left wondering, "25 percent off what?"

ALT attribute content is also used by search engines to help determine whether a page is relevant to a specific search term. Using descriptive ALT attribute text helps for this purpose as well.

Do use ALT text, but use it for the original purpose: As an alternative to the graphic for those who can't see it. People are becoming so inured to marketing messages that an honest explanation will probably make the user happier than hype anyway.

Here's a fully spelled-out version of an <IMG> tag with a source file and ALT text:

```
<IMG SRC="newcar.jpg" ALT="A shiny blue roadster">
```

IMG options with text

In the early days of the Web, designers spent a great deal of time exploring exactly how to align images with text. That's because there weren't many alternatives for doing so, and the ones that existed didn't work very well.

If you use table-based layouts, you may never have to worry about how text and images align with each other when they are placed cheek-by-jowl. However, if you don't use table-based layouts all the time, alignment options become a big concern. Also, if you know how to use alignment options, you can create more flexible layouts, table-based or not, that work well with a variety of different sizes of images.

Alignment options determine how an image is aligned relative to the text that comes before it and that appears after it. There are two types of alignment options: horizontal alignment, or the left-to-right alignment of an image within a page; and vertical alignment, or the way text is positioned at the top, middle, or bottom of an image.

Vertical alignment was offered in the earliest versions of HTML. It allowed only a single line of text to appear next to a graphic. The text could be aligned to appear at the top, middle, or bottom of a graphic. The options were ALIGN="TOP", ALIGN="MIDDLE", and ALIGN="BOTTOM".

Figure 2-4 shows the results of each vertical alignment option. These options were limiting and helped produce some truly ugly Web pages.

A little later, horizontal alignment options were added to HTML. Now text flowed around an image and could be positioned at the left, right, or middle of a page. (The "middle" attribute was called ABSMIDDLE to differentiate it from the old MIDDLE attribute.) Figure 2-5 shows these alignment options in use.

You can also specify a certain amount of white space around an image. Use the HSPACE and VSPACE attributes to specify the number of pixels of white space you want on the sides of an image (HSPACE) or above and below the image (VSPACE).

If you're going to be working directly in HTML, you should experiment on your own with these attributes to determine exactly how they work. You should do so even if you'll be using table-based layouts — you can make such layouts more flexible by judicious use of the ALIGN attribute.

If you're going to be working with a tool for creating Web pages, it will no doubt expose these attributes to you one way or another. Now that you understand them, you know better than to blame your tool — these are the options HTML makes possible, and you and the program's developers are stuck with them.

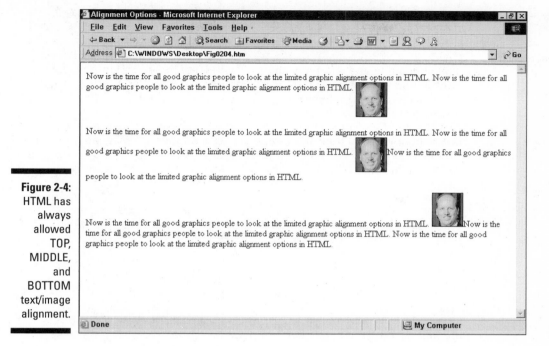

Figure 2-4:
HTML has always allowed TOP, MIDDLE, and BOTTOM text/image alignment.

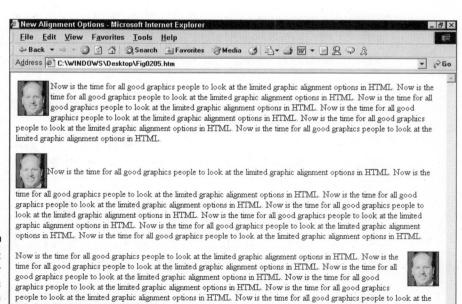

Figure 2-5:
Newer options allow text to flow around an image.

Thumbnail options

One `<IMG>` tag option supports a very creative use of images — as thumbnails that are linked to Web pages. This is the `BORDER` attribute. The `BORDER` attribute specifies the width of any border that appears around an image. If the image is used as a hyperlink, the border appears in the same color as text that's used as a hyperlink.

But wait, you say — how do I use an image as a hyperlink? The answer is simple after you've done it a few times. You create a Web link that is specified by the anchor tag, `<A>`, around the image link.

We're not going to get into the wonders of the anchor tag in detail in this section, or this book, because otherwise it would be just another HTML book. But here's an example of how to make an image a link to a Web page:

```
<A HREF="bigimage.htm"><IMG SRC="small.jpg" HEIGHT="70"
         WIDTH="50" ALT="Thumbnail image of blue car"
         BORDER="2"></A>
```

This code makes the image `small.jpg` a hyperlink. Because of the `BORDER` attribute, a border 2 pixels in width appears around the image. Because of the `<A>` and `</A>` tag pair, clicking `small.jpg` causes the page `bigimage.htm` to appear. Presumably, `bigimage.htm` is a page that highlights a larger version of the image found in the file `small.jpg`.

Figure 2-6 shows an example of a thumbnail image and the larger image linked to it.

As with other HTML tags, you should experiment with these tags if you'll be working directly in HTML. The `HREF` attribute of the `<A>` tag has the same purpose as the `SRC` attribute of the `<IMG>` tag. Like the `SRC` attribute, the `HREF` attribute requires you to specify where the file you're referring to is stored in relation to the HTML file that the `HREF` attribute is in. Otherwise, the `<A>` tag is pretty easy to use, considering how powerful it is.

If you're not going to be writing your own HTML, you need to be aware of the ability to link a small graphic as a thumbnail to another Web page, presumably one with a larger version of the image. Thumbnails allow you to offer large graphics as an option without imposing long download times on people who don't want to wait for them. Look for this capability in your Web page editing program and use it to the hilt.

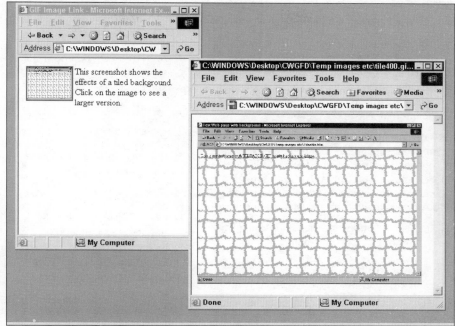

Figure 2-6:
Thumbnails give the user graphics and choices.

Seven Rules for Web Images

Keep these seven rules in mind as you use images in Web pages:

1. Be wary of using tiled background images; they tend to look amateurish.

2. Whenever possible, keep your image files in the same folder as the HTML file that uses them.

3. Be sure to set the height and width of your image in the <IMG> tag.

4. Be sure to provide ALT text to describe your image to people who can't see it.

5. Use thumbnail images to give people the visual interest of graphics without having to wait for large files to download.

6. Link your thumbnails to larger versions so people have the option of seeing the full image.

7. Be aware that graphics are stored and transmitted separately from the HTML page they appear in so you can make the whole page work well for the user.

Watching how images load

One of the oddest things about the Web is just how *decoupled* it is — how little about it is specified up front and how much just happens as users, computer programs, Web servers, and the Internet all work together.

A case in point is how a Web page with graphics is downloaded to your computer. It's natural to think that, when you type a URL such as www.dummies.com into a Web browser, the whole page is downloaded at once. Instead, something much more painstaking occurs:

1. User types URL into Web browser, clicks a link, or chooses a Favorite.

2. A request goes out over the Internet for a specific Web page.

3. A Domain Name Server (DNS) translates the name of the Web page into the DNS number of the Web server plus the path to the file.

4. The revised request is sent out over the Internet.

5. An HTML file, with no associated files, is sent to the client who typed the URL in the first place.

6. The HTML file arrives at the user's computer.

7. The user's Web browser program begins reading the HTML file and displaying the Web page.

8. As soon as the Web browser program sees an <IMG> tag, it makes displaying the image its first priority. The browser requests the file specified by the <IMG> tag. If the height and width are provided, the browser sets aside space and keeps going; if not, the browser may wait until the image downloads before proceeding further.

9. Step 8 is repeated for each <IMG> tag in the HTML file.

10. The page download process completes.

Chapter 3

Creating Great Web Graphics

- -

- -

*T*he rising popularity of the Web has driven the greatest increase in the need for graphics since the invention of hieroglyphics. Hundreds of millions of people now spend many hours each week surfing the Web, looking at page after page of text and graphics. Well-designed pages that load quickly and look sharp have a crucial edge over their less-attractive or slower-loading cousins.

Many graphics professionals bemoan the low resolution of computer screens versus print, the slow speed of most Internet connections, and even the lack of graphical sophistication of users. Don't buy it. Graphics is a more exciting field, with more producers (professional artists and amateurs alike) and more consumers (Web surfers) than ever.

In this chapter, we make clear all the limitations of Web graphics and how to work around them. But don't be fooled into thinking that everything is perfect in the print world. Getting a print job to come out the way you want it is extremely difficult. And when it's wrong, it's wrong big-time. You can easily end up paying for thousands of copies of something that's anywhere from slightly off to downright ugly.

The Web is flexible and fun. Today's mistake can be fixed tomorrow. You can mock up several designs in near-final form in the time it used to take to create one decent pencil sketch. So, as we show you the problems of Web graphics in this chapter, don't forget the good news: The Web is a great new delivery platform that will end up raising the practice of graphics and design to previously unheard-of levels of importance.

What Makes Web Graphics Great

Why is the Web the greatest platform ever invented for graphics? We take a look at some of the key reasons before we plunge into the difficulties you need to work around to show your graphics at their best.

The single best thing about Web graphics is how inexpensive it is to create, store, and publish graphically designed pages full of pictures and other graphic elements. Although print is held up as the gold standard, printing is associated with a huge range of problems. (In fact, the Internet helps solve some of them by making it far easier to transmit large files.)

The Web is also great for graphics because the creation platform is the delivery platform as well. For print, the original is on paper or on the computer screen; the original must somehow be made into a printable master. The final deliverable is printed, by a process the individual designer can't duplicate or test, on paper.

Figure 3-1 shows the process of creating print graphics versus Web graphics. Not only are more steps involved in creating print graphics, but also the time required for each step is greater, costs are greater, and the risk of a mistake is greater. If you've worked with print before, you probably have a horror story about each step; if not, just be glad you're working in a less-troublesome medium. You can even reduce costs and risks by using your Web site as a testbed for materials that end up in printed collateral.

For Web graphics, the original and final versions are both on the computer screen, making it far easier to manage the result. (One caveat, though: The designer or artist is likely to have a bigger and better screen attached to a faster computer and a faster Internet connection than your typical user.)

Unlike print projects, you can work on Web projects quickly and easily across geographic barriers and barriers of time. Many people can collaborate, all ready to see the most current version of the project as it moves closer to general release.

The Web also reaches a much broader range of people than most print projects. Because the Web brings them so much content, most of it free, people who don't speak English as a first language and who may never get to see your work do struggle through it (and gradually learn more English).

The Web also allows you to combine graphics with other media with ease. You always combine graphics with text on the Web, and hyperlinks are always part of the picture as well. You can also add sound, animation, and video to your project. Print supports text, of course, but not hypertext or multimedia.

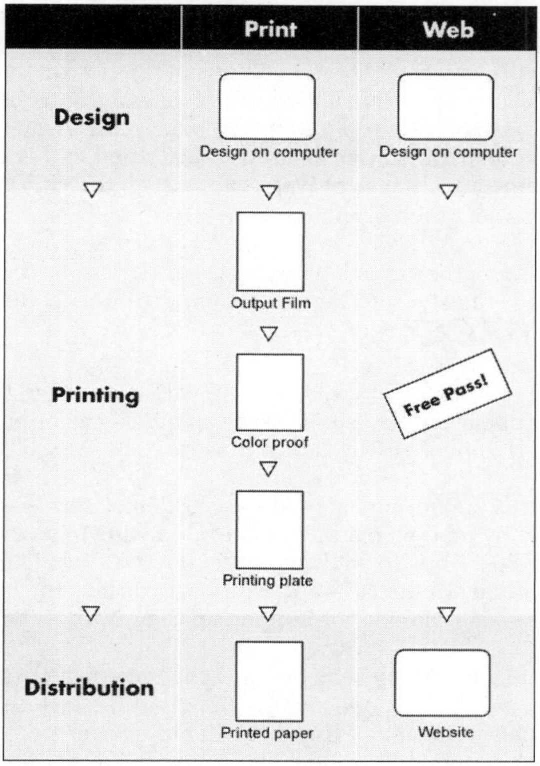

	Print	**Web**
Design	Design on computer	Design on computer
Printing	Output Film Color proof	Free Pass!
Distribution	Printing plate Printed paper	Website

Figure 3-1:
Web graphics are cheaper and easier to create and reach more people than printed graphics.

In addition, people find Web images very attractive. The glow of a computer screen, projecting light through your page designs and graphic images to the user, makes your pages and images attractive in a way that light reflecting off a printed page doesn't.

The Web is also good for the environment. Both creators and recipients of printed literature end up throwing away stacks of expensively produced paper laden with inks, glues, and so on. The Web lets thousands of people view a given piece of information with little adverse environmental impact.

The final immense plus about the Web is that it's great for feedback. After your work is out there, people can just click a feedback link or open an e-mail message and send you feedback on your work. It's much harder to know what people think of your work when it appears in print.

So, as you battle slow download speeds, low-resolution monitors, and other problems, you know that your page designs and Web graphics are much easier to create and publish than they are in print, that you can constantly check the appearance of the work-in-progress against the intended finished product, that your work can easily reach millions of people, that you can collaborate with others across borders and time zones, and that your work will look great. It's not easy to create top-notch Web pages and sharp-looking Web graphics and to overcome difficulties like those described in this chapter. But when you realize all the advantages of Web graphics, all the effort quickly becomes worthwhile.

The Need for Speed

The key problem when creating graphics for the Web is the need for speed. Web pages need to appear on the user's screen as quickly as humanly possible. All too often, they appear slowly rather than quickly.

The usual villain in this melodrama is the lowly modem. Users who have to dial in to the Internet by modem over a regular phone line have modems with speeds ranging from 28.8 Kbps to 56 Kbps, with effective download speeds of 2–4 Kilobytes per second. Modems — and users who access the Internet via modem connections — get blamed for holding up the whole ball of wax.

But this is a simplistic view. Many, many delays can take place between the time that a user requests a Web page and the time that the last pixel of the last graphic in that page appears on the user's computer screen. Users on corporate LANs often experience modem-like delays because of overcrowding on their corporate networks. Internet Service Providers (ISPs) and the architecture of the Internet cause delays, failures in file downloading, and many other problems.

Delays happen to everyone, not just modem users. Even if we all acquired T1 lines tomorrow, the Internet still wouldn't be fast enough. Few people involved in the Internet are ready to accept just how quickly users want things to appear. Users notice delays of three-tenths second or so and feel seriously inconvenienced if they press a key and have to wait longer than one second for the response to appear. That's right — one second. It sometimes takes longer than that just for someone's laptop to find a stored image on the user's hard drive and get it on-screen, let alone to get the image off a server and to transmit it down the wire.

Table 3-1 shows how users experience response times based on research by IBM a few years ago. It's pretty easy to remember: The Holy Grail is response time of .3 seconds or less. Response time under 1 second is pretty good. 1–10 seconds is bad. Anything over 10 seconds, and the user checks out and has to be lured back into thinking about what you're showing them. (An original reason for the popularity of the IBM PC since its introduction in 1980 was the quick response it gave users who were tired of waiting for slow mainframe responses.)

Table 3-1	System Response Times and User Experience	
Time	*Perception*	*Effect*
Less than .3 seconds	Instantaneous response	User has uninterrupted productivity.
.3–1 seconds	Fast response	Brief interruptions in workflow.
1–10 seconds	Slow response	Serious interruptions in workflow.
Greater than 10 seconds	Very slow response	User starts doing some thing else while waiting; returns to system when other task is completed.

If you're having trouble absorbing this tremendous need for speed, you're not alone. Web designers feel pretty good if they create a graphically interesting page that downloads in 15–20 seconds. But users are accustomed to instantaneous response in nearly everything else they do. When you turn a page in a magazine, graphics appear instantly. When you change the channel on a television set, the changeover happens in a fraction of a second. If your TV takes 2–3 seconds to warm up after you turn it on, that seems like a long time.

So even users on fast corporate networks or on other fast connections are frustrated if they have to wait 5, 10, or even 15 seconds for a Web page to appear because it's heavy with graphics or involves network delays or both. However, because their problems are not as great as those of modem-based users (who wait 20, 40, and even 60 seconds for the same pages), the delays that users with fast connections experience are ignored.

The point here is that the pressure for faster Web pages is not going to stop for a long, long time. Web pages are created to be used by people. If people feel like 2 seconds is a long time to wait for a Web page to appear, then it is — no matter how unreasonable that might seem based on today's computer and networking technology. As a Web graphics creator, you're like a greyhound, and the need for fast pages is like a mechanical rabbit — you're going to be chasing it for quite a while.

Why graphics slow pages down so much

There's an old saying that "a picture is worth a thousand words." Unfortunately, a picture takes a lot longer to transmit over the Web than a thousand words takes.

A typical Web page full of text might contain 250 words, with about 6 characters per word. Each character takes 1 byte, so that's about 1.5K total for a page of text. This amount of data takes less than 1 second to transmit over the Web, even over a slow connection. (It actually takes 3–4 seconds after clicking a link to receive an all-text page because of the time it takes to send the request and set up the file transfer.)

A small JPEG image used as a thumbnail or a photo illustration for a story might take up as little as 3–4K. That's more space (and time) than a thousand words consume. This adds a couple of seconds of transmission time over a modem. A large picture takes up 30–40K, and that means 10–15 seconds of transmission time.

If you're creating graphics for use on an existing Web site, you may be doomed before you even start as far as total download time is concerned. Many sites have navigation graphics — perhaps a left-hand navigation bar plus a couple of other navigation elements that contribute 20–30K of files that need to be downloaded before any text or graphics appears in the Web page. Every picture you add in the main part of the page simply increases the size of a page that's already on the way to being too large.

In addition to file size, there are two other tolls on the user that grow with the number of graphics in a page: request overhead and file transfer risk. Each link to a graphics file that you include on a Web page, no matter how small the graphic, must be deciphered by the Web browser, formatted into a request, sent out onto the Web, decoded by a domain name server, sent to the Web page's file servers, queued, processed, and then fulfilled by transmitting the file. The request and the file might each make five to ten stops at various routers on their way from your computer to the Web server and back. The miracle is that it all works as well as it does.

There's also a risk associated with file transfers. Each file transfer has a risk of failure, and each failure causes a lengthy delay while the request is re-issued and fulfilled. Unfortunately, the more separate files that appear on a given Web page, the more risk there is of a time-consuming file transmission failure.

The point here is not to avoid graphics in creating Web pages — otherwise, this would be a very short book. The point is that you always have to be mindful of file size and — a point most people are unaware of — file count when designing Web pages. Simple, clean page designs that use white space liberally as a design element aren't desirable only from an aesthetic point of view; they're also likely to load faster and more reliably than fussier, more complicated designs.

How to speed up your Web pages

The most important secret to creating fast-loading Web graphics lies in the design of each Web page on your site. If the navigation for your site is heavy with large graphics files, each page is going to load slowly, no matter how severely you compress that JPEG image of the boss drinking champagne at the company party. Similarly, if the navigation is light but you include four large photos on a given page, there's no way that page is going to load quickly.

So make sure that the pages of your site are designed so that it's easy for the page to load quickly. Here are a few rules that will help you achieve that goal:

- **Make navigation and overall Web pages light.** Light means less than 10K in size, including graphics and the HTML file that defines the page. (JavaScript and badly written HTML can balloon the size of the HTML file well over 10K.)

- **Make navigation consistent.** *Consistent* means reusing as many images as possible, which increases the odds that the page will update faster due to *caching,* which we discuss in detail later in this chapter in the section, "Caching helps and hurts."

- **Make all repeated page elements light and consistent.** We were consultants for a company that kept banner ads below 10K in almost all cases to guarantee fast page loading. You should put all repeated elements of your Web page on a budget of this type.

- **Define small areas for images.** Set up page templates so that image slots are small; for example, shots to illustrate a news story might be 50 pixels wide by 70 pixels tall. You should also have templates for big images in your hip pocket, but make the small areas the starting point.

- **Define flexible areas for images.** If you or someone you work with has the skill, create templates that allow for a variety of image sizes. People often put a larger-than-necessary image in because the template doesn't allow for a tall but narrow image or a short but wide one. Make templates flexible.

- **Link to large images.** If it's important that an image be large, provide a small version initially as a thumbnail. Then give users who are on a fast connection, or willing to wait for a download, the opportunity to click and see the full-size image.

✔ **Experiment with image creation and compression.** Try using a mono-chrome or grayscale image in place of a color image. Replace a color gradient with a flat background that compresses better. Try several levels of compression on each JPEG file and use the smallest file size among the decent-looking results.

Tricks like these can help you create great-looking pages that download in half or even less time than they previously did and that give you greater freedom to drop in a big image of that Ferrari when nothing else will do.

Figure 3-2 shows a page from the Zanzara Web site. It uses light, consistent navigation throughout and uses small images as highlights to the text, not as opportunities for artistic expression by the photographer. It's visually interesting and fast to load.

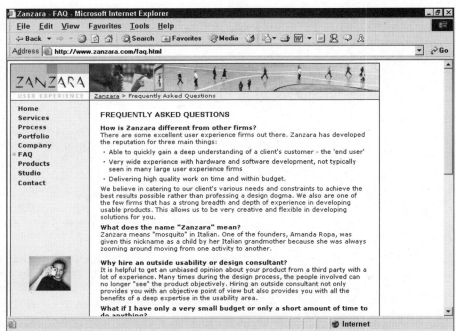

Figure 3-2:
The Zanzara site does it right.

How to make waiting almost pleasant

Page design sets the stage for success or failure in achieving rapid Web page download time. Good page design can make the waiting that does occur almost pleasant. On the other hand, poor page design can make your site almost impossible to use, even if the result looks good and works well when fully downloaded.

The secret is to take advantage of the fact that text downloads much faster than graphics. If you do things right, users will be able to see the text on your page and start reading it almost instantly. On a well-designed page, the text appears quickly, and then it stays stable as graphics download in and around it. Users can even find and click links well before graphics begin to download.

Protecting your <IMG>

There are two levels at which page design affects the user's experience of the graphics on your page. The first, lowest level is the level of the individual graphic. When you place a graphic on your Web page, you have the opportunity to specify its height and width (in pixels) in the HTML code you're writing or in the tool you're using to create the Web page. The resulting HTML code looks something like this:

```
<IMG SRC="joegrins.jpg" W="50" H="70">
```

This code causes the Web page to create an area 50 pixels wide and 70 pixels tall in which to display the graphic joegrins.jpg and then to request the graphic and display it as it appears. The Web page requests the graphic without having any foreknowledge of its dimensions or its file size. The only thing the browser knows is the size of the box in which to display the image — and it knows that much only if you tell it, via the WIDTH and HEIGHT attributes.

If your browser doesn't see these attributes, it just requests the graphic and gradually displays it in the spot just after the previous thing it was told to display. If it does see the WIDTH and HEIGHT attributes, though, interesting things ensue.

First, your Web browser sets aside a box of the right size, say, 50 pixels wide by 70 pixels high, using the preceding line of HTML code. Then it sends a request for the graphic, but because it was warned of the correct proportions, it can also keep right on displaying the rest of the page. The Web browser can usually display all the text and fire off several more requests for images if needed before much of the first graphic even appears.

If the image is the right size — again, 50 x 70 in this example — everything is great. People are usually careful with their images and <IMG> tags, so this is usually what happens: The page downloads smoothly, the image displays correctly, and you and the user are both happy.

If the width and height are not actually 50 x 70 — a mismatch you need to try hard to avoid — what happens next depends on how the image varies from the stated display size:

- ✔ **Image is too small but in proportion (with a 5 to 7 ratio of width to height):** The image is stretched gracefully to the needed size. Pixelation of the image occurs because of stretching.

- ✔ **Image is too small but out of proportion:** The image is stretched disproportionately to the needed size. Pixelation occurs because of stretching, and a funhouse-mirror effect occurs because the stretching is disproportionate.

- ✔ **Image is too large but in proportion:** The image is shrunk gracefully to the needed size. The effect is usually invisible to the user. However, the user has to wait for a large image to download, yet only gets to view a small one.

- ✔ **Image is too large but out of proportion:** The image is shrunk disproportionately to the needed size. Extra download time is incurred because the image is too large, and a funhouse-mirror effect occurs because the stretching is disproportionate.

Pixelation is not the same thing as *pixilation*. Pixelation occurs when manipulating a graphic causes chunky or blotchy areas — chunks of pixels of the same or very similar color — to appear. Pixilation is what occurs when someone has had too much to drink. Be careful to whom you're speaking before you point to a badly compressed photograph of someone and say, "she's pixelated."

Figure 3-3 shows all the possible things that can happen to a 50 x 70 image that's displayed at various height and width attributes specified by the <IMG> tag. Watch out that these problems aren't happening to you!

It's embarrassing when you specify that an image that's, say, taller than it is wide must be displayed so that it's wider than it is tall. The image will be stretched, in one dimension or the other, almost beyond recognition. But at least this mistake is easy to see and fix.

Specifying that a small image should be displayed larger than its actual size but more or less in proportion is anywhere from a minor embarrassment to a good thing. If the stretch is too great, the picture will look bad. (Of course, most pictures on the Web, being more or less heavily compressed, look somewhat bad anyway.) But the user only had to wait for a smaller file to download before seeing the somewhat ugly result. The enlargement is proportional, and if the stretch is too great, the mistake is again easy to see and easy to fix.

The big disaster, and one that happens all too often, is the third problem in the preceding list. A large image is shrunk, more or less proportionally, to fit in a smaller space. The problem is that the user has to wait while a big file downloads. Most of the information in the file is then wasted as the image is squeezed into a small onscreen space for display. And you may never realize this has happened. We recently visited a Web page where a 500K full-page image was being displayed in a slot about 80 x 80 pixels in size — a slot that can usually be filled by a JPEG image of 10K–20K. Users dialing up via modem were being forced to wait several minutes for a file that should have been resized to download in 10 seconds!

The only way to ensure avoiding this problem is to check the properties of each image in your Web page after you publish it on the Web. To do so, just right-click the image in the Web page and choose Properties. The image's properties, including its file size, appear. This might seem like an overly cautious thing to do, but it is the only way to ensure that what you get (via the file download process) is what you see on-screen and not something that's more than you need.

If you test your Web page only on your own machine before the uploading process, you can't know whether a different file replaced your carefully crafted masterpiece of compression. Testing file sizes on your own machine is important, but testing after the page and its associated graphics are live on the Web server is vital. Just right-click any image on a Web page and choose Properties; when the information box appears, check the image's file size and dimensions.

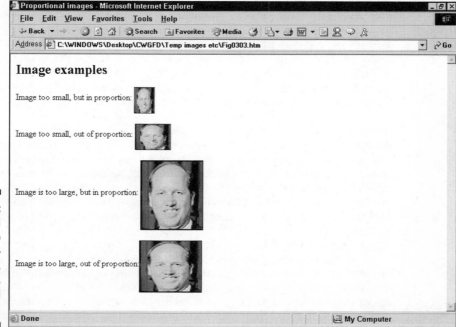

Figure 3-3: When IMG tags go bad — stretching, scrunching, and shrinking!

Get yourself to a machine that's connected to the Web via a modem and check your site on it as often as possible during the development and deployment process. This helps you spot errors, such as images that aren't resized, and also makes you painfully aware of the whole issue of download time. It's great to take everyone involved in a Web site's development to someone's home and have them try this. It makes people "get religion" about file size and page weight issues.

Table-ing the motion of shifty pages

Incorrectly sized images are fairly easy to avoid, though they're a big problem when they do occur. Bad table sizing is much harder to avoid, and it can be an even worse problem.

Tables, as you probably know, are often used to lay out Web pages. A typical Web page may be made up of three large cells — a wide strip across the top to hold a company logo and perhaps a banner ad, a narrow strip down the left edge to hold navigation, and a big blob of an area in the middle-right to hold the main content of the Web page. Each of these cells can hold text, formatting, graphics, and additional tables.

The width of each table cell can be set explicitly or implicitly. That is, you can explicitly specify a WIDTH attribute, which will probably be respected as the table downloads. (You may need to place a special graphic to hold the table cell open if the user narrows the browser window; more on this and other table tricks in Chapter 15.) Or you can simply allow the table cells to resize themselves as content downloads. This sets the table width implicitly — the width of each cell, and of the table as a whole, is set by the contents of the cells. If you're designing and implementing your own Web pages along with your own Web graphics, see *Web Design For Dummies,* by Lisa Lopuck (Wiley Publishing, Inc.) for details on how to make your pages work properly.

The trouble with allowing the table cells to resize themselves as content downloads is that the process of resizing is often very visible to the user. We've all started to read the text of a Web page as the page downloads, only to see the page lurch disconcertingly as some new chunk of content appears. This process is worsened if you have images in your Web page with no WIDTH and HEIGHT attributes; as the images download, the table cells go through real contortions as they resize to accommodate the new content.

It also makes a great deal of difference how wide the user has set the browser window. Many table layouts are partly or completely flexible; one or more columns are allowed to float in width, depending on how wide the user sets the browser window. You can actually make yourself seasick by widening and narrowing the window of a flexibly laid-out Web page as it downloads, especially if it's one that lurches into a new shape each time new content appears.

Some Web pundits have recently ventured the opinion that tables should be locked down and fixed in size so that users are obligated to set their window width wide enough to show all the content — so that making the window extra wide gets the user nothing but extra, empty space on the right margin. The rationale has two parts: First, that it's very hard to create a Web page that resizes well in response to anything and everything a user might do to the window size; second, that users will be confused by a resizable page when they're used to fixed-width pages in books, magazines, and many Web sites. We sympathize with this view. Unless you have a good reason for floating the width of your page, use tables to create a fixed-width, consistent, attractive, and highly usable Web page.

We believe that, in most cases, you should completely "lock down" your page layouts by making them a fixed width and by specifying the size of each element of your page in advance. Use the WIDTH and HEIGHT attributes of the <IMG> tag, the WIDTH attribute of the <TABLE> tag, and careful planning, calculation, and testing to make sure that all the elements of your Web page are predetermined and consistent in size.

Designing for the first panel

You can design your page so that the area visible to typical users before they scroll down — the first screenful of content — loads first, giving users an attractive initial image relatively quickly. Possible, but not easy.

The basic technique is to define the width of all table cells and the height and width of all graphics within a table that extends down to the level at which the first screenful of content ends. Content "below the fold" goes in a second table. The user sees the area above the fold fill in quickly.

However, there are several problems with this. The first problem is specifying how big the first screenful is. A full-height Web browser window running on a monitor set to 1280 x 1024 allows almost four times as much vertical space as the tiny Web page area left within the AOL client on an 800 x 600 laptop. If you optimize for one, you're going to miss the boat on the other.

Another problem is the mechanical difficulty of implementing and maintaining such changes. Web pages are changed all the time. The clever trick that made the visible part of a page load quickly one day becomes more of a stupid human trick when a change to the page leaves you with a mixed bag in terms of smooth page downloading.

The concerns of a Web page designer can quickly overlap with the concerns of a networking engineer! Don't try to do too much here, at least not until you are working on a very successful site where optimizing specific pages for various platforms becomes worthwhile. Just be aware of the concerns and tradeoffs and try to avoid the worst design and downloading pitfalls in your own Web pages.

If you're the beneficiary of — or, as it may seem when things don't work, the victim of — page layouts that are imposed on you by the organization in which you work or by a template-driven Web page tool, you may believe that there's nothing you can do. But, actually, quite a bit is in your power.

First off, you need to realize that creating templates that work on a wide range of browsers and with various user settings is hard work. It may seem very controlling that someone makes you crop, resize, and modify your square photo into a tall rectangle, but often that's the way it is, at least in the short term.

You can request changes to the template that make it more dependable and useful for a wider range of content. It takes creativity on your part and on the part of your organization to make templates better. You can also modify the template after you get it to make it work better. And above all, you can test, adjust, and test again to make sure that the Web pages you're responsible for work well.

Caching helps and hurts

Caching is the practice of storing Web files locally so that they don't have to be retrieved from the Internet every time they're needed in a Web page. Caching can be your best friend as a graphics designer — and your worst enemy when it comes to actually getting information to your users.

First, imagine: Wouldn't it be great if any file you downloaded once stayed on your hard disk forever, so that it would pop up quickly on your screen when needed? Only changed files would be downloaded. Because text files (small) change much more than graphics files (large), even changes would usually be downloaded quickly. Such an approach would greatly reduce Internet traffic and total page download time for millions of users.

The trouble is that the Web doesn't have a standard way of tracking changes in a file between one time the user visits a Web page and the next. So everybody caches — ISPs, your online program, your Web browser, Windows and other operating systems, and even custom utilities you can download and use while surfing the Web. And everyone messes it up. It's very common for users to download files they already have or to access a cached file and see old information when new information has replaced an older file of the same name in the meantime.

As a Web author and graphics designer, you benefit tremendously from caching. When a user visits a Web page on your site with, say, ten files on it — the HTML file with text and formatting, plus nine graphics files — some or all of them may be retrieved from a local cache on the user's hard disk, the ISP's cache, or elsewhere, greatly speeding the appearance of the Web page in the user's browser.

But you'll also suffer. Every time you update an existing page, you have to worry that only some users will see the new information; others will find old, cached versions of the page for hours or even days after you've published the update.

Users can get around caching by clicking the Refresh button in their browsers or even holding down the Shift key and then clicking Refresh (which means "update everything, darn it"). When they do, they receive all the files sent all the way from the Web server — and wait all the time it takes all the files to download. The trouble is, users often don't know that they need to reload, or they do so when it's not necessary.

So don't count on caching to reduce the impact of large graphics in your Web pages. It's a mixed blessing at best, and it doesn't help users whose caches have dropped the offending files or who click the reload button to ensure that they see the latest and greatest version of your Web page.

You Say You Want a Resolution

If you, as a creator of graphics for the Web, are a painter, then the PC screen is your canvas. The position you're in is much, much different than that of someone who creates graphics on the PC for later printing on paper. Your delivery platform is known in advance, and it has quite a few benefits, idiosyncrasies, and problems.

The resolution will not be televised

TVs don't really have resolution in the same sense as PC monitors. You can't separately address the points on a TV screen one pixel at a time as you can on a PC. The electron beam on a TV sweeps across the monitor in such a way that the color of one pixel affects the possible colors of the next pixel over.

A personal computer monitor is a marvel of precision compared to television. (And you'll miss PC monitors very much if you ever have to design Web pages or other static content for TV.) Each pixel on a PC monitor can have its color controlled independently. You can put white pixels next to black next to green next to orange ones without worrying about the order of creation or display. (You may have to worry about your paycheck after putting white, black, green, and orange together, but that's another issue.)

Today's PC monitors — even most laptop monitors — are *multisynching* monitors. The effect of this is that such monitors can display multiple resolutions. Users are not always aware of this, but most of them can run at 800 x 600 or 1024 x 768 resolution, even on a laptop; and many desktop PC users can run at 1280 x 1024 or even 1600 x 1200 as well. Many laptop users can hook up an external monitor as a replacement for their built-in laptop screen, and some can even run both the built-in screen and the external monitor as one connected, two-part Windows or Macintosh desktop.

These various resolution possibilities have strong implications for Web graphics. Table 3-2 shows the total number of pixels that are available on the screen at various resolutions. You can imagine the download time needed to deliver a high-resolution graphic that uses every one of the 1,920,000 pixels on a 1600 x 1200 resolution screen!

Table 3-2		Pixel Counts on Various Screens			
Resolution	*Total Pixels*	*@256 Colors*	*@Thousands*	*@Millions*	*w/Alpha*
640 x 480	307,200	300K	600K,	900K	1.2MB
800 x 600	480,000,	469K	938K,	1.37MB	1.83MB
1024 x 768	786,432,	768K	1.5MB,	2.25MB	3MB
1280 x 1024	1,310,720	1.28MB,	2.56MB	3.84MB,	5.12MB

In taking resolution into account, not only the absolute size of the screen but also user habits must be considered. Users with big, high-resolution desktop monitors tend to surf the Web with tall, relatively narrow browser windows so that they can use their monitor as a two-page display. These users often have to squint to make out text that appears tiny on their high-resolution screens. Users with screens limited to 800 x 600 — or who prefer to use that resolution so that they can easily make out text — often run in full-screen mode, and their browser windows are short and squat. If you display your text in a large font or use too much white space, these users may see only a few hundred words before having to scroll.

Many users running at 800 x 600 use ISPs, such as AOL or CompuServe, and view the Web through a window running in the overall AOL or CompuServe client software. This software takes up much of the top of the monitor space with control buttons and menus for the client software program. It also pops up Instant Messenger, news, and advertising subwindows that the user has to close or try to work around. Very few of the pixels on an 800 x 600 screen are left for your Web page after the AOL or CompuServe client software is accounted for as well!

Figure 3-4 shows a Web page being displayed on the AOL client on an 800-x-600-resolution screen. You can imagine how many times a user on such a system has to scroll down to read a long article or how carefully they have to scroll to make a large table or graphic fully visible.

DPI and resolution

Artists don't generally think of resolution in terms of the total number of pixels; they usually prefer to think in dots per inch, or dpi. A low-resolution color laser printout is 300 dpi; most home inkjet printers today print at 600 or even 1200 dpi. High-quality professional presses go even higher.

A computer monitor, by contrast, typically works at a measly 72 or 96 dpi, depending on the monitor size and the total number of pixels being displayed on-screen. At 72 dpi, you have one-sixteenth the pixels per square inch as are available on that low-resolution color laser printout; at 96 dpi, about one-ninth, just over 10 percent. The limited resolution available on a computer monitor is one of the main reasons artists complain so much about the low quality of Web graphics.

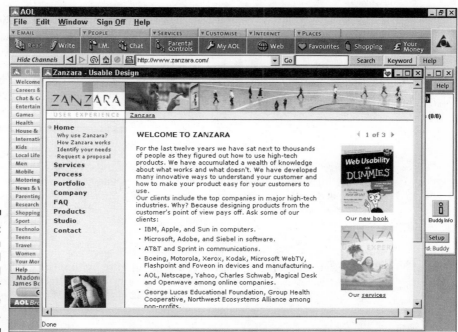

Figure 3-4:
Put AOL on a small monitor and watch your Web space disappear.

An immodest proposal

Let us make a proposal right here and now: A few additional Internet standards should be adopted to speed up graphics transmission.

Under this proposal, HTML files would never be cached; they're relatively small and are far more likely to contain recent updates than graphics files.

Graphics files would always be cached: After a user downloads a given graphics file from a given Web site, he or she would never have to wait for that file again. If the Web publisher wanted to update a graphics file, the publisher would have to replace it with a different file with a new name rather than modifying an existing file. This change would be reflected in the HTML file, which never gets cached, and . . . ta-daa! . . . suddenly no one would ever get an out-of-date Web page again.

Graphics files would also be compressed and packaged using ZIP or another popular algorithm. Web authors could deliver one, two, or more graphics files for a specific Web page in a single ZIP package. The ZIP file would be slightly smaller and, more important, its use would reduce the number of file requests and file transfers zipping back and forth over the Internet.

The relationship between the ZIP package and individual graphics files could be worked out by file-naming conventions or be statements in the header area of a Web page. Server administrators or site engineers could manage this with no effort on the part of individual Web page authors.

These proposals would eliminate the problem of users seeing out-of-date Web content and would free up huge amounts of bandwidth on the Web. Web graphics designers and Web authors would be free to do more in their Web pages without imposing long download times on users.

What are the odds of such proposals being adopted? There are strong vested interests on the side of not changing anything about the Web, and the standards process has ground almost to a halt as the influence of commercial interests on the Web has increased. So the odds are very low. But it's good to dream — and to think creatively about ways you can reduce download times for users of your own site.

Another problem is the wide variation in color and overall quality between various computer monitors. Desktop monitors vary widely in color and brightness. Laptop screens, based on a totally different display technology, are different still. Both types of monitors degrade with age, getting darker and often shifting toward purplish tones.

There are some compensations, however, for these problems. The first is that computer screens are *backlit,* with light going from behind the image toward the viewer. This gives all but the dimmest monitors more light coming from the image than a typical printed graphic, which is illuminated by reflected light.

Another is that the low resolution of computer monitors makes the problem of downloading Web graphics to the screen much easier. Because the monitor can display only 72 dpi or 96 dpi anyway, there's no point in downloading a multi-megabyte, print-ready, high-resolution graphic. The relatively low-resolution graphics that a PC screen can display match up well with the need to use graphics with small file sizes that download quickly.

Buying images is also much cheaper at low resolutions, and retouching them is easier as well. The dots that make up an image aren't truly cheaper by the dozen!

The final point is somewhat depressing, but important. The low resolution that computer users are accustomed to lowers expectations for Web graphics. Your graphics may be, by the standards of even the cheesiest printer, awful; but computer users are accustomed to that. Someday, we'll all have fast Internet connections and ultra-high-resolution monitors; but until then, users don't expect much from typical Web graphics. If you can create Web pages that are well designed, sporting graphics that look good, your site will be way ahead of most of the Web sites out there.

Is there life after (color) depth?

You've probably heard of the Web-safe color palette with its 216 colors. We believe that so few users face this limitation today that you can safely ignore it. But let us quickly spell out why it exists, why it's becoming less important, and when you might still want to take it into account.

The maximum color depth at which users can run their monitors is inversely related to the maximum resolution at which they can run. Almost any computer monitor today can display millions of colors, but the computer driving the display is more limited. If the computer dedicates one byte (8 bits) to each pixel on the screen, that allows up to 256 colors to be displayed on-screen.

256 colors isn't enough for everything you'd like to do with computer-generated graphics, and it's not nearly enough for photographs. A photograph uses thousands of shades of color to create the subtle gradations that your eye translates into information about depth, shading, and lighting angles. To support thousands of shades of color requires 2 bytes per pixel. To support millions of shades of color per pixel — which is best for high-resolution, naturalistic images — requires 3 bytes. Special effects, such as transparency or text overlays, can bring the total up to 4 bytes per pixel.

Graphic artists and designers always like to have a wide color palette to work from and typically have computer systems that offer them a palette of millions of colors. However, in the early days of the Web, many users were running at 256 colors. Many computers, especially laptops, could support no more; other systems were purposefully set to 256 colors so that they would run faster or so that a game or other graphics-intensive program would work correctly.

When a computer system that can display only 256 colors attempts to display a graphic that contains millions of colors, it uses a technique called *dithering* to replace the unavailable colors with patterns composed from among the 256 colors. Dithered graphics are usually pretty darn ugly compared to the originals.

In order to avoid dithering, designers began to limit themselves to 256 colors. Then they found that not all computer systems could show the same 256 colors. A safe set of 216 colors was defined that worked the same on Windows-based PCs as well as Macintosh computers. The Web-safe color palette was born.

These days, only about ten percent or fewer of the typical Web surfers are running a computer that's limited to 256 colors, and dithering, while less than optimal, is not that bad. So, many designers are again working from the "thousands of colors" palette to offer more attractive Web pages to most users at the expense of dithered patterns appearing on the screens of a few. It's quite possible that people you work with, or clients, have strong and differing opinions about this issue. Ask around before choosing an approach. In this book, we discuss the Web-safe color palette as an option to consider when creating Web graphics, but we don't recommend that you use it as an absolute limitation on the number of colors with which you work.

Part II
Discovering and Using Cool Graphics Tools

The 5th Wave   By Rich Tennant

In this part . . .

An artisan is only as good as the tools that he or she accumulates over the years. But now all-in-one tools mean that you can get hold of a great tool set very quickly and affordably. What you do with the tools is what makes the difference. In this part, we show you a free tool and some very good, very affordable tools, and how to use them.

Chapter 4

Cool Tools for Web Graphics

. . . .

In This Chapter

▶ Choosing Web graphics tools

▶ Identifying keys to using a bitmap tool

▶ Touring Microsoft Paint

▶ Using Paint Shop Pro

▶ Using Photoshop and Photoshop Elements

. . . .

*T*his chapter is about how to use a few specific graphics tools to make graphics ready for the Web. These graphics can be images you create in another program, images you capture with a digital camera or scanner, or images you create in the Web-specific tool itself. The source of the graphic doesn't matter; what's important is getting the graphic ready to be published on the Web.

In this chapter, we discuss a free program, Microsoft Paint; an affordable program, Paint Shop Pro; and an expensive program, Photoshop, and its affordable sibling, Photoshop Elements. We introduce these programs and begin to describe how to use them to create or modify graphics expressly for the Web.

Why focus on these three from among the other available graphics programs? Because they're all bitmap-oriented — adapted to working with pixels one at a time, rather than with smooth, idealized lines and curves — because they all have Web-specific features, and because they may be the three most popular Web graphics programs.

Choosing Your Tools

You may have one or more graphics tools on your system already. Figuring out what each one does and whether you should use it can be frustrating. We're here to make it simple for you.

Why are there so many tools?

Many tools exist for creating graphics, including object-oriented drawing programs like Adobe Illustrator, CorelDraw, and Macromedia FreeHand. Such tools make it easy to draw, change your drawing as you go along, and save it in a variety of formats — including, these days, the Web image formats GIF and JPEG. But the tools don't make it easy for you to work with your graphic at the level of individual dots, or pixels.

Figure 4-1 shows a screenshot taken from Adobe Illustrator. The program has a drawing area, a range of tools, and palettes for choosing things such as the current color. It's like a painter's studio, with a big canvas ready to be painted on.

There are also specific tools for Web graphics. You can convert files into JPEG or GIF format, create GIF animations, and much more.

There are so many tools because there are so many different needs. Sometimes you need to create, in which case, you need to work with a tool that reflects what you're thinking. Other times you need to model, so you want to use a tool that creates an image to represent something that will be produced in the real world, such as a dress or a building. And at other times, you need to edit — to maybe fine-tune an image, perhaps for printing, perhaps for display on the Web.

Figure 4-1:
Illustrator lets you create freely.

When should you use a bitmap editor?

A *bitmap editor* is a graphics program that makes it easy for you to work on graphics one pixel at a time. The name comes from thinking of a graphic as an array of dots — a bitmap. A bitmap editor gives you fine control of each pixel on the screen.

Using a bitmap editor for Web graphics makes good sense because of two limitations of working on the Web: the low resolution of the user's screen and the long download times that many users endure for graphics. Every pixel in your graphic has to count.

Bitmap editors are great for photographs because photographs are just collections of dots; a photograph doesn't know an arm from a leg from a tree. A bitmap editor lets you edit the dots.

Many of the best graphics programs are not bitmap-oriented. There isn't one catchy overall name for these programs, but we'll call them *illustration programs.* These programs store images as groups of objects. The objects are built from vectors — lines or curves that can be completely described mathematically. Another name for illustration programs is *vector drawing programs.*

If you draw a 2-inch square in an illustration program, your drawing will be stored just that way. When you display your square on the screen, print it on a cheap printer, or print it on a fancy printer, the program looks back at its original description and does its darnedest to output something that looks like a 2-inch square. A bitmap editor, on the other hand, displays or prints a certain number of pixels, even

if that means you have a 2-inch square on one screen, a 3.7-inch square on another, and a ½-inch square on a printer.

Illustration programs are great for drawing; they enable you to draw all sorts of wild shapes, colors, and fills. But a bitmap editor can do that, too. Where an illustration program shines is in editing your graphics, which you do while you're drawing in the first place and when you come back later to make changes.

Illustration programs work better for editing because they remember the separate objects you created as part of building up the object. If you draw a circle and then fill it with red, the illustration program lets you grab the circle and stretch it or shrink it. The filled area stretches and shrinks with the circle. You can draw a square that overlaps your circle and still grab and edit the square or the circle separately.

A bitmap editor gets confused when you try to edit overlapping objects. It thinks of everything you draw as a bunch of pixels. So when you draw a circle, then overlap it with a square, you can no longer grab one or the other. You have to get in there and select and move the pixels you want by their location on the screen — or give up and start over.

It's best to do creative work in an object-oriented drawing program like Adobe Illustrator or Macromedia Freehand. But when it comes time to prepare your drawing for display on the Web, use a bitmap editor. That's why — no offense to other programs — nearly all professional Web designers have a copy of Photoshop on their desktops.

At a given point in the process, you may have a range of needs. You don't want to start six or seven different programs to draw an image in order to add color, edit, and print. You want to use a single program that can do it all. Yet you don't want to have to buy an expensive, full-featured program to convert a bunch of graphics from one format to another, let alone go through the process of opening and resaving each file from within the expensive program. You want a simple converter that will do the whole job in one or two steps.

We recommend that you work in an illustration program to produce original graphics that involve creativity. We also suggest that you use one of our recommended bitmap editors, or similar functionality in a program you already own, to prepare your graphics for the Web.

Keys to using a bitmap editor

Before you decide to use a bitmap-editing program, consider the following:

- ✔ **Think about how bitmap works.** Bitmap editors don't remember objects. If you draw a line bisecting a circle, you can't select that line again; the line and the circle are a mish-mash of pixels. You also can't fill the circle with a color; you can fill the area within the top half of the circle and then the bottom half, but you can't select the bisected circle and fill the whole thing. Something that may be easy to do at an early stage of your work becomes nearly impossible a few minutes later. You may find yourself giving the Undo option a real workout, or giving up on an effect that you want to create out of sheer frustration.

- ✔ **Envision the final result.** In order to make good use of your time and money with a bitmap editor, you have to plan ahead. (You save time by planning ahead because doing so enables you to accomplish tasks in one or two tries; you'll save money because you won't throw your computer through the window in disgust.)

- ✔ **Make a rough sketch.** Do a quick and dirty sketch with the major elements in place — wrong colors or no colors, approximate shapes, basic fonts — and show it around or try it on your Web page. Then do the same with other concepts, saving each one in turn, before you commit to one approach. Give yourself a chance to figure out the right thing before you spend several hours doing the wrong thing.

- ✔ **Budget time before you start.** Spending hours working on things you never use or optimizing things that end up nearly invisible on the screen when you put up your Web page is easy. Likewise, don't get distracted by a new tool that can tempt you to experiment for hours. Experiment all you want when you're not working on a project.

✔ **Realize time and effort rise exponentially with the complexity of the image.** An image with ten elements is not twice as hard to get right as an image with five elements; it's ten times more complicated. Each element you add is likely to make you want to tweak some existing element, which is now hopelessly enmeshed in pixels from other elements, making it impossible to edit cleanly. Think carefully before setting out to create a complicated image in a bitmap editor; consider working in an illustration program first. As your skill level increases, you may be able to get the same flexibility in a bitmap editor by carefully using layers to separate various elements of your work.

✔ **Start with a clean original image.** Whether your starting point is a file imported from another program, a screen capture, or a drawing done in the bitmap program, you should always save using a complete original copy. Then save additional copies as you go along. You'll gradually learn to sense a group of changes coming and to save just before that happens, enabling you to get back to where you started.

✔ **Delay adding text.** Add text late in the process and save a version of your graphics file before clicking the text button. Check your time budget before you start experimenting with text.

✔ **Keep your text simple and readable.** Fancy fonts that look striking to you at the time can easily look cheesy after a project is out the door. Use italics and bolding sparingly, and underlining rarely or never — on the Web, an underline indicates a link, so don't use underlining for emphasis. If you keep things simple and develop a consistent approach, you can create professional-looking text elements in your graphics.

Introducing three top tools

Here are details about three tools you can use for your Web graphics. Each is at a different price point and each meets different purposes.

✔ **Microsoft Paint:** Paint, as we'll call it, is a free tool that comes with every copy of Windows. It's a simple bitmap editor that handles a variety of graphics tasks quickly and well.

✔ **Paint Shop Pro:** Paint Shop Pro is an affordable and highly capable tool. It costs about $100 for a full license, and it can do most daily graphics tasks quickly and well.

✔ **Adobe Photoshop:** Photoshop is the king of computer graphics tools. Photoshop's list price is $595. Photoshop alone can handle a huge range of tasks, and the program supports thousands of add-ons that can do many more things. If you don't have a copy of Photoshop, consider Photoshop Elements, which we use in this book. It does most of what Photoshop does for around $100 a copy.

Trial versions of Paint Shop Pro and Photoshop Elements are available on the CD-ROM that comes with this book. These are fully capable versions of the software, but they work for only a few weeks each. To keep using the programs after that time, you must buy fully licensed copies.

Using a screen capture as an example

Windows includes support for capturing the current screen image in Windows — you just press the PrtScrn key. (It may have a slightly different name on your keyboard, but the name will be something like PrtScrn.) Pressing PrtScrn copies the current screen image to the Windows clipboard in 24-bit bitmap image format (the default Windows format for graphics). From there, you can paste it into almost any Windows program, including such seemingly unlikely candidates as Microsoft Word and Excel.

Of course, people rarely use the whole screen from a screen capture. They usually just want one window or part of a window. That's where our bitmap graphics programs come in. We describe in the following sections how to use each tool to copy part of the screen image and save it as a separate file.

Capturing an image of the current screen turns out to be a surprisingly important function when creating Web graphics. You often want to show people just what you're doing — a screen capture of a Web page or part of a Web page does that beautifully. People can even mark up the captured image with comments. You also may want to capture others' Web pages as inspiration for your own or for guidance on what not to do on your own page.

Doing a screen capture is also useful for capturing other peoples' Web pages. You often see something on the Web that you'd like to use for inspiration, for comparison, even for derision (a particularly awful color combination, for example, that you want to be sure to avoid). The ability to quickly and easily capture an image from the screen, crop the image to just the piece you want, and save it is a vital capability to have in creating graphics for the Web.

You must be careful in doing so, of course, to avoid moral or legal issues regarding plagiarism and copyright protection. So don't capture images from the screen and then reuse them. Just use them the same way you would something you see in a magazine — as inspiration for your own original work.

Capturing a screen is such a valuable tool to have in your bag of tricks that we recommend following these steps for each bitmap editor you're considering. In addition, capture something interesting even if you don't have a specific need to at the moment. Practice makes perfect, and practicing now will make you perfect when you need to capture a screen image in the future. It also begins to give you a feel for the plusses and minuses of each program.

An image of the entire screen saved as a bitmap is a big file! A full-color, 24-bit bitmap of a 1024 x 768 screen image takes up about 3MB of disk space — as much as an MP3 music file, and the MP3 file is probably more interesting. The bitmap image is also physically too large to fit in the browser window if you use it as a Web graphic. Crop and compress the image before using it on the Web (and be sure to avoid copyright infringement).

If you just want to capture a specific graphic from the Web, you can do so quickly and easily in Windows by right-clicking it and choosing Save As from the menu that appears. Use screen capture to grab graphics in bitmap format or to grab combinations of several graphics or text and graphics together.

Paint versionitis

Versionitis is the condition you get when you're trying to manage various versions of the various computer programs that you use on a regular basis. Versionitis is usually accompanied by sweaty palms, shallow breathing, and chronic anxiety about whether the person you just sent a file to will be able to read it, and vice versa.

Versionitis is not that significant a problem with Paint. That's because all versions of Paint have the same default file format — the 24-bit, or full-color, version of the standard Windows bitmap format. So you can always share files from one version of Paint to another, and you can move files between Paint and any Windows program that supports graphics because they all support the standard Windows bitmap file format.

Microsoft Paint has evolved a little bit over the years, but not nearly as much as programs like Paint Shop Pro or Photoshop. Unlike those programs, what you see is what you get — there's no way to upgrade your current version of Paint to a more advanced version, at least not unless you upgrade your entire version of Windows as well. So the descriptions that we give in this book should work equally well for all versions of Paint.

Paint doesn't even have version numbers of its own. Instead, it's simply referred to as "Microsoft Paint Windows 98 Edition" or what have you. It's very hard to find much documentation or other information about Paint; in fact, the descriptions in this book may be the most complete Paint documentation you ever see.

While you can't upgrade Paint without upgrading Windows, you may be able to enhance it. That's because Paint can inherit GIF or JPEG filters that you install in Windows during the installation process or when upgrading Microsoft Word or other Microsoft Office programs. So, if you find that your version of Paint cannot open or save files in GIF or JPEG format and if you have Microsoft Office, get out that old install disk and try to install the missing filters.

Otherwise, don't worry about Paint versions too much. If you're spending a lot of time in Paint, it's almost certainly worth your while to spring for a copy of Paint Shop Pro or one of the versions of Photoshop for your work. Your results will be better and your work easier.

If you need to save a whole Web page, the Save As command in any recent version of Internet Explorer works wonders. Internet Explorer saves the Web page as an HTML file and a folder, with the same filename as the HTML file, containing all the images from the Web page. The HTML file is automatically modified so that its graphics links all point to the new images folder rather than to the Web server from which the images came.

Using Microsoft Paint

Microsoft Paint is a great program because it makes basic Web graphics capabilities available to everyone with a Windows PC. If you have little or no Web graphics experience, Paint is a great place to start. Even if you're an expert with tools like Paint Shop Pro or Photoshop, Microsoft Paint is handy.

Paint loads quickly, doesn't overtax even the slowest machine, and handles things like screen captures with the greatest of ease. And unlike Photoshop, which is found mostly on the machines of serious graphics types, nearly every Windows PC already has Paint — even that beat-up old machine in the back corner of an Internet café that you get stuck with while on a trip.

If you don't have much experience with graphics programs, spend a good amount of time experimenting with Paint. Because it's so simple and basic, using it forces you to absorb the core functions of any bitmap editor. With this knowledge in hand, you'll be ready to do more with a more advanced program such as Paint Shop Pro or Photoshop.

Finding your way around Paint

Paint has a very narrow range of features. It's lacking all sorts of cool things you find in Paint Shop Pro or Photoshop. But the lack of features makes the program agreeably small and simple. A tour takes only a few moments. See Figure 4-2 for a look at Paint's menus. Here's an overview of the most important ones:

- ✔ **File:** The File menu has typical Open, Save, Print Preview, and Print features, plus a surprise — the ability to import a figure from a scanner or camera. This feature only lights up when a scanner or camera is connected. You can save a file as a bitmap and, with the right filters installed for Microsoft Office, as a GIF or JPEG file — a pretty nice capability for a free program.

- ✔ **Edit:** With Edit, you can complete typical operations like cut, copy, and paste. You can also copy to a file or paste from a file, simplifying some operations.

✔ **View:** The View menu allows you to turn the tool bar, color box, and status bar on and off, though why you would want to do that is beyond us. You can also zoom in and out, which is crucial for detail-level work in any bitmap editor.

✔ **Image:** You can rotate, stretch or skew the image, among other operations. You can also set the size of the background area that controls the overall size of the image and specify whether to work in inches, centimeters, or pixels.

✔ **Colors:** Colors simply lets you choose the current color from among 48 basic colors and to set an additional 16 custom colors, giving you 64 colors with which to work. Unlike other programs, there's no guidance as to which colors are Web-safe for cross-platform use between a PC and a Macintosh.

✔ **Tool box:** The Paint tool box is very simple, and unlike many other graphics program, there's only one tool box. You can draw simple lines and shapes, select an area, erase, select colors, and fill with a color.

The bar at the bottom of the Paint window is also an important feature. It contains the color box, which gives you one-click access to 28 colors and displays the current cursor coordinates and the size of the current object you're creating.

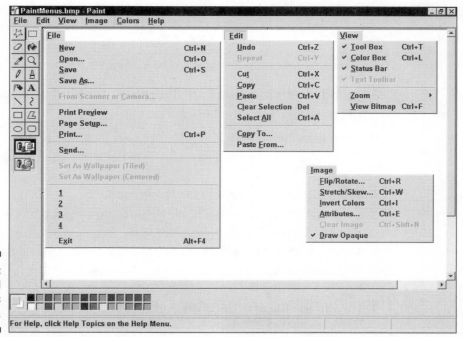

Figure 4-2:
Paint and
Paint's
menus.

Installing GIF and JPEG filters

If you just have Microsoft Windows and not Microsoft Office, you won't be able to open or save GIF and JPEG files with Paint. That's because Paint uses GIF and JPEG filters from Microsoft Office if they've been installed in Windows, but if the filters don't get installed, Paint can't use them. Without these filters, Paint can only work with bitmaps.

If you have Office, but don't have these filters installed so Paint can use them, use the Office installer to add them to Office. The specific instructions will vary depending on what version of Windows and of Office you have, so we can't step you through it in detail, but it should be a fairly easy process.

Because so many Windows users have Microsoft Office installed these days, we'll assume that if you have Paint, you have GIF and JPEG capability. If not, feel free to use Paint to edit files in Windows bitmap format, and use Paint Shop Pro, Photoshop, or another program to save files in GIF or JPEG format.

Using Paint for a screen capture

In this section, we provide specific steps for using one of Paint's most helpful capabilities: Capturing an image of a screen and editing it (we describe the advantages of doing so in the section, "Using a screen capture as an example," earlier in this chapter). In doing so, we can briefly demonstrate many of Paint's key features. In the next chapter, we show you how to create a new image in Paint, thus demonstrating many of its remaining capabilities.

Follow these steps to use Paint for a screen capture:

1. **Open Paint by choosing Start⇨Programs⇨Accessories⇨Paint.**
2. **Get the image you want onto the computer's screen.**
3. **Press the PrtScrn key.**

   The entire current screen image is copied as a bitmap and placed on the Windows clipboard.

4. **Bring the Paint program to the foreground.**
5. **Click the Maximize button in the upper-right corner of the Paint window to maximize it to fill the screen.**
6. **Choose Edit⇨Paste or press Ctrl+V to paste the image into Paint.**

   The image appears. Note that the Select rectangle is highlighted in the tool box and that the entire image is selected.

7. **Use the scrollbars to bring the portion of the screen capture that you want to use on-screen.**

8. Press the Esc key to clear the current selection.

If you don't clear the current selection, your efforts to drag a selection box around a new selection will just shift the entire bitmap around the screen — not the effect you're looking for.

9. With the selection rectangle, drag across the area that you want to copy, as shown in Figure 4-3.

Note that the numbers in the lower-right corner of the status bar denote the current width and height of the selected area. Remember the size of the image.

One of the frustrations of working in Paint is that it's hard to select an area larger than what's currently visible on-screen. This makes it hard, for example, to select all of an Internet Explorer browser window, including the top and bottom borders of the program window. One workaround for this problem when making screen captures is to switch your screen to a lower resolution, do the initial screen capture using PrtScrn, and then switch back to a higher resolution to do the editing. Doing so allows the entire captured area to fit on-screen at once.

10. Choose Edit➪Copy or press Ctrl+C to copy the selected area.

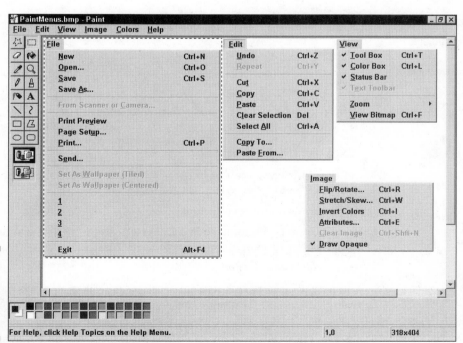

Figure 4-3: Selecting part of an image in Paint.

11. **Choose File⇨New to create a new file.**

    Paint brings up a dialog box asking, "Save changes to untitled?"

12. **Click Yes if you want to save the original screen shot and then save it in a folder of your choice; click No if you don't want to save it.**

    Paint opens a new window.

13. **Choose Edit⇨Paste or press Ctrl+V to paste the selection into Paint.**

    The selection appears in Paint.

14. **Choose Image⇨Attributes or press Ctrl+E to set the image attributes — that is, the size of the background area in which the image rests.**

    The Attributes dialog box appears, as shown in Figure 4-4.

Figure 4-4: Setting image attributes in Paint.

Paint regards the white canvas that your image rests on to be the image itself. You usually want the canvas to end up at the same size as the image so that there's not a big white border on one or more sides of the image.

15. **Set the Width and Height to the size of the area pasted in. Set the Units to Pixels. Click OK.**

    The canvas will resize to fit the image.

16. **Save the file by choosing File⇨Save or pressing Ctrl+S and navigating to the folder in which you want to save the file.**

    Save it as a 24-bit bitmap to preserve all color information.

    You may want to save it as a GIF or JPEG as well, but always save files from Paint as 24-bit bitmaps first in order to have a clean, uncompressed original.

17. **Choose File⇨Exit or click the Close button for the program's window if you want to exit the program.**

What about the Mac?

Apple introduced the idea of free drawing tools as part of a computer purchase years ago with MacPaint, long available for free with any Macintosh, and MacDraw, which more quickly became a paid-for, separate software program. Now the Macintosh comes with neither tool.

There isn't a direct equivalent to Windows Paint on the Macintosh, nor to Paint Shop Pro. However, not to worry — Macintosh computers will very often be found running Photoshop or, since it became available a couple of years ago, Photoshop Elements. Photoshop began life as a Macintosh program, and the Mac has been considered the best platform for Photoshop. Many add-ons for Photoshop run only on the Mac.

Windows is now so popular that Photoshop runs just about equally well on Windows as on the Macintosh, and all the add-ons a non-professional is likely to need are available for Windows. But if you have a Macintosh, your choice is clear — get Photoshop or Photoshop Elements and start learning how to use it. You can find plenty of Macintosh users who are also Photoshop users to help you.

You can condense Steps 10 through 16 into two steps by choosing Edit⇨ Copy To rather than choosing Edit⇨Copy. The Save As dialog box appears, enabling you to save what you're copying directly to a file. The image's attributes also will be set automatically to the size of the copied area! If you just want to capture a specific graphic from the Web, you can do so quickly and easily in most versions of Windows by right-clicking the graphic and choosing Save As from the cursor menu that appears. Use screen capture to grab graphics in bitmap format, or combinations of several graphics, or text and graphics together.

If you need to save a whole Web page, the Save As command in any recent version of Internet Explorer works wonders. Internet Explorer saves the Web page as an HTML file and a folder, with the same filename as the HTML file, containing all the images from the Web page. The HTML file is automatically modified so that its graphics links all point to the folder rather than to the Web server that the images came from.

Using Jasc Paint Shop Pro

Jasc Paint Shop Pro is the next step up from Microsoft Paint — and a big step it is. Paint Shop Pro is a worthy all-around graphics program that has a robust free trial version and sells for only $100. You can do just about anything with it that you need to do in Web graphics.

To stay on this theme for a minute, you're far better off buying Paint Shop Pro than using a bunch of different free tools to try to get the same things done. Just look at some of the major functions of Paint Shop Pro for which you would otherwise need separate programs:

- ✔ Bitmap editing
- ✔ Illustration tools
- ✔ Full set of GIF save options
- ✔ Full set of JPEG save options
- ✔ GIF animation support
- ✔ Special Web features such as slicing, image maps, and rollovers

Paint Shop Pro's broad range of features and low price have led to its being extremely popular. About ten million people have downloaded trial versions from CNET's Download.com service alone — more than ten times the nearest competitor, Ulead PhotoImpact. Jasc claims to have 20 million users for the program.

PSP versus Photoshop Elements

The other bargain-priced, full-featured image editor out there is Photoshop Elements. We recommend Paint Shop Pro if you're new to serious Web graphics work and Photoshop Elements if you have Photoshop experience or work with people who use Photoshop.

Paint Shop Pro is somewhat easier to use and more approachable than Photoshop Elements. With Paint Shop Pro, you're more likely to get your work done quickly and easily. The entire program is simpler and more accessible than either Photoshop program. Although Photoshop (and Elements) does have some shortcuts for specific Web graphics tasks, it's still all too easy to make a wrong turn in Photoshop and get stuck in a profusion of options. In Paint Shop Pro, your path to success is usually shorter.

Paint Shop Pro is also a more compact program than Photoshop or Photoshop Elements. For example, the download for the trial version of Paint Shop Pro is about 30MB. For Photoshop Elements 2, it's over 100MB. Photoshop and, to a slightly lesser extent, Photoshop Elements, are graphics platforms that don't always play well with other programs running on your machine. Paint Shop Pro is a powerful program, but you don't feel like it's taking over your computer.

Adobe has made life interesting for entry-level graphics users with Photoshop Elements. If you're stuck between the two, it's because both are great options. Use this book and the sample versions on the CD-ROM to check out both programs, but if you're still uncertain after doing all that, we recommend that you invest your initial efforts in Paint Shop Pro.

This means that, along with formal support, you're likely to find a lot of informal support for Paint Shop Pro as well. You probably already know someone who uses it, and it's easy to find others who do, which means that you can get quick answers to your questions.

Paint Shop Pro is the ultimate example of a program that's cheap — in the sense of being inexpensive — and easy. It's not quite as easy as Windows Paint, but it does so much more that it's worth the extra trouble. It's both easier and cheaper than Photoshop, though it does somewhat less. (Ease of use is its big advantage over the less expensive version of Photoshop, Photoshop Elements.) In other words, Paint Shop Pro is a great bargain.

We don't want to claim that the program is perfect, however. If you're used to industry-standard, relatively expensive software like Microsoft Office and Photoshop, you'll find a few rough edges in Paint Shop Pro. For example, the installation program is a bit rough around the edges, using generic Microsoft Windows wizards with seemingly extra steps and odd font combinations in the dialog boxes. Not serious problems, but it is a graphics program, and people who do graphics work usually appreciate attention to detail.

If you want to make it easier to use Paint Shop Pro, find the shortcut that was left on your Windows desktop by the installation program and drag it onto the taskbar to create a clickable icon you can use to start Paint Shop Pro at any time.

There's nothing to prevent you from switching back and forth between Paint Shop Pro and Photoshop or Photoshop Elements. The important thing is to experience some success with basic Web graphics tasks. When you get to that point, you'll have the confidence and ability to do your Web work in just about any graphics program.

Touring Paint Shop Pro

Paint Shop Pro has a large range of features — right in there between the bare-bones toolset of Microsoft Paint and the bewildering plethora of options in Photoshop. Paint Shop Pro does more than either program to guide you to a successful conclusion in your drawing efforts. Figure 4-5 shows the most important menus in Paint Shop Pro.

Here's a quick overview of the key options in each menu:

>   ✔ **File:** In addition to typical open, save, and print options, Paint Shop Pro allows you to import and export files, to save a working environment as a Workspace, and to do batch conversions of images. These additional

options encourage you to work in Paint Shop Pro's lossless, native format while experimenting with various ways to optimize your images for use on the Web.

✔ **Edit:** The Edit menu supports typical cut, copy, and paste commands, plus it has the capability of accessing a command history and sending updates you make to a graphic into the Animation Shop product.

✔ **View:** The View menu supports full-screen editing and previewing — less important for the Web than for print — and the ability to zoom in and out and to manage toolbars, rulers, grids, and guides. It also supports the ability to preview an image in a Web browser from within the program, acting as a control center for working on Web graphics.

✔ **Image:** You can flip, mirror, rotate, or resize the image, and much more. You can also resize the canvas on which the image rests and set placement of the image on its canvas. You can perform arithmetical operations on groups of pixels and even add a watermark to assist in copy-protecting valuable images.

Most Web images aren't worth watermarking, unless you like to post artistically inspired 1024 x 768 uncompressed images of your dog. But if an image is high-quality enough to deserve protection, consider using the watermarking capability.

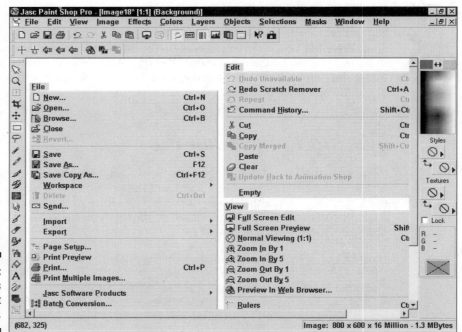

Figure 4-5: Key menus in Paint Shop Pro.

Paint Shop Pro versionitis

Versionitis is not that big a problem with Paint Shop Pro. For most people with older versions, it's worth upgrading.

At this writing, the current version of Paint Shop Pro, Version 7.0, is significantly improved. For one thing, it includes Animation Shop 3, a $39 program, for the first time. That addition alone offsets most of the $49 cost of upgrading from an earlier version of Paint Shop Pro.

It's also always nice to have the latest version. The only problem is that earlier versions of Paint Shop Pro were so darn cheap that even paying $49 for an upgrade may seem like a lot of money. But don't worry; it's worth it. If you're gnashing your teeth over paying a high price to upgrade a software program that was, in its earlier versions, shareware, just remember that Adobe used to give away Photoshop with scanners and digital cameras, and now it retails for over $500.

- ✔ **Effects:** Like Photoshop's filters, Paint Shop Pro's effects allow you to do all sorts of cool things to images, especially photographs. There are 11 photo-specific effects, and several of the others, such as Blur and Sharpen, are useful for photos as well.

- ✔ **Colors:** The Colors menu lets you add color to gray images, convert color images to grayscale, manage color palettes and color depth, and more.

- ✔ **Other menus:** Additional menus, which you won't need much until your images become more complex, include Layers (a recently added, powerful capability), Objects (for flexible editing), and Masks, as well as Window (for window management) and Help.

- ✔ **Tool palette:** Paint Shop Pro's tool palette is more robust than the Paint tool box, but not overwhelmingly so. You can draw simple or more complex lines and shapes, use an airbrush, select an area, erase, select colors, and fill with a color.

Paint Shop Pro is, at first blush, a lot like Paint — five of the first six menus have the same names and most of the same features. But Paint Shop Pro is broader, offering twice as many menus in total, and much deeper, offering a full range of adjustments to things such as JPEG compression in areas where Paint often offers no choices at all.

As we said when discussing Paint, simplicity can be an advantage. When the number of options grows, you have to exercise self-discipline in using or eschewing them. Spending an hour fooling with airbrush options and colors or with various effects is easy, but that's no good if the image in question just needs ten minutes of touching up. Take advantage of ease-of-use features such as the ability to preview your image in a Web browser before delving deeply into the finer artistic abilities Paint Shop Pro offers.

Using Paint Shop Pro for a screen capture

In the previous section on Microsoft Paint, we talk about capturing and saving a screen capture in Paint. In this section, we describe how to do the same thing in Paint Shop Pro, taking the opportunity to show off any tips, tricks, or gotchas in the operation of the program. In the next chapter, we show you how to create a new image using Paint Shop Pro.

Follow these steps to use Paint Shop Pro to capture part of the current screen:

1. **Open Paint Shop Pro by choosing Start⇨Programs⇨Jasc Software⇨ Paint Shop Pro.**

2. **Get the image you want onto the screen.**

3. **Press the PrtScrn key.**

   The current screen image is copied as a bitmap and placed on the Windows clipboard.

4. **Bring Paint Shop Pro to the foreground.**

5. **Press the Maximize button in the upper-right corner of the Paint Shop Pro window to maximize it to fill the screen.**

6. **Choose Edit⇨Paste or press Ctrl+V to paste the image from the Windows clipboard into Paint Shop Pro.**

   The result should resemble Figure 4-6.

   Unlike some other programs, you don't have to open a canvas or document area in Paint Shop Pro before pasting into the program. You can paste into an empty workspace; Paint Shop Pro will create a canvas of the appropriate size for the image.

7. **Use the View menu to make the image large enough so you can see its features, and use Paint Shop Pro's scrollbars to bring the portion of the screen capture that you want to use on-screen.**

8. **Click the Selection rectangle in the tool bar area to make it available.**

   The Selection rectangle is the sixth tool down in the tool bar area, not the first tool as it is in Windows Paint and Photoshop.

9. **With the selection rectangle, drag across the area that you want to copy.**

   Note that the numbers in the lower-right corner of the status bar denote the corners of the selection rectangle, the size of the selection, and the ratio of the selection's width to its height.

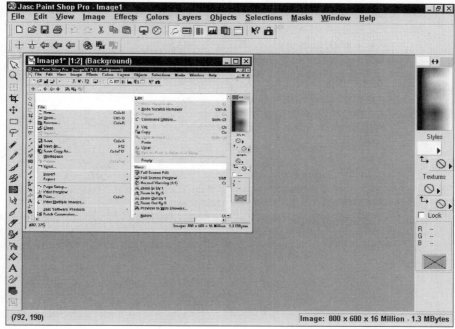

Figure 4-6:
Pasting a
screen
capture into
Paint Shop
Pro.

Width is more important in Web graphics than height. Many carefully designed Web page templates have tight restrictions on column width, while allowing height to vary. This is because it's considered acceptable for the user to have to scroll vertically (up and down) but not horizontally (left and right). So always know how wide you want your Web graphic to be and then vary height for aesthetics or other purposes.

10. **Choose Edit⇨Copy or press Ctrl+C to copy the selected area.**

11. **Choose Edit⇨Paste or press Ctrl+V to paste the selection into Paint Shop Pro.**

    The selection appears as a new window in Paint Shop Pro.

12. **Choose File⇨Save or press Ctrl+S to save the selection.**

    The Save As dialog box appears.

13. **Click the Options button to examine the save options for Paint Shop Pro format. The Save Options dialog box appears, as shown in Figure 4-7.**

    The options that are available for this format are Compression and Version. For Compression, Run length encoding compresses the file about 25 percent and allows the save to proceed quickly; LZ77, the default, compresses the file as much as 75 percent but can take longer. Both of these options are lossless, so all the data is retained. Uncompressed allows the file to be saved fastest but results in the biggest file size.

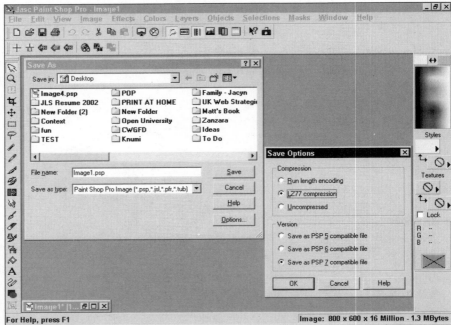

Figure 4-7:
Setting save
options in
Paint Shop
Pro.

Computers are becoming faster and faster; the amount of time it takes to save a file in Paint Shop Pro format using LZ77 compression is unlikely to be an issue for most images that are eventually destined for the Web.

For Version, the options are a PSP 5, PSP 6, or PSP 7 compatible file. If you have colleagues who use one of the older Paint Shop Pro versions, you may want to make a habit of using their version — or encourage them to join you in the brave new upgraded world!

14. Leave the default options in place and click OK to accept them. In the Save As dialog box, navigate to the folder in which you want to save the image and click Save.

You just saved your first file in Paint Shop Pro format. In Chapter 5, we show you how to export images from Paint Shop Pro to GIF or JPEG format.

15. Close the window for the image you just saved.

The file appears in the File menu in the recently used file list.

Choose File⇨Preferences⇨General Program Preferences to increase the size of the recently used file list. Choose the Miscellaneous tab and go to the first option within the tab. You can increase the length of the list to as many as ten filenames (recommended).

16. **Save the remaining image — the full screen capture image — if you want. Then close the window. Choose File⇨Exit or click the Close control for the program's window if you want to exit the program.**

Windows Paint is actually quicker for screen captures than Paint Shop Pro. However, it offers far fewer options, so if you want to do anything interesting with the image, Paint Shop Pro is by far the better choice.

Paint Shop Pro Version 7.0 has its own built-in screen capture program. It's too complex for us to go into here, but it's worth a try if you have complex screen capture needs. Choose File⇨Import⇨Screen Capture to examine the options and start experimenting with it.

Using Adobe Photoshop and Photoshop Elements

Photoshop isn't just a program, it's an environment. You can pretty much live your computing life in Photoshop and rarely need to be concerned that there's anything else going on outside.

Photoshop is a demanding program that was long known for taking over computers on which it was running. Computers today are powerful enough to run Photoshop without buckling, but it's still a big program. Both Photoshop and Photoshop Elements cram the screen with tools and dialog boxes; you need a large monitor with 1024 x 768 resolution or higher to run it. (Many Photoshop users run their large monitors at 1600 x 1200 resolution and complain that it's still not enough.)

Photoshop has been around for many years, since its debut in the early days of the Macintosh. It's hard to say how many people use the program because it's been placed on so many PCs in one version or another, but it would be safe to say that it has tens of millions of users.

The Photoshop world includes Photoshop and its slightly less powerful cousin, Photoshop Elements, in both Windows and Macintosh versions. Both programs are highly polished — installation is smooth, graphics are attractive, and documentation is complete and understandable. The programs are very similar, so almost anything you discover in one is useful in the other. Also, with either one, a huge network of people and products can help you work around problems. And both share a family resemblance with other Adobe products, making it easy to move from one to the other.

Photoshop and Photoshop Elements

Photoshop Elements is the latest — and the best — of several younger brothers or sisters of Photoshop that Adobe has created over the years. At this writing, Photoshop's current version is Version 7.0, and Photoshop Elements is at 2.0. (The 2.0 version of Photoshop Elements is much closer to the full Photoshop than the previous version was.) Expect the programs to be upgraded in tandem — first Photoshop, then Photoshop Elements shortly afterward — in the years to come.

For Web graphics users, Photoshop Elements is nearly indistinguishable from Photoshop, because the differences are mostly in the non-Web areas of the program. Key differences include the following:

✔ **Color management:** Photoshop Elements includes more limited color management than Photoshop, including limited output controls. This affects printing pretty seriously, but the Web color management capabilities in Photoshop Elements are fine.

✔ **Smaller toolset:** Some tools and options are missing from Elements versus the full version of Photoshop. The most important one is the Healing Brush, a key tool for photographers who fix lines and wrinkles.

✔ **Help system:** The Help system for Photoshop Elements is intended to be easier to use than in Photoshop proper.

Otherwise, Photoshop and Photoshop Elements are nearly identical. Which is not all good because Photoshop Elements is not much easier to use than Photoshop. You'll be bedazzled by somewhat fewer options, but core tasks are no more intuitive in one program than in the other.

Still, Photoshop Elements is a great deal; it's a worthwhile tool and a great on-ramp to full Photoshop. If you plan to use Photoshop in the future or need to work with Photoshop users or Photoshop files, Photoshop Elements is a great choice.

Photoshop is by far your best choice if you're a Macintosh user; you'll find a very high percentage of fellow Macintosh users who also use Photoshop, and a plethora of add-ons and tools that work with Photoshop for the Mac.

If you're a PC user, the scene is much more cluttered. Windows Paint is a good utility program, but not a serious graphics tool. But Paint Shop Pro is easily available, easy to learn, less demanding on your computer, widely used, and did we mention it's easier to figure out?

If you're planning to be a graphics professional, or work closely with graphics professionals, or use a Macintosh, either Photoshop or Photoshop Elements will be on your desktop eventually, so you might as well start using one or the other now. But if graphics is going to be just part of what you do or if you use a PC — especially an underpowered one — then Paint Shop Pro, covered in the previous section, is certainly a great place to start, and it may be all the program you ever need.

Getting acquainted with Photoshop Elements

A free trial copy of Photoshop Elements 2.0 is on the CD-ROM at the back of this book. To try the program, install it, following the installation instructions in the CD appendix.

Photoshop and Photoshop Elements are so similar that you can use either to follow along with the description and steps in this section and elsewhere in this book.

Photoshop Elements has a very broad range of features, and the full version of Photoshop adds a few more. In fact, part of the challenge of using either version of the program is finding the key features that you need at the moment and ignoring the hundreds of capabilities that you don't need.

Thoroughly touring Photoshop Elements or Photoshop could take hours, but identifying the key features for Web graphics work takes only a few minutes. See Figure 4-8 for a look at the key menus in Photoshop Elements — at least, all the key menus we could fit in a single screen shot!

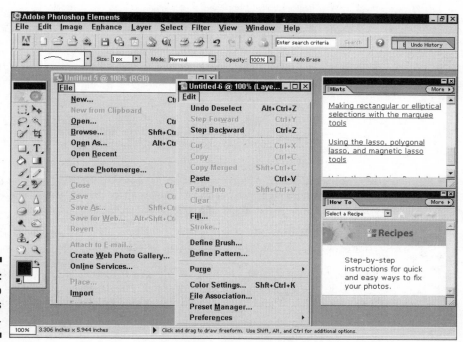

Figure 4-8: Photoshop and it's menus.

Here's an overview of the most important features:

- ✔ **File:** The File menu has the typical Open, Save, Print Preview, and Print features, plus many others. You can access Web and online features, import and export images, set up batch processing, and create automation tools. Take a close look at the Save For Web feature and the Import and Export options.

- ✔ **Edit:** Don't think the Edit menu in Photoshop and Photoshop Elements just supports cut, copy, and paste! There's a multilevel Undo/Redo feature with the ability to step backward and forward through changes, brush and pattern options, Color Settings, Preferences, and more. (You can spend a good deal of time just figuring out the various Preferences options, what they mean, and how you'd like them set.)

- ✔ **Image:** Every image option you can think of is not only present, but also in most cases is the topic of at least one menu or dialog box with multiple options. You can rotate an image or a selection using any of 14 different commands; transform an image in several ways; crop an image or resize the image or the canvas it rests on; and perform sophisticated adjustments or view a histogram or graph of the intensity of various primary colors.

- ✔ **Filter:** This is the crown jewel of Photoshop — the capability to apply filters to selections or entire images and thereby make subtle or egregious changes. In Photoshop Elements there are 13 types of filters, each with five to ten specific filters. The full version of Photoshop has more filters, and you can buy additional add-in filters as well.

- ✔ **View:** Less robust than the others, the View menu allows you to zoom in and out, fit things on-screen, look at an image at the pixel level, and manage rulers and a grid.

- ✔ **Window:** A key menu in Photoshop and Photoshop Elements alike, the Window menu lets you turn on and off the program's 17 windows and manage the numerous windows you're bound to generate as you work on your images.

- ✔ **Tool window:** The Photoshop tool box is uncomplicated, and unlike many other graphics programs, there's only one. You can draw simple lines and shapes, select an area, erase, select colors, and fill with a color.

Like many Photoshop or Photoshop Elements windows, the Tool window can float outside the main program window.

The Photoshop status bar is also an important feature. It contains the Color Box, which gives you one-click access to 28 colors and displays the current cursor coordinates and the size of the current object you're creating.

Using Photoshop elements for a screen capture

Earlier in this chapter, we talk about the advantages of using screen captures for Web graphics. You can show people your work and ideas and capture useful images. Follow these steps to perform a screen capture in Photoshop Elements:

1. **Open Photoshop Elements by choosing Start⇨Programs⇨Adobe Photoshop Elements 2.0.**

   If you don't have other Adobe programs, notice how Adobe cleverly puts Elements at the top level of the Programs list, not down in a folder.

2. **Get the image you want on-screen.**

3. **Press the PrtScrn key.**

   The entire current screen image is copied as a bitmap and placed on the Windows clipboard.

4. **Bring Photoshop Elements to the foreground.**

5. **Press the Maximize button in the upper-right corner of the Photoshop window to maximize it to fill the screen.**

6. **Choose File⇨New from the Clipboard to paste the image into Photoshop.**

   Practice using this command; it's a great shortcut, but you won't use it if you don't work at remembering how to do so.

7. **Use the scrollbars to bring the portion of the screen capture that you want to use on-screen.**

8. **Click the Marquee tool. Then click and hold to see the Marquee options. Select the Rectangular tool (not the oval one).**

   You can also change the type of Marquee tool you're using in the Tool Options window, the narrow horizontal area above the Tools window, which is a vertical strip on the left-hand side.

9. **With the selection rectangle, drag across the area that you want to copy, as shown in Figure 4-9.**

   Keep an eye on Tool Options as you change from one tool to another. Looking at Tool Options is a quick way to learn about hidden features of the program.

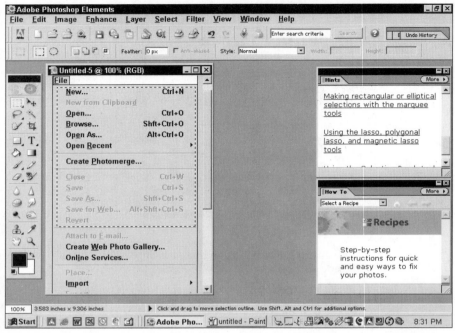

Figure 4-9:
Selecting
part of an
image in
Photoshop
Elements.

After you make a selection, you can hold down the Shift key and make a new selection that will be added to the first. Having multiple selections available simultaneously is a real plus for Photoshop.

10. **Choose Edit⇨Copy or press Ctrl+C to copy the selected area.**

11. **Choose File⇨New from the Clipboard to create a new file using the clipboard contents.**

When you choose New from the Clipboard, Photoshop automatically sets the area of the canvas in the new drawing to the size of the image being copied.

12. **Save the selection by choosing File⇨Save or by pressing Ctrl+S and navigating to the folder in which you want to save the file. Save it as a Photoshop file (`.psd`) to preserve all color information.**

You may want to save the file as a GIF or JPEG as well, but always save files from Photoshop as native Photoshop images first in order to have a clean, uncompressed original and to preserve layers. (As you become more adept with the program and start using layers more, preserving them becomes crucial.)

13. **Leave the default options in place and click OK to accept them. In the Save As dialog box, navigate to the folder in which you want to save the image, enter the filename you want to use and click Save.**

    You just saved your first file in Photoshop format. In Chapter 5, we show you how to export images from Photoshop to GIF or JPEG format.

14. **Close the window for the image you just saved.**

    The file appears in the File menu in the recently used file list.

    Choose Edit⇨Preferences⇨Saving Files to increase the size of the recently used file list. Choose the Miscellaneous tab and go to the first option within the tab. You can increase the length of the list to as many as 30 filenames (recommended).

15. **Save the remaining image — the full screen capture image — if you want. Then close the window. Choose File⇨Exit or click the Close button for the program's window if you want to exit the program.**

Photoshop versionitis

Versionitis is a big issue with Photoshop. Photoshop is an expensive program to buy and upgrade, so many users stick with the first version they get. There have also been several Photoshop lite programs over the years, and each now has a substantial user base.

We recommend that you upgrade to the most recent version of either Photoshop or Photoshop Elements, whichever you plan to use. Photoshop has a steep enough learning curve that you should make sure that your software is as feature-rich and easy to use as possible, and that means getting the latest version. Web-related features have improved and changed a great deal as of late, so for the best

Web features, you need the latest version. You also want to be sure you can open files from all versions of Photoshop, which means you have to have the latest version yourself.

If you are using an earlier version of Photoshop, Photoshop Elements, or some other Adobe Photoshop lite program while reading this book, most of the general graphics commands will be the same. However, the Web-related features are likely to be weak or, with really old versions, non-existent. Follow along as best you can, or use the free Photoshop Elements try-out that comes on this book's CD-ROM as a "taste test," and consider upgrading as soon as possible.

Chapter 5

Compressing Photos with JPEG

- -

- -

*J*PEG, pronounced *jay-peg,* stands for Joint Photographic Experts Group, the standard for photographic image compression. The term JPEG has also become a shorthand term for an image that's been compressed using the JPEG standard. We think JPEG is wonderful! When you use JPEG to compress an image, you reduce its file size by about 90 percent while still retaining high quality. Because JPEG makes it possible to use photographs widely on the Web without undue waiting for the images to download, it makes the Web far more rich and interesting than it would be without JPEG.

If the best things in life are indeed free, JPEG might qualify. You don't need to pay anyone a royalty to create, distribute, or view an image created using the JPEG standard. You may have to pay a royalty or fee to use the image itself, but applying JPEG to compress the image (in an application like Photoshop or Paint Shop Pro) and view the image (in an application such as Internet Explorer) comes at no cost to you.

In the early days of the Web (pre-90s), JPEG images were displayed in a separate viewer because Web browsers only supported GIFs (Graphics Interchange Format). But in the mid-90s, just as the Web really took off, browsers were created with JPEG decompression built in, and JPEG images appeared integrated into the page — just like GIF images. Now JPEG and GIF images can be used simply and easily in Web page design.

In this chapter, we describe the JPEG standard in detail and tell you how to use JPEG compression in major bitmap-editing programs — Windows Paint, Paint Shop Pro, and Photoshop and Photoshop Elements. In later chapters we cover creating, editing, and placing photos on the Web.

What's a photograph?

The word *photography* comes from the words for light and writing. So photography can be described as writing with light.

The photograph that you receive from the photo processor is simply a bunch of dots of chemicals that reflect different colors. The photograph is created by exposing chemically treated paper to light — the more light, the better, at least up to a point. More chemicals are then applied to the paper to bring natural-appearing colors from it.

The resolution of a photograph is limited by how close together various sensitive chemicals can be layered on photographic paper to support the production of different colors; by the amount of light that can be directed to each area of the paper; and by interactions among the chemicals that make it hard for one saturated color, for instance, to appear directly adjacent to another. Different kinds of film have different resolution.

A photograph displayed on the computer screen is different. A typical computer monitor can support resolutions ranging from about 70 to 100 dots per inch — far fewer than a printed photograph. However, unlike a photograph, each individual pixel can be any available color — the fact that one pixel is red doesn't make it more difficult for an adjacent pixel to be blue. And also unlike a photograph, you don't need external light to view an image on a monitor; it has its own light. If we were all smart enough to do our computing in darkened rooms to reduce glare and reflections, and buy better monitors and get them color-calibrated, viewing images on a computer screen would actually be a pretty good experience.

However, a carefully taken, expertly processed, and properly mounted photograph is still the gold standard for image quality (and will continue to be until we have better computers and far better monitors, plus better network connections to bring data to them).

We also discuss JPEG, the key compression standard for photographs; in Chapter 6, we discuss GIF and, briefly, PNG, both of which work best for illustrations with 256 or fewer colors. Both JPEG and GIF are supported by almost all browsers and are supported by the HTML <IMG> tag. PNG is supported by some browsers, but has not, at this writing, emerged as a credible alternative.

Compression Basics

You need to know a few basic ideas about compression to use it effectively in Web graphics. Here are the key elements of compression:

- ✔ Image size
- ✔ File size

  ✔ Lossless compression

  ✔ Lossy compression

  ✔ Transmission

Two big differences exist between Web graphics and print graphics: Web images are displayed at low resolution, and many of the images are compressed. Because low-resolution images require less disk space and transmission time than high-resolution ones, and because compression further reduces disk space requirements and transmission time, these facts are closely related.

We describe the key ideas of compression in detail in the following sections. Take the time to read through this — you'll run into these ideas every time you prepare a graphic for the Web.

Image size and file size

The image size is simply the dimensions of an image when displayed on the screen, in pixels. A 1-inch square on a high-resolution display is about 96 x 96 pixels. The total number of pixels in the square, therefore, would be a little fewer than 10,000 pixels.

The file size is closely related to the image size. The bigger the image size, the bigger the file size is likely to be. Without compression, a black-and-white image requires 1 bit per pixel to store — each pixel is either black (0) or white (1), which can be stored in a bit. You can specify 8 bits in one 8-bit byte, or the entire image in 1,250 bytes — just over 1K, a very small image file.

A grayscale image requires 1 byte per pixel — a byte is 8 bits and allows up to 256 shades to be stored. The human eye can't distinguish many more shades of gray than that, so 1 byte per pixel is enough to create a very attractive grayscale image. In grayscale, a 1-inch-square image would require 10,000 bytes — about 10K, a much larger file. (A 10K file takes about 4 seconds to download over a 56 Kbps modem.)

You can keep a color image file small by restricting it to the same number of colors as a grayscale file — 256. With this limitation, you keep the file size small, but you've limited your palette to 256 colors. If the original image is, for example, an outdoor photograph with a wide range of colors and shades, you'll do some violence to the image to portray it with only 256 colors. Even a close-up of a human face, which is nearly all skin tones, suffers when reduced to this small a range of colors. But with 256 colors, you can at least keep your file size to that small 10K size.

You can get that face right by using more colors. If you allow 2 bytes per pixel, you can have thousands of colors — about 65,000, to be exact. That's enough for a typical face, but now the file size is up to 20,000 bytes, or about 20K — a 5-second modem download.

But suppose that you want something more colorful than a face — a panoramic shot early or late in the day in the Amazon rain forest. You need more colors to capture all the shadings — the human eye can distinguish among millions. To support millions of colors, you need at least 3 bytes per pixel. Now the file size is 30K, a 10-second modem download — very large, when you consider that's only for one square inch of screen space.

Some file formats even use 4 bytes per pixel. The fourth byte is used to hold just one or two bits of information about transparency, an alpha channel, and so on. A fourth byte may also be used just for efficiency's sake — computers operate more efficiently on 32-bit, or 4-byte, chunks than on smaller pieces of data, so why not assign 4 bytes to each pixel? Assigning 4 bytes per pixel makes a 1-inch square, 96 x 96 pixel file almost 40K in size.

Keep in mind all the figures we're discussing are for uncompressed files, and files for the Web are typically compressed in one way or another. The most important form of compression that you can achieve is, oddly, more about art (compressing the image itself) than about computing power. The smaller the image you use, the smaller the resulting file will be, both before and after compression.

Compression happens in several ways, all of which may not be obvious to you. But think about it: When you trim an image by 25 percent in both height and width, the number of pixels needed for the image drops by almost 50 percent. That's right — while a 96 x 96 pixel image requires almost 10,000 pixels to display, a 72 x 72 pixel image requires just over 5,000 pixels, a reduction of almost 50 percent. So you can use two images that are each three-fourths of an inch square and have the same total file size as a single image 1-inch square.

Figure 5-1 shows an image shown in progressively smaller sizes and the number of pixels for each image. You can see how the pixel count drops off very quickly with image size.

When you reduce the size of an image, you should consider trimming its background as well. In trimming, you cut out background that doesn't convey much information but that may have some extra colors in it. Compressing an image is easier when fewer colors are in the image.

Full-size
176 x 144
25,344 pixels

3/4-size
132 x 106
13,992 pixels
(50% reduction)

Half-size
88 x 72
6,336 pixels
(75% reduction)

Quarter-size
44 x 36
3,168 pixels
(nearly 90% reduction)

Figure 5-1:
Slightly
smaller
pictures use
many fewer
pixels.

After you shrink the image size and trim out background, compression actually does less damage than before. In a small image, there's less room for the user's eye to pick up irregularities in a straight line or discrepancies between, for example, one expanse of green and another. Shrinking the image size not only reduces the size of the uncompressed file, it allows you to be more aggressive with compression.

Big files are worse, in terms of download time, than they appear. The software and hardware that run the Internet often lose, or drop, a chunk of data from a file, called a *packet*; if too many packets are dropped during transmission, the transmission is aborted and started over. As file size rises, the odds increase sharply that enough damage will occur in transmission to require resending the file. Small files not only transmit faster, they're significantly less likely to require time-consuming retransmission.

The smaller the image, the less background you can afford — zoom in on the subject! For very small images, you should include as little background as possible — just a few pixels around the subject at the top, bottom, and sides of the picture.

Consider trying GIF format for small photos. By the time you reduce the size of the image on-screen, sharpen it up in Photoshop or some other program, and put a border around it, it might not leave many colors in the image. Using dithering to cut the image's color count down to 256 and then saving it in the otherwise lossless GIF format may do less harm to the image than compressing it in JPEG. See Chapter 6 for details on how to use GIF.

Lossless compression

Lossless compression, a type of compression that makes an image smaller without removing any data from the image is rarely achieved for photographs. Lossless compression is used regularly for illustrations; the GIF format is lossless, as we explain in Chapter 6. But if you think about lossless compression in the context of photographs and JPEG, you can better understand the tradeoffs you make when using lossy compression to achieve acceptable file sizes for photographs displayed on a Web page.

Lossless compression involves finding regularities in the file that allow you to store it in less space than usual. For example, suppose that all of the background of an image is the same shade of red. If you store that one fact, background = bright red, you save yourself from storing different color values for thousands of pixels. Unfortunately, the computer is, in a way, stupid — it doesn't know what is background or the shade of red you'd like to use.

In lossless compression, the computer uses *run length encoding.* Run length encoding works like this: The computer looks at pixels one row at a time. Every time it finds a few pixels in a row that are exactly the same shade, the computer stores the number of pixels that have the same color, then the actual color value. The more runs (the rows of pixels) there are, and the greater the length (the number of pixels) of each run, the better run length encoding works. A color drawing of a Stop sign encodes very well — because it has lots of long runs of one shade of red, several short runs of pure white, and so on.

Unfortunately, lossless compression doesn't work as well on photographs because depth and lighting information in the photo is conveyed by having different variations on a single color. Look at a person's cheek in a photo, for instance. It's all brown or tan — but there are dozens of different shades of the main color due to a highlight at the cheekbone, shading as the cheek curves away from the camera, and so on. If you were to render the cheek all in one identical shade of tan or brown, it would look like a big blotch. (Just the effect you get when you compress a photo heavily, but we cover this later in the section, "What JPEG does to images.")

Eye and brain and Web graphics

How do people see? When you open your eyes, light is focused by the eye and falls onto little clusters of rods and cones in your retina. Many hundreds of thousands of these rods and cones are so sensitive that, in complete darkness, they can pick up a single photon. Yet in normal use, the eye is awash in millions of photons per second, at energy levels corresponding to millions of colors. The eyes are constantly making slight movements to pick up subtle angular variations in the light falling on them, and this shifting plus the simultaneous use of two eyes allows depth to be inferred fairly accurately.

A photograph doesn't have much hope, let alone a computer monitor, of having enough resolution and fidelity, let alone depth cues, to accurately mimic reality. But, fortunately, you use your brain as well as your eyes to process colors, so there's more hope for us graphics types than a dumb computer monitor.

Small clusters of neurons in the brain process the input from the eyes and detect various features — horizontal lines, vertical lines, angled lines, specific shapes, and so on. A full, detailed natural image isn't needed to trigger these tiny detectors; just a few pixels on a computer screen in the right arrangement will do the trick. The brain then assembles an image from all this information, compares incoming data to its memories of people, objects, and events, and then assigns meaning to the images; all of which goes into what you see. Ever think something was close up and then realize it's actually far away? The visual data coming in was the same throughout — but the meaning your brain assigned to it changed with further thought.

Even very sketchy representations — a hurried glimpse, a bad photo, or a small image on a computer screen — can trigger the brain to pull up the intended person, object, or event. Because even a distorted or low-resolution image is still recognizable, you actually have a lot of room to maneuver in trading off image size, file size, and image quality in Web graphics. A typical photograph found in a Web page may not be the world's most beautiful image — but it still can be very effective.

Even a simple photo like a photo of a real Stop sign doesn't encode well — the lighting source and the presence of shadows and of natural variations in the colors means that the sign is made up of shades of red and white rather than one red and one white. And that's not even counting the background behind the sign, which is likely to have thousands of shades of its own. Lossless compression tends to not be able to compress a complex image of this sort enough to make the image usable on the Web, with its premium on small file sizes and fast file transmission times.

Part of the reason lossless compression works with GIF is because of the 256-color limit itself. If you only allow 256 shades, the odds of having long runs of pixels be the same exact shade are higher, making run length encoding more efficient. If you allow more shades — or even if you have a strong mix of different shades from among the 256 colors, as occurs in dithering — then the degree of compression you achieve may be quite small. You can even end up with a compressed file that's larger than the original!

Lossy compression

Lossy compression is any kind of compression that involves removing some of the data from the image as part of compressing it. JPEG compression is lossy compression; GIF compression isn't unless colors have to be dropped to fit the 256-color limit.

Why would anyone use lossy compression? Because the penalty for not compressing images is great in terms of transmission time. As we mentioned previously, an uncompressed, 1-inch square full-color image can take up about 10K, which takes about 5 seconds to transmit over a modem. And you still have dozens of square inches to fill!

GIF compression is lossless, but GIF compression only supports 256 or fewer colors in an image. If you use GIF compression for an image with more than 256 colors, some of the colors get changed to colors that are in the 256. Some GIF compressors can create a palette on the fly so that the right 256 colors are used; others have a fixed palette of 256 colors of their own, and every color in the original image gets replaced by the closest value from among the 256. Even with fixed parameters such as GIF's 256-color limit, details in how compression is implemented can make a big difference in the results.

But we're mainly talking about lossy compression right now in the context of JPEG. In what way, you may wonder, is JPEG lossy? And how lossy is it? The answer is simple — it's up to you!

Most lossy compression follows a rigid formula for simplifying an image. JPEG, however, allows you to specify the degree of compression and thereby the impact on an image.

Figure 5-2 shows a file compressed with JPEG to varying degrees. The results of compression don't show up as much on a grayscale image, but take our word for it: The first two, less-compressed, images of the four JPEG images have very few visible problems.

Transmission

Transmission used to be a safe harbor for files in terms of compression, but no more. Once upon a time, the Internet was designed to make sure that files were received with exactly the same data that they started out with when they were sent. Then big ISPs — Internet Service Providers, such as America Online, Earthlink and others — noticed how much money they were paying for transmitting gigabytes and gigabytes of data.

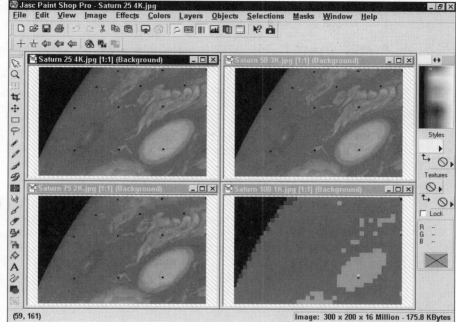

Figure 5-2:
Some lossy
JPEG
compression
doesn't
show much
loss.

So what did the ISPs do? They started compressing data during the transmission process. Text is compressed losslessly, but images are compressed using a lossy process. That's right — your JPEG images, artfully compressed to the maximum degree possible while still retaining almost all their original beauty — may be compressed further in transmission by the ISP. The graphics may arrive at the destination — the user's Web browser, running within the ISP software — a shadow of their former selves.

All about JPEG

In this section, we delve briefly, but deeply, into the details of JPEG algorithm and how it's used on the Web. Then we show you how to use JPEG in three key programs — Windows Paint, Paint Shop Pro, and Photoshop.

The JPEG algorithm

The JPEG algorithm works like this: A JPEG compressor examines the image in 8 x 8 pixel chunks (64 pixels per chunk). It then describes the color pattern in that 8 x 8 chunk via a mathematical formula, using a mathematical technique called Discrete Cosine Transform, or DCT.

The DCT has two options: The DCT can come up with an exact description of the 64-pixel chunk every time — in which case JPEG is lossless, but not very effective — or the DCT can operate in a more or less approximate fashion. The more the DCT approximates the setting for JPEG's quality, the smaller the file — and the less accurate the result.

But for JPEG to work correctly, it takes into account a human factor as well. For instance, most people can distinguish many shades of red and green, but only so many of blue. In compressing an image, JPEG can reduce the many possible blues to a few dozen shades without visibly affecting the image. The basic operation of the DCT algorithm and tricks like this make JPEG effective at compressing an image by 75 percent or more without greatly affecting its quality.

But the best thing about JPEG is that you can set the quality of the compression. Some images can be compressed more severely than others without much visible damage. Others are far more sensitive to compression. And your own tolerance for distortion varies depending on what the image, and the Web page it appears in, is used for. JPEG doesn't try to make these trade-offs for you; it simply allows you to experiment with various quality settings until you find the best one for the image in question.

What JPEG does to images

JPEG does a fantastic job of compressing graphics without messing them up much. But it does have discernible effects.

At various degrees of low quality, more severe tradeoffs are made. Compression is definitely visible — it's just a matter of how bad you want the image to be versus how long you want the image to take to transmit. Remember, though, that up to about 6x, compression is virtually free; it's only when choosing between 8x, 10x, and 12x compression that you have to make serious tradeoffs.

Figure 5-3 shows some of the artifacts that show up when you push compression a bit too hard. The leftmost figure is uncompressed; the rightmost figure is about 40 times smaller. The rightmost figure is definitely recognizable, but is too pixelated to be useful in most contexts.

What exactly is happening to an image that's been compressed by JPEG, and why? Higher levels of compression tend to average out colors, brightening lows and lightening highs. JPEG also eventually succumbs to the bane of all compressors, creating small areas of banding — blotches of the same color — due to repeated use of the same color in what had been a delicately shaded area.

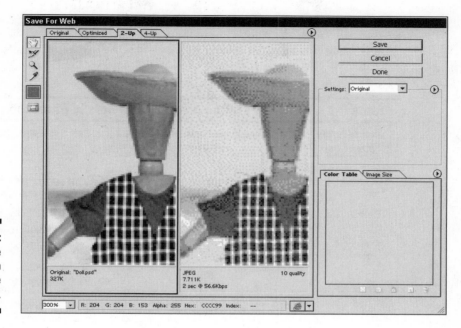

Figure 5-3:
More
compression
means more
artifacts.

Given the power of JPEG compression, we recommend that you tread lightly on key images after achieving compression of about 6:1. Further compression often saves you very small amounts of file size at significant cost in image quality.

Be ready to experiment with each and every image you compress under JPEG to make sure that you've made the best possible tradeoff between file size and image quality. Some images can be compressed much further than others before showing much effect of compression, leaving more room in your Web page for images that are more sensitive to compression. By experimenting, your pages can look significantly better at little cost in total page weight.

Finding the right tradeoff between quality and size

Finding the right tradeoff between image quality and file size in JPEG can be maddening. Although JPEG does a great job, you still all too often end up wringing your hands, wondering whether saving one or two seconds of modem download time is worth making your image just a little bit uglier.

We did an experiment, compressing a highly detailed, 200 x 100 pixel image we borrowed from the Adobe Photoshop Elements 2.0 splash screen. We compressed the image at a quality rating of 100 (the highest) down 10 points at a time to 0 (the lowest). Table 5-1 shows our results.

Table 5-1		JPEG Compression Example in Photoshop	
Quality rating (Photoshop)	*File size*	*Seconds to download (56 Kbps modem)*	*Size and appearance*
Uncompressed	172K	34	
100	59K	12	3x compression; no visible artifacts
90	40K	8	4x compression; no visible artifacts
80	27K	6	5x compression; no visible artifacts
70	20K	5	6x compression; slight loss of detail
60	15K	4	10x compression; slight loss of detail
50	11K	3	16x compression; slight blockiness in background
40	8.6K	2	18x compression; slight additional loss of detail
30	7.2K	2	24x compression; some blurring, loss of crispness
20	6.1K	2	28x compression; additional blurring
10	4.5K	2	38x; significant blurring, blockiness
0	3.4K	2	50x compression; visible chunkiness and noise

In Table 5-1, all the new problems occur between quality ratings 50 down to 0. The file size decreases, which looks impressive, but only means about 1 second of download time saved. (Maybe not even that, since establishing and ending a connection often takes longer than actual data transmission time for small files anyway.)

What we believe, from this table and our own work, is that the sweet spot of JPEG compression for medium-sized and small images is in the Medium range, at quality ratings of around 40 or 50. These images are small enough that additional compression yields little benefit in file transfer time but has significant cost in terms of visible artifacts.

Some images allow you to go lower without visible damage, but in these cases you should only stick with the lower quality rating if it truly makes no visible difference in the file's appearance; saving 2K or so just isn't worth it.

How much compression is too much?

By using techniques we describe in this book to lay out your Web pages, you can make the text in a page appear quickly and lock into place before images begin to appear. By doing so, you eliminate some problems that are caused by a combination of large image downloads and poor page design, such as text shifting around as the user begins to read it.

For images, especially photographs, you need to consider the impact you want an image to have versus the amount of time it takes to appear. For users on fast connections — nearly all users at work and a growing proportion of home users — a few K more or less makes no noticeable difference. For these users, it's certainly better to err on the side of quality.

Most home users, however, are still on slow modems. To them 5–10K in size makes a big difference in waiting time. But 1–2K or so, amounting to one second more or less in the speed with which an image appears, may be less important than a significant improvement in image quality.

Many Web page creators spend far too little time worrying about the download speed of their pages. Others go the other way and spend too much. Be willing to give back 3 to 4K of the possible compression you could get out of an image if that buys you visibly better quality. Your users will enjoy your Web pages more in the long run.

Compressing an Image Using JPEG

In this section, we show you how to actually do JPEG compression in three featured programs — Windows Paint, Paint Shop Pro, and Photoshop

Elements (which works almost exactly like full version Photoshop in this way). These instructions really cover the range of JPEG compression options you're likely to find in all programs — from no options, in Windows Paint, to a solid range of features in Paint Shop Pro, to a full save-and-preview control panel in Photoshop Elements and Photoshop.

Some Photoshop users who had early versions of the program and hadn't bothered to upgrade in years suddenly got the latest version when Photoshop added ImageReady within the Photoshop program. Now ImageReady can be found in both Photoshop and Photoshop Elements. ImageReady includes quick, easy-to-use, and complete features for image compression. If you plan to spend much time creating either JPEG or GIF images, then you should consider using Photoshop Elements or Photoshop.

Compressing an image in Windows Paint

Compressing an image using JPEG in Windows Paint is easy, but not necessarily in a good way, because Paint does almost nothing for you. Paint just saves the file in JPEG, using medium compression. You have no opportunity to change the compression settings or preview the result. You just get a JPEG file created for you.

And there's more bad news: Saving a file in JPEG format using Windows Paint doesn't work for everyone. Only if you use Microsoft Office and have installed the JPEG filter will you be able to open or save files in JPEG format.

To find out if the JPEG filter is installed on your computer, open Paint and choose File⇨Save As. When the Save As dialog box appears, pull down the Save as Type drop-down list. If the JPEG option is listed, you're in good shape. If not, find the Microsoft Office installation disk and install the JPEG and GIF filters. If you don't use Office, you have to use Paint Shop Pro, Photoshop Elements, Photoshop, or another program for saving an image in JPEG format.

If you have the ability to save a file as JPEG in Paint, follow these steps:

1. **Open Paint by choosing Start⇨Programs⇨Accessories⇨Paint.**

2. **Open an image that you'd like to save as a JPEG.**

   If you don't have an image handy, consider doing a screen capture as we describe in Chapter 4 or use an image from the *Creating Web Graphics For Dummies* CD-ROM.

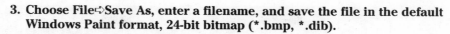

3. **Choose File⇨Save As, enter a filename, and save the file in the default Windows Paint format, 24-bit bitmap (*.bmp, *.dib).**

   Always save a file in a lossless format such as the 24-bit bitmap format before saving it as a JPEG file. If any problems or changes need to be made, you can edit the original, instead of having to edit the JPEG and then save as JPEG again, compounding compression artifacts.

4. **If you want to get a good look at the subtle, but visible changes that JPEG makes in an image, choose View⇨Zoom⇨Large Size before saving the file as a JPEG image.**

   The image appears close-up.

5. **Choose File⇨Save As.**

   The Save As dialog box appears.

6. **Enter a filename (don't enter a file extension such as .jpg or .jpeg).**

   Use a different filename from the one for the 24-bit bitmap so you don't confuse yourself.

7. **Click the Save as Type drop-down list. Choose JPEG File Interchange Format (*.jpg, *.jpeg) and click Save.**

   The file is saved with the extension .jpg.

8. **Inspect the image carefully; you'll see small changes that reveal the impact of JPEG on the image.**

   Look at Figure 5-4 for an example. The changes are almost invisible in a photograph viewed at normal size; they're much more visible in an illustration, or a computer-generated image such as a screenshot, as shown in the figure.

9. **To see the effects of JPEG on file size, navigate to the two files you just saved from Windows Paint. Right-click each file and choose Properties.**

   The Properties box reveals the image and file size of the uncompressed bitmap file and the JPEG version of the file.

Congratulations! You've just saved a file in JPEG format using a free program. The file is saved at a compression quality roughly the same as the Medium, or 40 percent, setting in Photoshop. Though other programs give you many more options, the Medium setting is not a bad choice, and Paint is free and very easy to use. Paint is a convenient choice for occasional use, for times when you're in a hurry, or when nothing else is available.

Figure 5-4:
An example
of JPEG
compression
effects from
within
Windows
Paint.

Compressing an image in Paint Shop Pro

Paint Shop Pro is a good intermediate choice overall, and the same is true of its JPEG compression abilities. Paint Shop Pro allows you to vary compression settings and see an interactive preview of part of the image. At the same time it doesn't do too much.

The best way to see what Paint Shop Pro can do for you in JPEG compression is to try it. Follow these steps:

1. **Open Paint Shop Pro by choosing Start⇨Programs⇨Jasc Software⇨ Paint Shop Pro 7.**

2. **Open an image to experiment with.**

   Although screen captures aren't very JPEG-friendly, they're good for experimenting with. Find out how to capture a screen shot in Paint Shop Pro in Chapter 4 if you need an image, or get one from the *Creating Web Graphics for Dummies* CD-ROM. Don't use a JPEG — compressing a JPEG image a second time creates serious distortion.

3. **Choose File⇨Save As, enter a filename, and save the file in the default Paint Shop Pro format, Paint Shop Pro Image (*.psp, *.jsl, *.pfr, *.tub).**

Always save a file in a lossless format such as Paint Shop Pro format before saving it as a JPEG file so you have an original to work from. Paint Shop Pro makes it easy to keep your JPEG version and your original separate, but saving prevents confusion or lost work if your computer freezes (which seems to happen more when working on large graphics files).

4. **Click the Export JPEG arrow in the upper-left corner of the Paint Shop Pro window.**

The JPEG Optimizer dialog box appears, as shown in Figure 5-5. Note the Uncompressed preview in the upper left of the dialog box and the Compressed preview in the upper right. For larger images, the previews are too small to give you a full picture of compression's effects. The buttons between them allow you to zoom out, pan, and zoom in.

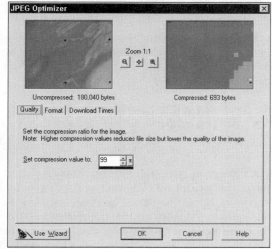

Figure 5-5: JPEG Optimizer helps you preview JPEG files.

5. **Click the Quality tab and adjust the compression value.**

To change the compression value, type in a value, use the up and down arrows, or hold down the pull-down arrow and drag the slider — not an easy thing to do.

Watch as you adjust the compression value; the Compressed preview updates to show you how the file will look and how large the file will be.

Paint Shop Pro uses higher compression values to indicate more compression and a smaller file size (1 = least compression, 100 = most); Photoshop Elements and Photoshop do the opposite. This can be very confusing if you switch between the programs, or use one and talk to people who use the other.

6. **Click the Download Times tab.**

A table appears showing you the download times at various connection speeds. Focus on the 56 Kbps and 128 Kbps settings. Most modems are 56 Kbps, whereas 128 Kbps or so is what many broadband users experience when taking into account shared T1 lines, busy traffic on cable or DSL lines, and other factors.

You can't access the Quality tab to adjust the compression setting while also looking at the download times preview. You have to switch back and forth to get the settings right.

Don't use the Wizard option in the lower corner unless you really want things simplified. It offers few options and no preview. Then, if you cancel it, the JPEG Optimizer dialog box disappears as well, and you have to re-open it.

7. **Toggle between the Quality and Download Times tabs, keeping an eye on the Compressed preview, until you get the settings the way you want them. Then click OK in the JPEG Optimizer dialog box.**

The Save Copy As dialog box appears.

8. **Navigate to the folder you want to save your file in, change the name to avoid confusion with the original, and click Save to save it.**

The JPEG file is saved.

You should preview your image in Internet Explorer, Netscape, and — if available — the AOL client. Not only does this let you see the JPEG-compressed image at full size, which Paint Shop Pro's small preview window does not let you do; it also lets you see how the different decompressors in the various Web browsers do with your image. Photoshop Elements and Photoshop offer more functionality in these areas, as we describe in the next section.

Compressing an image in Photoshop Elements

Photoshop Elements and Photoshop are almost identical in their Web image capabilities, and that's a good thing. Both include ImageReady, which used to be a separate program but which is now very usefully integrated into its bigger brothers. While the steps in this section are specifically for Photoshop Elements, you'll find very little difference between it and Photoshop.

With ImageReady — which is not noticeable as a separate program, being fully integrated — Photoshop Elements and Photoshop have the ultimate range of options for saving JPEG images. You may find that you spend extra time in these programs using all the JPEG-related options, but you won't mind the extra time, because you'll be going through just about every conceivable option and cross check you could imagine for a JPEG image.

Photoshop Elements and Photoshop make the entire process far easier than it used to be, and arguably easier than in any other program. But don't take our word for it; follow these steps to save a file as JPEG in Photoshop Elements:

1. **Open Photoshop Elements by choosing Start⇨Programs⇨Photoshop Elements 2.0.**

2. **Open an image to experiment with.**

   If you copy an image from the clipboard, choose File⇨New from Clipboard.

   If you don't have an image handy, grab a screen shot as described in Chapter 4, using File⇨New from Clipboard, or get an image from the *Creating Web Graphics For Dummies* CD-ROM. Don't use a JPEG as your starting image — recompressing a JPEG leads to poor results.

3. **Choose File⇨Save As (Ctrl+Shift+S) to save the original image.**

   Because Photoshop Elements saves the JPEG version of the image separately, you may not think you need to save the original before starting. However, there's always the chance of a computer crash during the process of optimizing the file for JPEG, so it's best to save the original before proceeding.

   Working with a memory- and disk-intensive process such as experimenting with various JPEG options seems to be more likely to crash your computer than most other things you might use it for. Save everything that's currently open, and consider closing some files or programs for maximum protection.

4. **Choose File⇨Save For Web (Alt+Shift+Ctrl+S) or choose the Save For Web icon in the Shortcuts bar.**

   The Save For Web dialog box appears, as shown in Figure 5-6. The Save For Web dialog box allows you to simultaneously view much or all of the original image, a preview of the compressed image, and relevant settings and download speed information.

5. **Inspect the settings contained in the Save For Web dialog box.**

   The JPEG quality setting is set to Maximum/100 by default. Look at the preview and check the estimated file size and file download time.

6. **Adjust the quality settings — High (60%), Medium (30%), and Low (10%) — in the Settings drop-down list and then fine-tune the numeric settings in the Quality text box.**

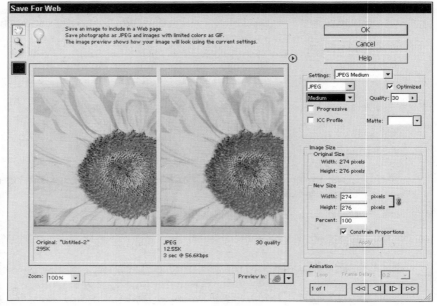

Figure 5-6:
The
Photoshop
Elements
Save For
Web dialog
box.

Watch the quality of the preview image change. Observe the estimated file size and download time changing. Type a number, such as 40 or 50 percent, to make additional changes to the numeric setting.

The availability of the rough settings — High, Medium, and Low — alongside numeric settings can be confusing, but can also be a time-saver. Get in the habit of trying the rough settings first to get your bearings before diving into changing the specific numeric settings.

Photoshop and Photoshop Elements use lower compression values to indicate more compression and a smaller file size (100 = least compression, 1 = most); Paint Shop Pro does the opposite. This can be confusing if you switch between the programs, or use one and talk to people who use the other.

7. **Click the triangle next to the preview window and change the transmission speed setting and observe the effect on the estimated download time. Experiment further using the Zoom tool and the Hand tool in the upper-left corner to inspect the preview image closely.**

The 56 Kbps setting represents the most common modem in current use. Cut the number of seconds needed at 56 Kbps in half to approximate the likely broadband download time — though most broadband pipes are wider than that, various choke points on the Internet usually prevent actual transmission speed from reaching its theoretical maximum.

8. **Experiment with the different options available next to the triangle to see how your image will look with a browser dither, or with uncorrected, PC and Macintosh color profiles.**

   The Browser Dither option shows what you can expect if your JPEG image is shown on a limited, 256-color graphics display subsystem, or on a computer that's been set to show graphics in 8-bit color.

9. **Use the Preview In area in the lower middle of the dialog box to preview your image in various Web browsers.**

10. **Click OK when you're ready to save your image.**

    The Save Optimized As dialog box appears. Navigate to the folder you want to save your image in, and then click Save to save the image.

    You're done!

You've successfully used some of the most powerful JPEG compression tools around for the first time. You can accomplish a great deal within the Photoshop Elements and Photoshop Save For Web dialog boxes.

Chapter 6

Creating GIF Images

*G*IF, short for Graphics Interchange Format, is the other major Web graphics standard along with JPEG. It's supported by every widely used Web browser and by a wide range of tools, several of which we talk about in this chapter.

You can pronounce GIF either with a hard G, so that it sounds like *gift* (minus the T), or with a soft G, so it sounds like a popular brand of peanut butter. We tend to use "GIF like gift" ourselves.

GIF was the first graphics format used for the Web. It's great for buttons, icons, dingbats, text displayed as a graphic, and all the hundreds of little images you see in even a short Web-surfing session.

GIF is *lossless,* meaning that it only compresses up to the point where it can keep all data intact — if your file has fewer than 256 colors to start with. If your image has more than 256 colors, most programs that create GIF files will more or less recklessly throw away all but 256 of them and render your file in the remaining colors. This produces very bad results with most photographs.

However, GIF is fantastic for just about everything else. It cuts the file size of suitable images significantly, usually in the range of 50 to 90 percent, and adds additional features, such as transparency and even simple animation, which we explain in this chapter. GIF definitely needs to be part of your graphics repertoire; in this chapter, we explain how it works and when is the best time to use it.

Knowing how to use GIF images effectively and when to use them versus JPEG images is basic operating information for anyone who wants to be effective with Web graphics. Yet most people only pick up a smattering of hearsay or folklore assembled from bits and pieces they see on the Web. In this chapter, we lay out the truth about GIF, what you can expect from it and what you can't.

All about GIF

GIF is a standard for lossless compression that is the most commonly used graphics standard on the Web. GIF was the first and, for a while, the only graphics standard supported by commonly used Web browsers.

As the Web became more popular, as average access times sped up, and as the average computer got faster, JPEG was added to GIF as a widely supported Web graphics standard. (Web old-timers can still remember when JPEGs were originally handled by an outside program, not inside the browser, just as a typical movie or sound file is today.) That allowed JPEG to handle support for photographs and allowed GIF to be used for the many other things it's good for.

The GIF algorithm

GIF is, at its heart, an *algorithm* — a mathematical procedure for manipulating data. GIF is also a *standard* — a widely agreed-on way of doing things.

If you really need to know the details of the GIF standard, the reference version used in the Web is called GIF 89a. Just type the term **GIF89a** in your favorite search engine, and you'll find a wealth of resources and documentation. The official specification is at this URL:

```
www.w3.org/Graphics/GIF/spec-gif89a.txt
```

To run the GIF algorithm, a graphic is viewed as a series of rows of pixels. Imagine an image of the word HELLO displayed on a computer screen. An example of this is shown in Figure 6-1.

The GIF algorithm looks for *runs* — areas in a row of pixels where several pixels in a row are the same. Every time it sees a run, it stores the length of the run and the color of the pixel used in the run. So if you were to read a GIF file, its core would alternate between two kinds of 8-bit numbers: Length, color; length, color; length, color. . . . (You can see why we have computers for this stuff; it's far too boring for humans.)

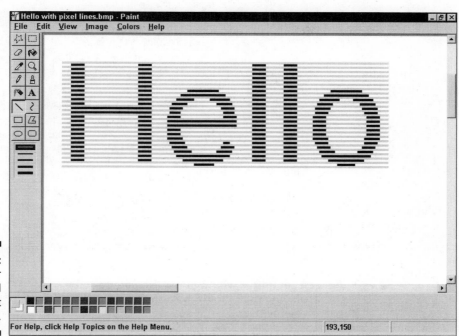

Figure 6-1:
Looking for
runs in all
the right
places.

For the word "Hello," the situation is great. Above and below the word is nothing but runs of white. In the rows that actually include lettering, there are still long runs of white interrupted by short runs of black. GIF compresses the file to less than 10 percent of its original size.

If an image has many different intermixed colors, a GIF file could be larger than the original image! That's because the length would always be 00000001, and the color would be the same value every time. An 8-bit bitmap file, on the other hand, would just have the color repeated all the way through, and would be smaller. However, bitmap files aren't universally recognized by Web browsers, so even for this kind of file you'd want to use GIF.

But most computer-generated graphics contain enough runs that GIF compresses them rather well. (And the others are usually suitable for compression by JPEG, as described in Chapter 5.)

So that's the core of a GIF file, but it can have other things as well. The GIF file can include a palette — a specific list of the 256 colors needed to reconstruct the original graphic. However, shipping a palette is not always a good idea for Web graphics. Here are some reasons why:

Isn't 256 colors enough?

Hearing that GIF has a 256-color limitation often confuses people who look at a photograph of a face and see maybe 6 or 7 colors — the hair color, skin color, eye color and the whites of the eyes, lip color, teeth if the person is smiling, and the background. Given the way people normally use the word color, that's accurate. But from a technical point of view, even a closeup of a person's cheek has hundreds of colors — subtly different shades of tan or brown that convey lighting and depth information to the eye. In an entire face there are thousands of shades, and in a naturalistic scene there may be millions of colors.

So think of only having 256 shades to use in a GIF image, and you begin to see a problem. If you understand that GIF normally uses a fixed palette, no matter what the original image looks like, you'll get even closer to understanding what happens. If you convert a photograph to GIF format, entire areas of the image become monochromatic blocks or blotches — not a very appealing prospect!

✔ **Not every computer would allow the palette to be used.** If the computer displaying the graphic is limited to 256-color display, either by design or by the user's color setting, then the palette can't be used — the computer's fixed 256-color palette is used instead.

✔ **The palette takes up valuable space.** Putting a palette with 256 3-byte colors into a GIF file takes up almost 1K of space. This is a bad thing for any file, but for simple files that compress well, it can make for a big percentage increase in file size. No big deal when it happens one time, but when you consider that a carefully designed page might include 10 or 12 GIFs. . . .

✔ **Designers need to know their colors.** Because a palette might be thrown out, it's fooling the Web page designer (that would be you) to ever allow it to be used or defined at all. A program that more or less forces you to use a fixed palette might be doing you a favor by only allowing you to create something that all users will see the same way.

✔ **Creating the palette adds complexity.** People who make graphics-authoring programs have limited time available too, just like you. If they can justify not taking the time to add the ability to create and modify a palette in their graphics programs, they will do so. The fact that the palette is likely to be thrown out some of the time gives them just that justification.

✔ **The Web-safe palette has acquired its own momentum.** The Web-safe palette, which we explain in the section, "The 216-color Web-safe palette," allows you to neatly step around most of these problems in the graphics that you create. If everyone uses the Web-safe palette, there's no need to ship a palette with most GIFs — and therefore no reason to support that capability.

So don't count on your GIF file including a custom palette. Consider simply using the Web-safe color palette to create files that you make up from scratch, or converting other files to Web-safe colors before including the GIFs in your Web page. Otherwise, get ready to spend some time worrying about palette use on the Web.

What GIF does to images

If you create your images using the 216-color Web-safe color palette — which we describe later in this chapter — GIF won't do anything to your images. But what about images that start in some other program?

The answer depends somewhat on the program you use to create the images. If you use a smart program, it will create a palette customized to the image — an adaptive palette. The program will then gently and carefully convert the many hundreds or thousands of colors in your image down to the 256 colors in the palette it just created. The result is often pretty good.

Mind you, a program is only so smart. It doesn't know that adding 2 or 3 more colors to better render a chin might be a lot more valuable than using the same colors to get all the leaves right in the tree in the background. But all in all, it does a pretty good job.

The trouble is that your nice adaptive palette may get lost in translation somewhere — in processing by another graphics program, by the browser on your user's machine, or by a 256-color limitation on the user's machine itself. In fact, in 8-bit mode, PCs and Macs use slightly different color palettes, so they can't support all the same colors, complicating matters further.

So your carefully crafted graphic just lost its adaptive palette. Then what happens? The answer is a word that throws fear into graphic artists everywhere: Dithering!

Figure 6-2 shows an example of *dithering*. Basically, in dithering, the graphics program creates patterns using colors it does have available to approximate the lost color. This actually works fairly well on large, dense images where the colors available are hand-picked to suit the image in question. But on low-resolution images where the colors used for dithering are fixed by the specific machine — and with different colors on Macs and PCs — the results can be surprisingly bad, even unintentionally funny.

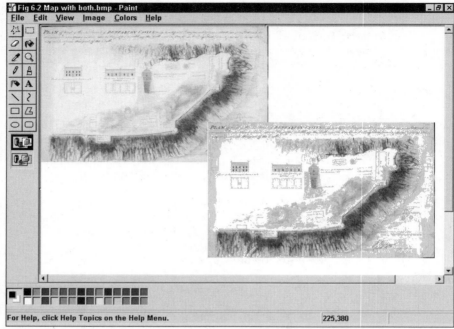

Figure 6-2:
Dithering
can make
your
graphics
ugly in a
hurry.

You may hear people say that you don't need to worry about dithering — that it isn't that bad, and doesn't happen all that often anyway. Unfortunately, it's still a big enough problem that you do need to look out for it. Later in this chapter, we show you how to preview the effects of dithering for yourself, so you can make the call about what to do next. See the sections on "Saving a GIF image in Paint Shop Pro" and "Saving a GIF image in Photoshop."

Mac versus PC on the Web

In the early days of the Web, designers agonized over having to reduce their images to 256 colors. (JPEG wasn't as widely supported then, so even photos often got saved as GIF files. Yuck!) Yet with an adaptive palette and some sweat and tears, they were able to create decent-looking, fast-downloading versions of most of their images.

Designers would create their images, upload them to a Web server, and test them. They might even have some of their friends look at them. They looked great! But the designers and their friends tended to be people on fast corporate networks, with bright, cheery, large Apple, Radius, or Supermac displays connected to a Mac.

Why would a user choose 256 colors?

Very few computers shipped today are limited to only 256 colors. However, you still have to allow for the fact that some of your users will see your Web page in 256-color mode. How do you account for these discrepancies?

First of all, for a busy Web site, even a small percentage of users with only 256 colors available on their computers can be a lot of people. If you haven't stuck to the browser-safe palette, these users may see a version of your Web pages that's anywhere from slightly different to very ugly. It's hard to predict without trying it yourself. And to get the full effect, not only would you have to set your own computer to 256 colors, but you'd have to find some people with older laptops or cheap monitors whose screens, bad from the beginning, have faded and had their colors shift with time.

Many users with more capable color systems either choose 256 colors themselves, or have 256 colors chosen for them, because the computer runs faster if it only has to deal with 8-bit colors. And computer games, which need to run fast, will often throw a system into 256-color mode without telling the user — or restoring the previous color setting when they close down.

So you can't count on your users having more than 256 colors. For JPEG, there's not much you can do, and it doesn't matter as much — dithering doesn't hurt JPEG images as much, because it's not obvious what colors were supposed to be used in the first place. The exception is larger images that you took some care to keep looking nice, but creating those with a 256-color palette in the first place would defeat your purpose.

But for GIF files, you can help yourself a lot by simply working in the Web-safe color palette. That way, you see what your user is going to see, monitor quality and PC versus Mac differences allowing. After you get used to doing this, you'll more or less think in Web-safe colors, allowing you to be creative even within these limitations.

In those early days, almost all Web design was done on Macs. The Macintosh was more popular then than it is now, and it was by far the better platform for any kind of graphics work. Programs like Photoshop and its thousands of add-on filters either didn't run on the PC at all, or ran poorly, frequently crashing the machine.

So our fearless friends would post their boldly designed Web pages with their carefully hand-tweaked GIF images to the Web, publicize the new or updated Web page, and watch as their e-mail inboxes filled with complaints. The pages were ugly, hard to read, and often had graphics or text spilling over into areas reserved for the other. While most Web designers at the time used Macs, most Web users then, as now, ran PCs. (Now most Web designers run PCs too, though Macs are found in higher proportions among the most experienced and best-paid.) And on those PCs, several bad things happened to images and Web pages:

- **Images got about a third smaller.** PCs tend to run at higher resolution than Macs. So a 100 x 100 image that would be a generous 1⅓-inch square on a Mac screen would shrink to 1-inch square on a PC screen.

- **Everything got darker.** PC screens tend to be tuned darker than Macintosh screens. More PC users also had laptops with the cheaper, dimmer screens common at the time. So color contrast that worked well on the Mac resulted in very hard-to-read pages on PCs.

- **Images got dithered.** Most Macs support thousands or millions of colors; most PCs at that time didn't. So the beautifully crafted, brightly lit images that looked so good on a Macintosh were dithered, often with ugly system colors, as well as darkened on the PC.

- **Pages got weird.** The Web browsers on Macs and PCs have subtle differences in default width, border width, and so on. That and the incredible shrinking images on PCs made pages carefully tested on one platform look funny on the other.

The PC territory was very much the wild, wild West, compared to the clean, paved streets of the Macintosh world. The 216-color Web-safe color palette developed as a kind of demilitarized zone between them — a small, grim, but safe place where both could come together.

The 216-color Web-safe color palette

You may have heard of the "Webmasters palette," the "Web-safe color palette" or something similar before. The Web-safe palette is simply the 216 colors that are always available as-is on both Macs and PCs, even on systems that are set to 8-bit color (that is, 256 colors). The color sets on Macs are a little different from those on PCs, so the shared palette is only 216 colors.

When you create a GIF image using Web-safe colors, it will display without dithering. This is likely to present a more attractive image to your users, and prevents your having to do a lot of testing on Macs and PCs running different browser software to see how images look with various amounts and styles of dithering.

The Web-safe color palette is on the CD-ROM. You can also find a version quickly on the Web by using a search engine with the term "Web-safe" or visiting the following URL:

```
http://the-light.com/colclick.html
```

You can easily use the Web-safe color palette in major illustration and Web graphics tools and even some HTML editors, such as Paint Shop Pro and Photoshop, as well as Illustrator, FreeHand, Dreamweaver, GoLive, and others. We show you how to use the Web-safe color palette in Paint Shop Pro and Photoshop later in this chapter.

In most cases, the Web-safe palette is not too limiting if you use it from the start. In fact, it can be somewhat liberating because it reduces the number of options you have to select from and because it reassures you that users will see something very much like the graphic you create.

If the audience for your Web site is relatively small and likely to have relatively new computers, you may be able to use the "thousands of colors" setting to create your GIF image without getting many complaints or giving anyone a bad experience. However, if you have a large audience or a less sophisticated one, using the 216-color palette is probably still a good idea in order to reduce support and user experience concerns.

GIF, royalties, and PNG

The whole idea behind GIF is its simplicity, and browsers decompress GIF quickly and easily. You don't need to worry about inaccuracies or speed in GIF decompression as with JPEG decompression.

However, one aspect of GIF causes problems — royalties. (No, we're not talking about princes and princesses.) Unisys owns some patents that apply to GIF, and collects fees from companies that make tools that create files in GIF format. No known plan exists yet to collect fees from browser makers whose browsers decompress GIF images or users who view Web pages with GIF images in them.

However, the whole idea of royalties being collected on a key Web technology makes some people nervous, creating interest in a rival format called *PNG*. PNG, which is pronounced *ping* and stands for "PNG's Not GIF," has gained some support in Web browsers and in tools. It promises no royalties, has better compression than GIF — about 20 percent better, in many cases — and has advanced features, such as more flexible transparency.

Sounds good so far, right? But further research is likely to scare you off. Visit the PNG home page at the following URL:

```
www.libpng.org/pub/png/
```

On this Web site, you find PNG described by its creator as "a turbo-studly image format with lossless compression." You find a link to a book about PNG which has, sadly, gone out of print. And you find news, links and references that, as of this writing, have not been updated in over a year.

Many reasons exist to not create graphics in PNG:

- Many older browsers don't support PNG.
- Web browsers that do support PNG have uneven support of advanced features such as transparency.
- Web graphics tools have uneven support for PNG.
- PNG, though created to replace GIF, doesn't support key GIF features, such as animation and interlacing, described in the next section.
- Though PNG was designed to be royalty-free, it may yet turn out to have patent complications just as GIF has.

You may hear more about PNG, but unless you're planning to create Web graphics tools and really want to avoid paying royalties to Unisys, we suggest you avoid it for the foreseeable future.

GIF Special Effects

One of the great things about GIF is its support for three key features that we discuss in great detail later in this book. The key features are

- **GIF transparency.** Although GIF images are always rectangular or square, you can make the background color around a GIF transparent. This makes the foreground of the image — the coffee pot, sports car, athletics shoe, or round button — that you're trying to bring attention to look like it's floating on the Web page, a striking effect.

- **GIF interlacing.** GIF files can be interlaced — that is, cut into 4 pieces, each piece having the rows of pixels 4 rows apart. The lines that are then downloaded one set at a time. First the first, fifth, ninth, and so on, lines download, then the second, sixth, tenth, and so on. This has the effect of making a very low-resolution image appear first, then the image sharpens a bit, sharpens some more, and finally becomes complete.

- **GIF animation.** GIF files can be animated by the simple trick of stuffing a bunch of images into a single GIF file, with the files then displayed as fast as the browser can replace one with another. (Yes, this makes animations run faster on fast PCs, a real sore point.) GIF animation is a very easy way to liven up a Web page.

For now, look for these special effects when you surf the Web, and let your imagination begin to roam as to how you'll use them in your own Web pages.

JPEG has no support for transparency and animation, but has recently gained an interlacing-like feature called progressive JPEG. It's only supported by newer browsers, so we don't discuss it in this book. The only fully reliable way to get a gradually sharpening image is by using GIF.

Saving GIF Images

Saving an image as GIF is easy and relatively straightforward, at least if you use our approach: Always use the 216-color Web-safe color palette, and use JPEG if saving an image in GIF format looks bad.

This implies a certain amount of experimentation — if you're not sure which file format to use, try GIF first, and then try JPEG. You should try the alternatives until they become second nature to you. In the next sections, we show you how to save a file as GIF in our three featured programs — Windows Paint, Paint Shop Pro, and Photoshop Elements (a workalike for Photoshop). These steps are fairly similar for all three programs; the differences come in the more advanced GIF options, such as transparency and interlacing, which we cover in Chapter 12.

Saving a GIF image in Windows Paint

Saving a GIF in Paint is a bad idea except when you just need a GIF file — any GIF file — for testing and experimentation. That's because Paint doesn't even use the full 216-color Windows-safe palette when it saves as GIF. Instead, it seemingly only uses the 48 basic colors it has available. The results can be good for some files, but horrible on others. If you're trying to save space by saving a small photograph as a GIF — something that can be a good idea when you're using other programs — the results are likely to be terrible in Paint.

As we describe in Chapter 5, if you don't know yet if your copy of Paint supports GIF file saves, open Paint and choose the File⇨Save As option. In the Save As dialog box, pull down the Save as Type drop-down list. If the GIF option is listed, good; if not, find your Microsoft Office installation disk and install the JPEG and GIF filters. If you can't do this, you'll need to use one of our other recommended programs — Paint Shop Pro, Photoshop Elements, Photoshop, or another graphics program — to save images in GIF format.

What makes GIF and JPEG standards?

The answer goes back to the early days of the Web. GIF was the first graphics format supported in a browser, and the use of GIF images seamlessly embedded in Web pages drove the Web forward rapidly. Web pages with GIF images represented the first easy-to-use way to combine text and graphics on the Internet.

But GIF is a really bad format for photographs, and pressure mounted to support JPEG, an excellent and already-existing format for photographs. JPEG was first supported by a helper application, but was soon built into Netscape Navigator, the only Web browser that mattered much at the time.

In HTML, the underlying language of the Web, the <IMG> tag is used to specify that a graphic will be displayed on the Web page. For instance, to show a map of the United States in the middle of a line of text, the HTML would look something like this:

```
We're from the good old<IMG
    SRC="usmap.gif"> U.S. of A.
```

When this HTML was displayed by the browser, a map would appear between "good old" and "U.S. of A."

When JPEG support was added to HTML, it went right in the same HTML tag, <IMG>. You can put a JPEG file in an <IMG> tag with exactly the same other attributes as a GIF file. (GIF features, such as transparency, interlacing, and animation, are specified within the GIF file, not through any special HTML code.)

Now in those days almost every Web user was an avid fan of the Web, and would download a new browser as soon as it came out. So early, GIF-only browsers were quickly replaced when newer, GIF- and JPEG-savvy browsers came out. Within a few months, just about every browser in use had both GIF and JPEG support, and Web page developers could use both formats with confidence.

During this time, more and more people were joining the Web, and the level of enthusiasm for downloading new browser software declined as the Web was taken more and more for granted. People would buy a PC with a browser already installed and, in many cases, continue using the same browser version until the PC wore out. So anytime someone had a new idea for Web graphics that required support from a browser, they had to worry about the huge number of people who didn't download new browsers. It meant that it would be years before a majority of people could use a new graphics format — and practically forever before all users could.

So graphics standards were pretty much locked in place from that point on. Although PNG got a pretty fair share of attention a few years ago, it seems to have slipped back off the radar. Expect GIF and JPEG to be the only two widely supported formats for Web graphics for a long time to come.

If you create the original image in Paint, it will save as GIF just fine from within Paint.

If you do have the ability to save a file as GIF in Paint, follow these steps to do so:

1. **Open Paint by choosing Start⇨Programs⇨Accessories⇨Paint.**

2. **Open an image that you'd like to try saving as a GIF.**

   If you don't have an image handy, consider doing a screen capture as described in Chapter 4, or use an image from the *Creating Web Graphics For Dummies* CD-ROM.

3. **Choose File⇨Save As, enter a filename, and save the file in the default Windows Paint format, 24-bit bitmap (*.bmp, *.dib).**

   Always save a file in a lossless format, such as the 24-bit bitmap format, before saving it as a GIF file so that you have the original handy. Given what Paint can do to a file when saving it as a GIF, this is particularly important.

4. **Choose File⇨Save As.**

   The Save As dialog box appears.

5. **Enter a filename with no extension (such as .gif). Click the Save As Type drop-down list, choose Graphics Interchange Format (*.gif), and then click the Save button.**

   The file will be saved with the extension .gif. If you get a warning about losing colors, click OK so you can see what happens. If the image is a photograph, or even an illustration that doesn't happen to have the right colors, you're likely to see a dramatic shift in colors.

   Inspect the image carefully, or open the original image and the GIF version next to each other so that you can see what changes saving as GIF has made. Zoom in, if it's a small image, to see the changes better.

6. **To see the effects of GIF on the image's file size, exit Paint and navigate to the original file and the GIF file; right-click each file and choose Properties to see the size in kilobytes of each image.**

If you really want to be clever, you can try creating custom colors in Paint to add the colors you need to save a file as GIF without undue color-shifting. However, we don't recommend this because the colors are unlikely to be Web-safe — so your image won't look as good on all machines.

Hopefully, your image saved as GIF just fine in Windows Paint. But Paint isn't capable enough to use as your everyday GIF program. Even if this image worked OK, you're likely to see fairly horrendous changes in using Paint to save other images as GIF. Not to worry! Paint Shop Pro, Photoshop Elements, and Photoshop are likely to do a much better job. Use the trial versions on the *Creating Web Graphics For Dummies* CD-ROM to get started with these programs, if you don't already own one of them.

Saving a GIF image in Paint Shop Pro

Paint Shop Pro works very well for GIF images — and it comes with an associated program, Animation Shop 3, which you can use for GIF animations. If you've tried saving a photo or other densely colored file as a GIF in Windows Paint, you'll be relieved to see what Paint Shop Pro can do for you.

Paint Shop Pro teaches you about GIF options even as it carefully saves your GIF file:

1. **Open Paint Shop Pro by choosing Start⇨Programs⇨Jasc Software⇨ Paint Shop Pro.**

2. **Open an image to experiment with.**

   If you need an image, use the steps in Chapter 4 to capture a screen shot in Paint Shop Pro, or get an image from the accompanying CD-ROM.

3. **Choose File⇨Save As, enter a filename, and save the file in the default Paint Shop Pro format, Paint Shop Pro Image (*.psp, *.jsl, *.pfr, *.tub).**

   Having a clean original that you can experiment on later is always a good thing!

4. **Click the Export GIF button (shaped like an arrow) in the upper-left corner of the Paint Shop Pro window.**

   The GIF Optimizer dialog box appears, as shown in Figure 6-3. As with saving a JPEG, the Uncompressed preview appears in the upper left of the dialog box and the Compressed preview appears in the upper right, with buttons between them that allow you to zoom out, pan, and zoom in.

Figure 6-3: GIF Optimizer gives you before and after views of GIF files.

Examine the transparency options on the Transparency tab. Experiment with the options if you'd like; we cover transparency in detail in Chapter 12. Also click the Partial Transparency tab, though you probably don't have any images with partial transparency to hassle with.

5. **Click the Colors tab, as shown in Figure 6-4.**

Note that the Colors tab enables you to choose how many colors you want, how much dithering, and which palette to use. Dithering is set to "full dithering," which produces a nicer looking image but a larger file. Consider setting dithering to a lower value or to zero to save file size. We discuss these options in more detail in Chapter 12, but you can see that the Standard/Web-safe option is the default.

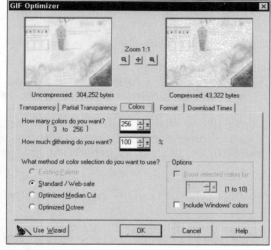

Figure 6-4:
Paint Shop Pro offers the Web-safe palette as a default.

6. **Click the Format tab and Download Times tab to examine the interlacing options and the estimated download times.**

The 56 Kbps and 128 Kbps settings are the speeds most likely to be experienced by home modem users and fast access users, respectively.

The Use Wizard option in the lower left on the Format tab is actually a pretty good bet, unlike the JPEG version of the same option. We recommend that you use the main GIF Optimizer interface for now, so you can see and consider all of the options, but consider using the wizard when you know your way around the GIF option settings.

7. **To save the file as a GIF, click OK in the GIF Optimizer dialog box.**

The Save Copy As dialog box appears. This dialog box saves a copy of your image, leaving the original file unchanged.

  8. **Save your file with the name and in the folder you choose.**

     The GIF file is saved.

If you use the Web-safe palette, your image won't look too different on any Windows or Mac machine out there. However, you may still want to see how it looks in various browsers and on different kinds of machines. Your image should only be affected by specifics of the type of machine in use, such as the tendency of the Macintosh to display files larger, or of the monitor in use, such as its brightness.

Saving a GIF image in Photoshop Elements

As is the case with JPEG images, described in the previous chapter, Photoshop Elements and Photoshop work about the same way in their GIF options.

Photoshop Elements and Photoshop actually use the same dialog box for both JPEG and GIF images, which makes experimenting with all possible options very quick and easy. The two programs also display not only file size but download time options all the while that you're in the dialog box. The only thing missing is a notepad area where you can take notes about the plusses and minuses of each approach you try! (But nothing's to stop you from opening a word processor or jotting down notes on an old-fashioned piece of paper.)

Here's how to use Photoshop Elements (and, by extension, Photoshop) to save a file as GIF:

  1. **Open Photoshop Elements by choosing Start⇨Programs⇨Photoshop Elements.**

  2. **Open an image to experiment with. If you copy an image in from the clipboard, use the File⇨New from Clipboard command to bring it in.**

     As a text image, you can get an image from the accompanying CD-ROM or capture a screen shot as described in Chapter 4.

  3. **Choose File⇨Save As (Ctrl+Shift+S) to save the original image.**

     Again, it's always nice to maintain the habit of saving a copy of the original image.

  4. **Choose File⇨Save For Web (Alt+Shift+Ctrl+S) or click the Save For Web icon in the Shortcuts bar.**

     The Save For Web dialog box appears — actually the same initial dialog box as for JPEG compression, shown in Figure 5-6 in Chapter 5.

  5. **From the Settings drop-down list, choose GIF Web Palette.**

The image on the right in the preview window will instantly be updated to using the 256-color Web-safe palette, with the file size and download time information updated to fit. Note that the default for dithering is set to "no dithering," unlike Paint Shop Pro.

You have many other GIF options, but the GIF Web Palette choice from the Settings drop-down list takes care of all your choices for many images. You don't even really need to use the Preview In option to look at the image in various browsers, though it's interesting to use the triangle above the preview image to see how it looks at PC and Macintosh levels of brightness. We describe all the options in Chapter 12.

6. **When you're ready to save your image, click OK.**

   The Save Optimized As dialog box appears. Navigate to the folder you want to save your image in, and then click the Save button to save the image. The image is saved and you're finished.

Though both programs offer a complete array of GIF options, Photoshop Elements and Photoshop are the easiest choice for quick, simple saves, and the most powerful choice for previews, for experimenting with both GIF and JPEG, and more. Although the programs put a lot of choices in front of you, they also offer shortcuts through them that are very helpful much of the time or, for some users, all the time.

Part III
Getting Photos in Your Web Site

In this part . . .

Having photographs on the Web has extended the capabilities of both photographs and the Web. Yet it's no mean feat to do a good job of photo publishing. This part shows you how to do the job right the first time and to take advantage of the full power of Web photo publishing.

Chapter 7

Preparing Photos for Your Web Site

*L*ong-time Web users may remember having to choose between having JPEG images appear *in-line* — within a Web page — or in an external viewer. For a while, the quality of JPEG images displayed by an external viewer was higher than the quality of images displayed by the browser. It was also nice to have photos displayed in separate little windows that lived after the page that had included them was closed. Eventually, though, rendering of JPEGs within the browser improved, and people stopped using an external viewer for JPEGs.

However, after technical standards improved, the other bugbear of photographs in Web pages reared its ugly head: the file size of images. Image size remains an issue with JPEG images. In this chapter, we tell you how to use images appropriately in your Web page without causing problems for the user. Chapter 8 includes step-by-step instructions on how to use graphics tools to process photos for maximum effectiveness on the Web.

We tell you how to use these factors to your advantage in creating Web pages that are generously illustrated with photos and other images, yet still work well for the user. First we discuss effective use of compression, because that topic is so compelling to us as well as to most people who work with images. But we also discuss two related topics that are possibly just as important: Effectively sizing an image, and effectively laying out a page to take best advantage of one or a few small images.

Avoiding Photo Compression Mistakes

Many Web graphics creators use an ineffective process for deploying photos on Web sites. The process involves doing something to a photo whenever it occurs to them and then fixing problems on the spot with whatever iteration of the image is currently at hand. Unfortunately, doing what comes naturally is often the worst way to proceed in getting photographic images ready for the Web.

In most cases, the easiest way to create Web graphics is also the worst way. Here are some common mistakes people make when putting photos on the Web:

- ✔ **Not using photographs.** Plain text is a bore, and text enlivened by little GIF graphics is only a bit better. Photos are among the most effective communications tools. Figure 7-1 shows an effective use of photos scattered across a Web page. Captions make photos even more powerful.

  If you use photos, though, respect their power — think through what you want to communicate, and what the user is interested in. Combine the two to make your point in a compelling way.

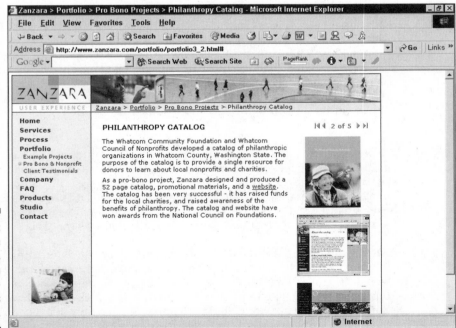

Figure 7-1: Whatcom County, Washington philan- thropists use photos.

✔ **Using large image sizes.** The main models for page design are books, magazines, and newspapers. Of the three, magazines are by far the most visually attractive, so people tend to use them as the main model for Web design. But magazines tend to use lots of large images, including full-page images.

Newspapers, excluding advertisements, are a better model. Newspapers tend to use lots of text and fewer photos and print on coarse paper, which gives them low resolution more like a computer screen. (One difference: Photons don't rub off and stain your fingers like newspaper ink does!) Newspapers place a premium on grayscale rather than color images. Consider using small images with few colors in your Web pages, like newspapers do, and don't implement a magazine-like model on the Web.

✔ **Resizing images using HTML.** Whether you create HTML directly, or with a Web page creation tool, you'll have seen that it's very easy to resize an image just by specifying new `WIDTH` and `HEIGHT` attributes. Don't! When you do this, the original image is downloaded to the user's browser, and then stretched or scrunched to fit the parameters. If you display a 100 x 100 pixel image as a 75 x 75 image, what happens is the big 100 x 100 image gets downloaded, but the user only gets to see the smaller 75 x 75 image.

Downloading a 100 x 100 image takes nearly twice as long as displaying a 75 x 75 image. We've seen Web pages with a few small graphics, over 1 megabyte each in size! They were beautiful full-screen images displayed in little windows about 200 x 100 in size. Use a graphics program to resize images to the size you want them displayed, and the file size reduces as well.

✔ **Not keeping the original.** Manipulating an original image to make it better suited for display in a Web page is easy. And it's very likely that at some point you'll wish you had that original image back.

In preparing an image for the Web, you're likely to resize, crop out unneeded background, fix problems like red-eye, add a blur to soften detail, and compress the image using JPEG. (See Chapter 8 for details.) Any mistake or change in what's needed within the Web page leaves you scrambling for the original — or taking a new photo and going through the whole process again!

✔ **Using JPEG compression on the same image twice.** JPEG is so effective that people often aren't aware that the original image they're working on is a JPEG image. Other times, people haven't saved their original, so all they have left is the JPEG they created. When the file needs to be resized, recropped, or compressed further, a JPEG ends up being used as the starting point, then recompressed using JPEG again at the end, with terrible results.

The JPEG algorithm tends to blur the image subtly. The eye compensates for this blurring to a large extent. But recompressing a JPEG image with a fresh round of JPEG compression is inefficient — the blurred areas don't compress well — and ugly. Always start with an uncompressed original; or if a JPEG has to be your starting point for editing, don't compress it again at the end.

✔ **Trying to fix errors at the pixel level.** It's a natural temptation: When you see a problem with an area of an image, you zoom in, find the problem area, and fix it. This works well on some problems, such as a diagonal line with lumps in it. But in photographs, with their thousands or even millions of shades of color, you're likely to cause new problems rather than fix existing ones. In most cases, you should use filters and other techniques to improve the image as a whole, or use tools to fix areas of an image, rather than trying the pointillist approach of fixing problems one pixel at a time.

✔ **Not making a large file available.** The reason for this book is that people love images — creative people love to use them, and users love to look at them. Why, then, do so few Web sites make the large version of an image available?

Many users have broadband connections, and have hardly any wait for even a very large image. And some users with 56 Kbps or even slower modem connections are patient, or skilled enough to surf other pages in the foreground while an image downloads onto a page in the background. Give your users the option of accessing a large, lightly compressed — or even uncompressed — version of each showpiece image.

✔ **Using JPEG for text and other flat images.** JPEG is really bad at compressing the things that GIF is good at compressing. GIF is good at text and images with large expanses of flat color. The blurry areas that JPEG creates tend to disappear within a photograph, but stick out like a sore thumb in areas with flat colors. Figure 7-2 shows the difference between a GIF-compressed and a JPEG-compressed area of a screen shot. Which would you rather look at?

✔ **Not creating a routine.** People who put a lot of photos on Web sites invariably end up establishing a routine. The sooner you do this, the better. Your routine can be in the form of a checklist, as we describe in the next section, or simply a set of habits you acquire to make handling photos easier. Either way, get used to a routine to guard against the sloppy habits that tend to accumulate when you do things in the order they occur to you. Be proactive, not reactive.

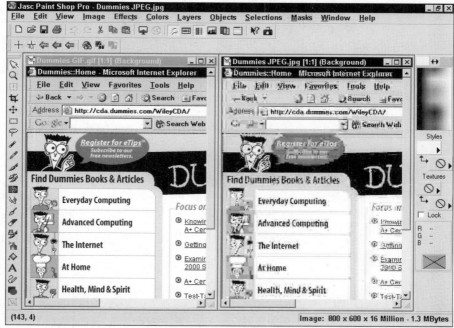

Figure 7-2:
GIF (on the left) versus JPEG (on the right) compression for a screen shot.

Planning Photo Compression

Devote some time to planning your compression session. (Chapter 9 details how you roll up your sleeves and actually do the work.) Before you begin, experiment with a few different images and approaches. Kick around ideas with others. Think about what you're trying to achieve and how you might best — and quickly — achieve it. If you don't brainstorm a bit at the start, you may work a lot on a specific solution only to have to begin again after you realize (or someone else convinces you) that you should have done something differently. Here are some suggestions:

1. **Set a time budget.**

   Think about how long acquiring, saving, and processing an image should take. Don't just say to yourself, "I can do it in 15 minutes." Think about the last couple of times you processed a similar image and use that experience as a guideline for the task ahead of you now.

2. **Acquire the image physically and get it into your computer.**

   And acquire it legally — make sure you have the right to use it. We describe different ways to do both of these in the Chapter 8.

3. **Archive a copy of the acquired image.**

   You may be able to use and reuse the entire image, or bits and pieces of it. Save a reference copy as soon as you have the image in digital form.

4. **Improve the image at full size and resolution by making changes that affect the image as a whole.**

   Color balancing and similar whole-image effects may work better at full size and resolution. You can also remove unwanted objects or people from the picture at this point. (Some changes will be easier after resizing; you discover which are which through experience.) Save a copy of this version as well.

5. **Make a loose crop of the picture at full resolution.**

   Frame the central part of the image to focus on the subject. Don't be aggressive here — leave yourself a little wiggle room in case you need to put the image in a predefined slot. For example, you may need to put a face shot of a person, which is naturally portrait-shaped, in a square photo area in a template. Save a copy — this is the version of the image you might print in a brochure or put on a T-shirt.

6. **Reduce the image resolution to 96 dots per inch (dpi), the standard for PCs.**

   At this resolution, what you see is what you get — a 96 x 96 image is about 1 inch square, at least for most PC users. People running medium-size screens at high resolution will see your images smaller than you intend, and people running larger screens at low resolution, such as many games players, will see your images larger. However, 96 dpi is a happy medium used by many Web designers. (Macs tend to be set at 72 dpi; your images will appear about one-third larger in height and width than you intended.)

   Funny things happen when you print on-screen images. Because the screen is about 96 dpi, and printers run at 300, 600, or 1200 dpi, a 1-inch square image on-screen may print at one-ninth, one-thirty-sixth, or even one-one-hundred-and-forty-fourth of the area you intended.

7. **Crop the image for the space you plan to put it in.**

   Consider very tight crops that keep the image recognizable even if you make it very small on-screen. (News sites often zoom in so tightly the subject's head and part of the chin is cut off. This is fine.) *Remember:* The number of pixels decreases with the product of the image's height and width, so small trims can produce big effects. As usual, save a copy.

8. **Blur, sharpen, and manipulate.**

   (See Chapter 9 for information about using specific filters.) Really work over the image — do all the things to it that will make it compress better while remaining recognizable. That includes simplifying the background and using filters, such as blurring and sharpening to make the image more compression-friendly. Save a copy of the manipulated image. You need to experiment to find the best image you can create before compressing it.

9. **Gently compress the image.**

At this point, you should have the image small enough and compression-friendly enough that it doesn't need to be stepped on hard to make its file size small. Stop compressing just before the point where visible artifacts occur — finding this point takes some experimentation. Chapter 9 gives more details about how to do that.

Don't compress the image further just to reduce its size by 500 or 1,000 bytes if that causes visible degradation to the image. Images lose much of their impact if they're visibly flawed.

10. **Sharpen again and make other improvements.**

If you're working with rigid file-size standards and heavily compressed the image, sharpening the graphic may restore its recognizability. And you may have changes to make that are easier now than they would have been on the full-resolution image. Turn to Chapter 9 to find out more on how to sharpen graphics.

11. **Consider adding a border.**

Sometimes background colors in an image match the background of your Web page closely enough that one blends into the other. You can prevent blending without undue worry, and further improve image recognizability, by adding a thin black border around the image. HTML can do this for you, but we prefer to add the border to the image itself, making it more immediately usable on various Web pages.

12. **Stop and think.**

You may be sick of this image by now, having spent many minutes — even hours, in some cases — looking at and working on it. But take the time to think about how the final image actually works in the Web page it's going into. Do you really need a smaller image? A larger one, or a different one? It's easier to experiment while you remember how the various versions of your image look, and where you stored them.

Communicate. If you learned anything new while working on this image, or if it could be useful beyond the immediate purpose you created it for, let others know. Take this opportunity to make sure the various versions of the image are named something useful and stored where you can find them again when needed. And look at the clock and see how close you came to meeting your deadline.

13. Find out how to batch-process your work.

Think about what steps you do repeatedly and experiment with ways to process images in batches. Paint Shop Pro and Photoshop Elements both have basic batch-processing features; Photoshop has a very complete set of them.

Figure 7-3 shows a flow chart of the core, repeated steps in this process. Vary it for your own purposes, and keep it handy as a reminder of all the important things you need to do to effectively process images.

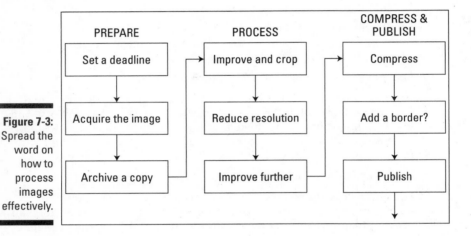

Figure 7-3:
Spread the
word on
how to
process
images
effectively.

Deciding on Image Size

Today, the phrase *use small images* is the watchword on the Web. We recommend it and we show you how to do it. But we think things are changing, and the trend is moving back toward using larger images in an interesting way.

More and more users are getting broadband connections, so download time is much less of an issue. At the same time, the standard of design on the Web is gradually rising, making high-quality images more important.

However, broadband adoption is very uneven within specific countries and across regions of the world. Some countries have more business use of the Web, others have more emphasis on home use. And some countries and regions have flat-rate, affordable broadband connections, while others have high prices that discourage use. In some cases, such as fast DSL availability in the United States, DSL may be readily available in a middle-class neighborhood, but an upper-class area a mile or two away is too far from the nearest switch and can't get DSL for love or money.

So what's a Web page author who wants to use graphics to do? We respond to this confused but interesting situation with two do's and a don't:

- ✔ **Do make your main pages download quickly.** Too many users are still on slow connections to do otherwise. Even business users who have fast connections at work may have slow access when at home or on the road. Fast download time remains the primary goal for all the important pages in your Web site, especially the home page — which is usually the most-visited page on your site, and makes the first impression on visitors.

- ✔ **Do offer extras for broadband users.** Give users the option to click a small image to see a large image or a multimedia clip. Make it clear what's going to happen so that dial-up modem users can make an informed decision as to whether to wait for a long download.

- ✔ **Don't split the difference.** You'll be tempted to go for the average, to create moderately heavy pages with medium-sized images, small video clips, and so on. However, this is called *splitting the middle of a bimodal distribution* — taking a middle-of-the-road approach that produces a page too heavy for modem users, yet without enough interesting, high-quality features for broadband users. Instead, work hard to create a light page with all the core information and functionality, and then offer heavy extras as an option.

Making Layout Effective

Photos in Web pages are commonly placed in a flow of text that wraps oddly around the image, to require the user to scroll horizontally to view the photo fully, or to have the image not visible to users who take in the initial view of the page but don't scroll down.

More broadly, images have to be used within an effective overall Web site to have much value. If your Web site has hard-to-use navigation, odd color combinations, misspellings, or other errors, no one's going to care about your images; they'll leave your Web site before they have a chance to look at them closely, if at all.

A number of good books exist about Web site design that you can use; we like *Web Design For Dummies,* by Lisa Lopuck (Wiley Publishing, Inc.). If you're creating your own sites, use this book or one like it to guide your efforts. If you're adding pages or images to a site designed by someone else, you're in luck — you can contribute ideas without having to be responsible for the overall design.

The following are some tips for using images effectively in Web site design:

- **Link to larger images.** Use small images less than 100 x 100 pixels in most of your Web pages. Then link the image to a large, relatively uncompressed version of the image. Amazon.com is famous for doing this — go to any book page on its site and you'll see a small image of a book's cover that links to a larger version of the image. Consider doing the same thing on your site.

People often refer to big Web images as being high-resolution. High-resolution can mean several things — large in size, high in quality, or both. Technically speaking, all the images in a given Web page are the same resolution when displayed on the computer's screen, whether they're big, small, high-quality, or low-quality. Usually, high-resolution indicates an image that's large in file size and slow to download.

- **Reuse images.** Use images to create a theme across your Web site, or in one area of your site. Use an image from within a story as an icon on the home page to link to the story. Done well, this kind of reuse saves you work while making your site more interesting and useful. It also reduces page load speed because the image may be cached the first time it's displayed, and then retrieved quickly from the hard disk when used again later.

- **Article template with one small image.** Consider creating a template for a story, article, or product description with a single photo. With clever Web page design using tables, the template can accommodate a photo up to 100 x 100 pixels without interfering with the flow of the rest of the story. If you can't create a single design that's flexible, consider creating templates that accommodate images of 50 x 70 pixels for a person's face, 70 x 50 pixels for a landscape, and 70 x 70 pixels for a pair of people or a square object.

- **Article or product page template with one large image.** Consider creating a page design that focuses on a photo as its central point of interest. Look at advertising-supported pages on sites such as CNET, as well as product sites, for examples of how to design around a large image area.

- **Article template with two images.** Consider creating a template with a small image above the fold — that is, within the first page view that the user sees — and a larger image below the fold. The first view of the page appears quickly, but there's something interesting to see farther down.

- **Additional designs.** Consider additional templates to fit your specific needs. Every time you need to do something that doesn't fit in your existing templates, create a custom page; then consider whether a template based on the new page is needed to support similar needs in the future.

Chapter 8

Getting Photos for Your Web Site

. . . .

. . . .

*W*here do you get photos for your Web site? From a piece of film inside a camera is only one answer. You can scan a photograph, ask a photo processing shop to create a digital image from a negative, use an online photo library, buy a CD-ROM with stock photos, and more.

This chapter focuses on all the steps to get a photo (with all rights issues cleared) into digital form and onto your hard drive, ready to clean up, compress, and put onto your Web site. The things that you need to do after you have the photo are covered in Chapter 9.

Acquiring Images

Getting photos and other images onto your hard drive can be easy or difficult, inexpensive or expensive, and legally simple or a legal minefield. A little planning up front can keep you on the cheap, easy, and lawsuit-free side of the road.

The following is a list of the most common ways of getting photos:

✔ **Taking photos yourself with a digital camera.** After you have the downloading process from the camera working, this is the easiest way to get photographs. *Remember:* You have to consider the cost and hassle of getting a signed model release from anyone recognizable in your photo, though.

✔ **Taking photos yourself with a regular (film-based) camera.** These days, you can order a Photo CD from many photo processors when you have your film developed. The Photo CD approach is great because you have no download hassles and quality is high.

✔ **Scanning existing photos.** Scanning photos can result in good-quality digital images, but you have to consider the rights of the photographer and, if one or more people are in the photo, the subject(s). Unless you took the photo of yourself, you have to think through these issues.

✔ **Using photos in online stock libraries or photo sites.** Some of these images are available for free, others for a fee. Rights concerns vary considerably depending on the site; unless you see an explicit statement that you can use the images for your purposes, you have to assume you can't. Also, stock photos are usually JPEG-compressed already, making some editing difficult and limiting your choices in terms of compression.

✔ **Purchasing a CD-ROM of photos.** This can be a way to get high-quality photos, and rights issues are often handled for you. But previewing is difficult — you have to buy the CD-ROM before you need it, hoping that the exact photo you want happens to be on it.

Table 8-1 shows some of the many ways that you can get photos and compares them in terms of how easy and how affordable they are. As you can see, solutions tend to be either easy and expensive or affordable and difficult. It's often true that you get what you pay for in terms of ease of acquisition for photos.

Table 8-1	Cost and Difficulty of Acquiring Photographs	
Method	*Cost*	*Difficulty*
Digital camera	Moderate to expensive	Easy
Film camera	Moderate to expensive	Easy
Scanning printed photos	Inexpensive	Moderate
Buying a CD-ROM	Moderate	Easy
Online	Inexpensive to expensive	Easy

We discuss rights issues in the section, "Rights!" at the end of this chapter. Be sure to read about, think about, and take action on rights issues before putting any photograph on the Web. Get legal advice if you have any concerns at all.

Royalty-free and rights-managed stock photos

You can find two major kinds of stock photos on the Web: royalty-free and rights-managed. You pay once for royalty-free stock photos and can then use them freely. Rights-managed stock photos, which are likely to be of very high quality, are carefully limited as to their use, based on considerations such as the size, placement, length of time you use them, number of people who view them, and so on. Carefully study the license for any kind of stock photo you acquire to make sure that the rights granted fit your needs.

Taking Photos

The ability to distribute pictures to hundreds of millions of potential purchasers online is a big step forward in photography — a step that hasn't been fully taken advantage of yet. Too many photos available online are low-resolution or have complicated rights agreements, when high-resolution photos with simple rights agreements are needed.

On the other hand, taking photos can be an enormous hassle. Most work that you do on your Web site can be done by taking advantage of the power of the computer and of the Web itself. But if you're taking the photographs you put on your Web site, you usually have to go somewhere, interact with real people, and snap the right pictures. Then you have to bring the photos into the computer, which can involve delays of hours or days.

A million things that you do (or don't do) can affect the quality of your photographs, but we're not going to go into all of them here, only the aspects that relate specifically to using your images on the Web. Just be aware that there's a big learning curve involved in becoming a skilled photographer, and those of us who lack any discernible talent may never master all the details.

Taking photographs with film

A good way to get photos for a Web site is to grab a plain old film camera and start taking pictures. You don't have to be as careful as when taking a real photograph because you're only going to be displaying the image at 96 dpi or so and, for any serious problems, there's always Photoshop or another tool. (Although a minute or two of planning your photo may save you an hour or more of work in a bitmap-editing program.)

Can computers be great photo machines?

In some ways, the best way to see a photograph is as a slide or as an image within a movie because vision, and therefore photography, is so dependent on light. Backlit or projected images like slides and movies can be very bright or very dark, just as in real life. Printed images, on the other hand, depend on reflected light, and so can't be as bright as backlit or projected images.

Images on the Web are backlit, and therefore have the same potential range of brightness as slides or movie images. The disadvantage of the Web is that bandwidth concerns and resolution limitations prevent truly outstanding images from being distributed and shown.

If you take your own photos and bring them onto your computer as digital images — either by using a traditional camera and getting a Kodak Photo CD made of the negatives, or by using a digital camera — you get the advantage of this backlit effect, so the potential quality of your images is higher than with a scanned image. If you scan a printed photo, however, some brightness has been lost in the printing process, and there's no way to get it back. And you still have the disadvantage of low-resolution display of the image.

We're going to make a prediction here: Sometime in the near future, increased attention will be paid to the quality and consistency of brightness and color reproduction of computer monitors (traditional and flat-panel both). And more effort will be put into delivering high-quality images within Web sites. Over time, computers may become a favored method of distributing outstanding, high-impact photos.

You can use several output options to speed the passage of images to your Web site:

- ✔ **Traditional prints.** Get large prints and scan them into your computer. (See the "Using a scanner" section, later in this chapter.)

- ✔ **Picture Disk.** You can get the scanning done for you and get the images returned to you in low-resolution Picture Disk format. This is fine for many Web uses of images.

- ✔ **Photo CD.** You can get your images returned to you on a Kodak Photo CD in addition to, or instead of, as prints. Quality is high, but there's a problem here: Kodak compresses the images for you. The compression is pretty good, but it can interact in odd ways with JPEG compression to cause strange effects. (And Photo CD images are large enough that you still definitely need to compress them with JPEG.)

Many pros still get prints and scan them to avoid problems with Picture Disk and Photo CD and to have maximum control over every step of the process. For higher quality, they scan negatives, which contain more detail that can be used as input for editing on the computer. And for higher quality yet, they scan positives, that is, slides, so brightness is never lost. Whichever way you go with taking your own photos using film, the photographer's credit is taken care of!

Consider making full-size images available to your Web site visitors. Warn them about the download time required for users with dial-up modems. Figure 8-1 shows a high-quality image that nearly fills the browser window at 800 x 600 resolution.

Taking pictures digitally

Taking pictures with a digital camera is a lot of fun and is the quickest way to gather hundreds of images that you can easily use on your Web sites, model release and property release forms permitting. (See the "Rights!" section, later in this chapter, for details.) Modern digital cameras capture far more data than you need to produce a 100 dpi or so image on your Web page.

The only caveat we're concerned with is compression. Digital cameras often offer you a choice between JPEG-compressed and uncompressed TIFF images. You may want to start with the TIFF image (which can be up to 10MB in size), clean it up, apply JPEG compression, clean it up some more, and then use it on your Web site. The trouble is that unless you buy a large memory card (for example, 128MB or 256MB) for your digital camera, you may only be able to take a handful of TIFF images before you fill up your camera's memory. You may prefer to use the JPEG-compressed setting instead, so that you can take more pictures before filling up the memory card.

Figure 8-1:
Bigger can be better with high-quality Web images.

The temptation is great to use the highest compression setting the camera offers to fit more pictures in memory. But, as we describe in Chapter 11, you really want to start with an uncompressed image and preview different levels of compression before making a choice. You can't do that when you're out taking photos.

Using light compression all the time may not be a great choice, either — if the image can stand a lot of compression, you no longer have the option to use heavy compression, because compressing your lightly compressed image again will produce more problems in the image than if you'd compressed it heavily in the first place.

Some of the current high-pixel-count digital cameras produce such good images in the high-quality JPEG mode that visual quality is high and further JPEG compression can be done without too many problems. Cameras in the 1 megapixel range and below, however, are subject to problems in these areas.

Yet another complexity: Compression needs can change greatly after you clean up an image, especially if you crop tightly, simplify, or even remove the background. You have to choose compression for the original image before you've had the chance to do any of these things (though zooming in a bit when you take the picture can reduce the need for cropping).

All of this adds a whole additional set of concerns to the process of taking photographs. You'll eventually develop a feel for how much compression you should use on each image, given its makeup and how you want to use it. But the process is imperfect compared to the luxury of having an uncompressed, high-resolution original image on your PC to play with.

Consider using medium compression rather than a high degree of compression as your default setting when taking digital pictures. It's hard to undo lossy compression such as JPEG, and if you use a high degree of compression as standard practice, you'll end up wishing you could get some of that data back.

To get the most out of digital cameras you need to know a lot about them. *Digital Photography For Dummies*, 4th Edition, by Julie Adair King, (published by Wiley Publishing, Inc.) is a good source. Also consider doing research on these Web sites:

```
www.dpreview.com
www.steves-digicams.com
www.dp-now.com
```

Other Sources for Photos

You don't have to take photos yourself to get photos onto your computer. Scanners and image libraries allow photos originally taken for use in other media to be recycled for the Web.

You certainly don't have the same control of the process with photos that other people take as you do with your own. But when you're using smaller photos, or using photos for spot illustration purposes, this is likely to not matter too much. Getting the image yourself may only become a necessity when you need a large, high-resolution shot.

Using a scanner well requires creativity and expertise; using image libraries requires time and money, with one substituting to a certain extent for the other. Keep at it, though; experience allows you to more often get the image you need quickly, easily, and affordably.

Using a scanner

For many Web graphics practitioners, a scanner is a vital part of their toolkit. You can use a scanner to bring in all kinds of material — photographic prints, magazine pictures and illustrations, even a handprint! (See the "Scanning images directly" sidebar for details.)

If you don't have one already, though, getting and using a scanner can be a hassle. Scanners aren't too expensive, usually less than $100, but they take time and hassle to set up. Many of us are already short on USB ports, which is the most popular scanner interface. The desk space a scanner takes up is substantial. And scanning can be a time-consuming process.

A good intermediate alternative is to use someone else's scanner. Many workplaces have scanners set up and don't mind occasional personal use. And copying centers, such as Kinko's, have scanners all set up and ready to go, along with helpful staff who can save you time and effort in doing your first few scans.

Here are a few tips on using a scanner:

  ✔ **Do test scans first.** Do a few low-resolution scans of small areas to get a feel for what your results will be before you wait many minutes for a high-resolution scan that turns out to be in the wrong part of the scanning area. And take an image through the whole process, from scanning it in to the finished, Web-ready image, to get a feel for any issues before you start scanning a ton of images.

✔ **Scan at 100 dpi when possible.** 100 dpi is a good round number for scanning that will produce on-screen images that roughly match the real-world size of the original. If you need a smaller image on-screen than the original, then scan at 100 dpi and downsize in Photoshop, Paint Shop Pro, or another program. However, if you need a larger image on-screen than the original, double the scanning resolution to 200 dpi to get a scanned image twice as large as the original, scan at 300 dpi for and image three times as large as the original, and so on. We recommend that you approximate at this stage — you can get the exact size you need in Paint Shop Pro or Photoshop.

✔ **Set the scanning area carefully.** Scanning can take a while. Set the scanning area so you only capture the area you need. This may take a little trial and error, but it can save you a great deal of time, both in image capture and in working with the captured image.

✔ **Get the image square on the glass.** Aligning the image on the scanner's glass so that it's at perfect right angles can save you a lot of hassle later in trying to rotate the image exactly. It might take a couple of tries, but the time you save later will be worth it.

✔ **Be mindful of file size.** Every 1-inch square that you scan at 100 dpi at full color produces approximately 40K of data. So if you scan half a page, you bring in about 1.6MB. At 200 dpi, a 1-inch square is 160KB, and a half-page scan is 6.4MB. You might begin to notice your PC slowing down as you open, pan, or rotate a file this size. So do all you can to keep scanned images under 10MB or so or risk long, difficult, and crash-prone editing sessions.

✔ **Clean the scanner glass and the scanned paper.** It's amazing how much trouble a little dirt, even just a fingerprint, smudge, or smear, can cause you. It can take a great deal of effort to clean it up in Paint Shop Pro or Photoshop, and dirt doesn't compress well! A little cleaning up front can save you a lot of time and effort later.

✔ **Block outside light.** One of the greatest advantages of scanning is the consistent and bright light that the scanner applies to each part of the subject as it's scanned. Outside light can ruin the consistent results you would otherwise expect. For photographs and other small, flat objects, the scanner's cover works fine. But for electronic devices, toys, and other unwieldy objects, use a drop cloth to cover the scanner and the scanned object. This will eliminate outside light that can ruin the edges of the scanned image and cause you hours of work in Photoshop or another program trying to put things back to rights.

These tips just touch the tip of the iceberg; you may have a lot more to figure out to do really good scans. For more information, read the manual that comes with your scanner. Look online, or buy a book such as *Scanners For Dummies*, by Mark Chambers. In addition to the scanner manufacturer Web site, a couple of good online scanning resources are

```
www.scantips.com
http://desktoppub.about.com/cs/scanning/
```

Scanning images directly

For certain kinds of images, you can use a scanner as a camera — a very flexible and very high-resolution camera — by just putting a plastic wrap over the scanning surface, and then putting the stuff you want to photograph right on it. A cereal box, a pile of marbles, all sorts of things can be scanned right into your computer.

Lighting is excellent — each part of the subject is brightly and directly lit as the image is captured — and resolution is just about whatever you want it to be. (Of course, your image is going to end up being displayed at 96 dpi, so don't waste hours scanning piles of sugar at 300 dpi.)

You don't need to do this every day, but it's a great way to get unexpected images onto your computer quickly and easily.

Getting stock photos

Stock photos are a great resource for Web page use. Rights should not be an issue — you can usually count on sellers of stock photos to have taken care of rights issues (described at the end of this chapter), or at least to be the target of choice for a lawsuit if an image isn't truly free and clear in terms of availability for resale.

Stock photos also give you ease of use, variety, and availability. You can search online databases before buying; CD-ROM-based stock libraries usually offer a great many images for the price.

You don't have much to worry about technically with stock photos, except you need to pay attention to whether they're compressed before you get them. If so, be careful; not only do you not have the opportunity to choose how much compression you want to use, but images don't resize as well after compression as before. Because the image provider has no way to know just what size image you need, this can be a big issue, so pay attention to it.

So many images are available for free on the Web that it's odd to think of paying for a photo you download. However, it can make a great deal of sense. One prominent site sells many of its photos for wide-ranging use for $19. If your time is worth $19 an hour, then you only have to save one hour by downloading an image instead of taking it yourself — or save the lawyers' fees you might otherwise pay in a rights dispute — to make buying a photo worthwhile.

The biggest publishers of photographs that are available for free use are governments, especially the United States government. (The theory being that citizens paid for the photos to be created through taxes, so go ahead and use them.) Government-created photos are great if you need a beautiful full-color image of a super-nova; selection is limited otherwise.

Having said that, the best way to learn about stock photos is to get to know what's available, then use one or two when needed to get a feel for them. The following is a list of some top stock photo resources, online and on CD-ROM:

- **Corbis.** Corbis is a large and easy to use library with separate professional and personal access points. Corbis is constantly improving their site and their collection.

  www.corbis.com

- **Getty Images.** This may be the leading online image catalog. Getty Images has photos for just about every need, and it has been buying up image libraries (or access to them) and related products.

  www.gettyimages.com

- **Associated Press photo archive.** This is the best archive we know of for photos of public figures, places, and events. Fees vary, depending on who you are and what you're trying to do, but you should at least know of this resource if you do anything at all with news on your site.

  http://photoarchive.ap.org

- **Free Stock Photos site.** This site lists many of the top stock libraries on the Web, including government sites (where photos are largely free of copyright).

  www.freestockphotos.com

- **About.com list of photo sites.** About.com has a very useful list of photo sites and CD-ROM providers, kept regularly updated.

  http://webdesign.about.com/cs/photos

Most people's eyes glaze over when they see a Terms and Conditions page — the *T & Cs* — on a Web site, on a CD-ROM, or in a printed manual. However, you have to read the terms very carefully before using stock photos on your Web site. Many stock photo collections, especially free ones, are limited to non-commercial use, and the definition of non-commercial is something someone with a smart lawyer might love to take you to court over. Other T & Cs include additional restrictions or limitations on the publisher's liability that leave you open to unwanted attention from the photographer or the subject of a photo. Read carefully before using such photos; if you have a lot at stake, have a lawyer review the terms before you use the photos.

Rights!

The topic of rights is crucial, but less interesting than the hands-on processing stuff, so we put it after the others. Pay attention, though — it's easier to get rights issues wrong than, well, right.

Photographs can be highly prized objects, and everyone involved in a photograph may have some rights in it. Here's a list of the major parties to consider when it comes to photographic rights:

- **The subjects of the photo.** Any people recognizable in the photo have rights to the use of their image, though news organizations have special privileges, and famous people have fewer rights than others. The owners of certain objects and places claim rights to photos of their possessions as well, but these claims are often a matter of controversy.

- **The photographer.** A lot of people make money from taking and selling photographs, or they have non-financial interest in the use of their pictures, so the rights of the photographer always have to be considered before you use a photograph.

- **The developer.** If a creative or artistic process is used in the developing of a photograph from the original image, the developer could possibly claim rights to its use.

- **The publisher.** When a photo is published in any form — online, in print, or on CD-ROM — the publisher has many responsibilities and some rights.

- **The viewer.** The public at large has the right to be protected from certain kinds of images, although there is tremendous legal activity and controversy over the extent of these rights, and laws (and prosecutorial zeal) vary by nation, by state or province, and even by municipality.

You need to understand two concepts in order to use photos without risking legal trouble. The first is that, unlike other items you might buy, you can't just assume that someone who gives or sells a photo to you has all the rights to it that they need to in order to sell it. For example, if we give a friend a photo, and he gives it to you, then you publish it, we can sue him and you both for damages — almost no matter what our friend told you when you bought the picture.

The only way to protect yourself from these cascading rights concerns is through a scary-sounding legal principle called *indemnification*. As the purchaser, you need the seller to indemnify you — to agree to protect you from legal liability — from the subjects or photographer or previous publishers. This is a big burden for sellers to take on, and only a few sellers of images on CD-ROMs and stock image Web sites are willing to do so.

If you can't get indemnification from your seller, you have to get permissions from the models for any people recognizable in the image and from the photographer. (The seller may claim to be the photographer, but this can be hard to verify.)

Well-known people are just a little bit different from the rest of us when it comes to having their pictures taken. You can often use a photo of a public figure without a model release, even in circumstances where you would need one for a private citizen. Of course, the exact legal definition of a *public figure* can become the topic of litigation, but you're a lot safer putting a photograph of yourself shaking hands with the mayor on your Web site than of yourself shaking hands with a random passer-by.

For casual use, most Web publishers simply ignore these concerns and freely use photographs they copied from another Web site, or that they took themselves but lack model releases for. And this is so common that the odds of having trouble from it are low for personal or hobby Web sites. The problem comes when your Web site becomes popular, or if you use it for commercial purposes. Then anyone with a possible claim against you comes forward to get their share of the resources they assume you have. If you created a site for someone else, both you and your customer or friend could hear from the lawyers. Or a rights owner might contact your Web host and get your site shut down. So be careful — pay attention to rights issues from the start.

Chapter 9

Processing Photos for the Web

Getting photos ready for Web publishing has become a minor industry since the Web first exploded into popularity in the early 90s. It's a mysterious process to those who are new to it and a dreadful bore to many who are experienced at it.

In this chapter, we describe how to become really good at getting photos ready for the Web. But we go a bit beyond that by suggesting ways to take a creative, constructive approach to getting your photos ready for the Web.

Instead of seeing images as problems — overly large files that need to be compressed to the point of excruciating pain for the image's quality, and for the visual sense of the user who must view them — we encourage you to look at images as solutions to a couple of questions:

✔ How do you make your Web page stand out and serve the user?

✔ How can you raise, not lower, people's expectations of the quality of what they see on the Web?

Ansel Adams didn't become famous by just standing in cold dawns at Yosemite waiting for the light to strike El Capitan in an interesting way. He really is best known for his work in the darkroom. He regarded capturing an image as only the first step. The rest of the process (and often the most important part — the creative and enjoyable part) happened in the darkroom, where he used new and experimental techniques to bring everything possible out of the image.

As you prepare photos for the Web, you have the chance to apply your creativity in a digital darkroom (that happens to be the name of a now-little-used software program). You can take a hasty approach to this work — trying to get it done as quickly as possible, without letting the chemicals splash on your clothes — or an imaginative approach, in which you try to get the best possible image up on your Web page, space (on the page) and time (to download the image) allowing. We show you how to do a good job of processing 100 photos in a day, but also how to do a great job of creating striking images for use on the Web.

The Digital Darkroom program is an easy-to-use tool for fast photo processing with some neat advanced features. You may want to try it and use it for quick jobs or share it with a friend or colleague who has less demanding needs than you do. The demo version doesn't save, print, export, or copy, and is just capable enough to give you a feel for the program. The full version that does all these things costs $39.95 at this writing. You can download a demo version of Digital Darkroom for either Windows or Macintosh from the MicroFrontier Web site at:

```
www.microfrontier.com/products/digital_darkroom10/demo.html
```

Choosing Your Image Wisely

"You can't make a silk purse out of a sow's ear," the saying goes. Everyone knows about the wizardry that experienced designers can perform using programs like Photoshop.

Even with the power of Photoshop, you still want to start with a high-quality original image that exactly suits your purposes. You don't need a high-resolution original image for a small, illustrative photo less than (for example) 100 x 100 pixels in size. But if you intend to put up a larger photo, starting with a good original image makes a big difference.

We outline the various ways to acquire an image in Chapter 8. From best to worst, some popular sources for a high-quality digital image are as follows:

✔ A high-resolution Photo CD image produced from a film negative

✔ A high-resolution image from a digital camera

✔ A transparency or negative scanned with a film scanner

- ✔ A photograph (on photographic paper) scanned on a scanner
- ✔ A directly scanned image of an object from the faceplate of the scanner
- ✔ A photograph (on regular or magazine paper) scanned on a scanner (As former U.S. Senator Bob Dole once said, just don't do it.)
- ✔ A photograph (on newsprint) scanned on a scanner (What Bob Dole said above, only double.)

Stock photos can fit anywhere in this list. You usually have no way of knowing how a stock photo was handled between original capture and sale as a digital image. You simply have to trust your eye as to the attractiveness and interest of the image.

The key issues making one source of images better than another are resolution and contrast range. Backlit images can have nearly unlimited contrast range, while resolution varies from one technique to another. Slides are the highest-resolution backlit format. Movies are next, while computer monitors and TVs are quite poor.

Printed images have a much lower range of contrast because paper can be relatively reflective, relatively light-absorbent, or mixed. The paper that best suits one image may not be the best for the next one. Photographic paper has the widest range of contrast, with typical white or magazine paper much poorer, and newsprint the worst.

Because images on a monitor are backlit, and because both film-based and digital images can be made directly into backlit formats, one trick is to avoid having an image printed at any point between initial capture and display on the computer monitor. If you work from a printed image, you lose much of your contrast right off the bat.

Avoiding making a physical copy of any sort is important, though. (Making a copy of a file on your computer is fine because digital copies preserve all the information.) Every time you make a copy, there's some loss of information. Different media can also have different characteristics, such as type of color or different resolution support that can make you lose additional data.

So for high-quality images, get a Photo CD image from regular film or use a digital camera. If you have to start with a printed photograph, use the information in the section "Enhancing contrast" to increase the contrast in your image.

Preproducing an Image for the Web

Before you compress an image, you can do a number of things to make it better suited to display in your Web page. These steps are relatively easy, thanks to bitmap-editing programs such as Paint Shop Pro and Photoshop.

In this section, we describe how to handle the most commonly performed steps for getting an image ready for compression and point out where you can take things further if you want.

Here's what you need to do before compressing an image:

1. Rotate the image to the proper alignment for you to work on it.
2. Flip the image, if needed, so the focus of attention is where you want it.
3. Crop the image to the proper proportions.
4. Balance colors in the image to improve appearance.
5. Enhance contrast to make the photo livelier on-screen.
6. Sharpen the image to make it more recognizable.

You may want to use these steps as a checklist for each photo you prepare before publishing it on the Web.

In the sections that follow, we give you more details about the steps to take before compressing images. By the time you're done going through it, you'll know how to perform these steps for Paint Shop Pro and either Photoshop Elements or Photoshop, whichever you use. This gives you a framework of knowledge with which you can experiment and create a customized process of your own.

Most of the steps described in this chapter are irreversible. Although rotating an image is reversible, cropping and color balancing are not (unless you *immediately* use the Undo command). Be sure to save your original image under a separate filename before beginning, and consider saving additional copies along the way so you can go back to that version if a later step doesn't pan out.

Rotating and flipping

Given the complexities of using scanners, digital cameras, download programs and so on, you're likely to end up with an image that needs to be rotated every now and again. Understanding why you might need to rotate a photographic image is easy: Getting a photo of your cousin to look its best is tough if she appears to be standing on her head.

Deciding when you need to flip an image — to reverse it so that the parts on the left are now on the right, and vice versa — may not be as easy to determine. One reason you may want to flip an image is for accuracy. Another reason, which deliberately courts inaccuracy, is for effectiveness.

The left/right orientation of an image is an important part of its accuracy. If text is in an image, certainly having it backward is going to be a problem that your Web page users will take great pleasure in catching you out on. But even subtle differences in the layout and orientation of a place in an accidentally flipped image can nag at people who know, subconsciously if not consciously, that everything's backward.

Here's an anecdote to help you remember the importance of keeping left/right (or in this case, west/east) orientation correct. One of the most accidentally famous moments in the film career of actress Julie Andrews was when a movie began with her waking up one morning in California to watch the sun coming up — over the Pacific. The scene was filmed on the east coast, but it was supposed to take place on the west coast.

But sometimes deliberately courting inaccuracy is worth it to make a page more effective by purposely flipping an accurately oriented photo the other way. Why do that? Because your user's gaze tends to go to whatever the people or objects in a photo seem to be looking at or pointing toward. (We told you photos are powerful!) If you have a picture illustrating a story, it's better to have the person in the photo looking into the story text — leading the reader's eye there — than to have the person in the photo looking away. Other elements in a photo that "point" or lead the viewer's eye can be used in the same way.

Figure 9-1 shows an example of this from the Zanzara Web site. The photo in the lower-left corner shows a mobile phone held in a person's hand. The person is looking at the phone, and the strong diagonal line of the phone and the hand holding it leads up and into the text.

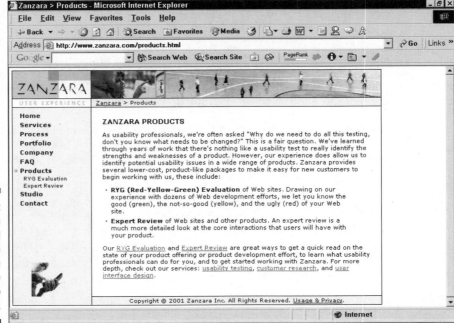

Figure 9-1:
The
diagonal
line of the
mobile
phone
points into
the text.

For photos of objects, realize that most photos have a *vanishing point* (a point that the lines in the image subtly converge to and the viewer subconsciously tends to look toward). Other converging lines in a photo also tend to lead the eye in one direction or the other. And, people tend to assume a story behind the location of objects and to look back to where the objects seem to have come from. Look at these elements in a photo and decide which way the eye is being drawn. Then, if needed, flip the photo so that the viewer's eye is drawn into the content of the page.

Of course, flipping a photo to make it draw the viewer's eye in the right direction may introduce inaccuracy, which may be obvious or not. No one except your friends and family may notice that your cousin's hair, after you've flipped a photo of him, is parted on the wrong side; many people will notice if you show famous model Cindy Crawford's facial mole on the left rather than the right side of her photo. (They're also going to ask how you secured rights to her image; we cover rights in Chapter 8.)

Rotating and mirroring photos in Paint Shop Pro

To rotate an image in Paint Shop Pro, follow these steps:

1. **Open Paint Shop Pro, and then open the image you want to rotate.**

2. **Choose Image⇨Rotate or press Ctrl+R.**

   The Rotate dialog box appears.

3. **Click OK.**

   The image rotates 90 degrees clockwise. Inspect the image to see if it's rotated to where you need it.

4. **Continue pressing Ctrl+R and clicking OK on the Rotate dialog box until the image is rotated to the correct orientation.**

   Now carefully inspect the image to decide whether or not to mirror it. If you know where it's going, think about whether the image will tend to lead the user's eye into the main part of the page content. If not, and if there are no obvious giveaways as to the picture's natural left/right orientation, consider mirroring it. If you don't know where the image is going, consider mirroring it now (or at the end of processing it) and saving both orientations.

5. **To mirror the image, choose Image⇨Mirror or press Ctrl+M.**

   The image reverses.

6. **Look at the mirrored image to see whether anything in it looks wrong. If you see a problem, mirror the image again to reverse the process.**

   You may see obvious signs, such as backward text, or more subtle signs. (Sometimes a flipped image looks more natural than the original, unflipped image!) Then decide which image to use for the best effect in the specific Web page; you may want to keep both versions to give yourself flexibility.

Be sure to name mirrored images in such a way that you can easily identify them. That way, you can revert to the naturally oriented image for situations where accuracy is the foremost concern.

Rotating and flipping photos in Photoshop Elements

To rotate and flip an image in Photoshop or Photoshop Elements, follow these steps:

1. **Open Photoshop, and then open the image you want to rotate.**

2. **Open the Rotate options by choosing Image⇨Rotate.**

   Rotate options appear, as shown in Figure 9-2.

3. **Choose the degree to which you want to rotate the image — 90 degrees left or 90 degrees right or another choice.**

   If you aren't sure which to choose, use 90 degrees left repeatedly until you get the desired effect.

   Before flipping the image, make a copy of it so you can compare the flipped and unflipped versions on the screen.

4. **Click the Title bar of the image window that you want to copy; then choose Image⇨Duplicate Image.**

   A dialog box appears, asking you to name the image.

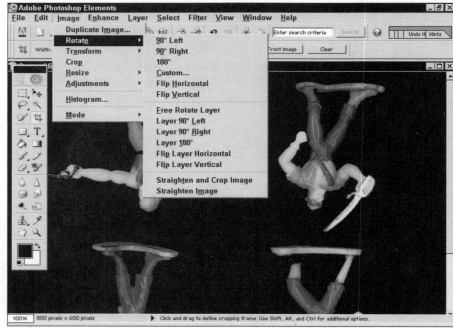

Figure 9-2:
Photoshop
Elements
has a full set
of rotate
options.

5. Enter a name; then click OK.

A copy of the image appears on-screen.

6. Flip the image by choosing Image⇨Rotate⇨Flip Horizontal.

The image flips.

7. Check the flipped image for obvious problems, such as backward text, or other things that look odd.

Inspect both images to see which suits your purposes better. Close the one you don't want, or save it so you have it as an option for later.

Include the word *flipped* or some similar indicator in the file's name so you always know which images don't have their natural orientation.

Cropping

Cropping robs your picture of information, which may make it seem like a bad thing. Perhaps that's why the children of graphic designers play "crops and robbers."

Seriously, cropping can be a great example of the old artist's saying, "Less is more." By removing extraneous information from a photograph, cropping makes the actual subject much more prominent and the effect of the photo much more intense.

Cropping is especially important if you're using poorly composed shots or shots with low contrast between the subject and the background. If such a shot is loosely cropped, it can be hard to make out the subject in the background. (If the subject is not at the center of the image, it can be nearly impossible.) Tightly cropping the shot and centering the subject in the image brings the subject to life.

Don't be afraid to crop really tightly, or even over crop for effect. Face shots cropped to the middle of a person's forehead and the middle of his or her chin are usually fully recognizable, even if made into very small images (for example, 50 pixels wide by 70 high). You can overdo this effect — one computer magazine had a columnist's photo cropped to show one eye, one cheekbone, and part of the nose, making the columnist look like a half-crazed Captain Ahab searching for the great white whale. But experiment freely in order to find just the right balance.

The dimensions your image must fit into may dictate how it's cropped. Depending on how much you rely on templates for your Web page layouts, you may know exactly, at the beginning of your editing session, how large an image needs to be. Or you may simply suspect that it needs to be wider than it is tall, or taller than wide, or roughly square.

Here are some scenarios to help you determine how to crop an image:

- **Exact dimensions known.** If you know the exact dimensions needed, you can either crop to those dimensions — for example, 50 x 70 pixels — or to some multiple of those dimensions. Just keep at least 50 x 70 pixels of data in the cropped version and maintain the needed aspect ratio that we describe in the next few paragraphs.

- **Approximate dimensions known.** Suppose that you know the image will be horizontal but you don't yet know the specific limits on its size. Cutting out some of the sky and ground, for example, is tempting, but how much do you cut? You may cut out too much and then have to size the image upward, or start again with the original, either of which can be a big hassle. Consider waiting to crop until you know the exact dimensions you need, or cropping to a square shape to give yourself maximum flexibility.

- **No particular limits on dimensions.** If you're the page designer as well as the graphics guru, or if you work closely with that person, or if the image is an important one, you may have no specific limits on the dimensions of the final image. In this case, experiment with all sorts of crops to find the most effective, and fit the overall shape of the rectangle — landscape, portrait-shaped, or squarish — to the proportions of the subject.

The aspect ratio of an image is the proportion of the width of the image to its height. For a 50 x 70 pixel photo slot in a Web page template, the aspect ratio is 1.4. You can figure out the aspect ratio by dividing the height by the width (for example, $70 \div 50 = 1.4$). Any cropping you do that results in an image more than 50 pixels wide and with the correct aspect ratio will be easy to resize to the correct dimensions. See the instructions for each program to learn more about cropping to the correct aspect ratio for your images.

Cropping photos in Paint Shop Pro

Be sure to save the uncropped image before you start cropping in Paint Shop Pro; when you complete the cropping, the remainder of the image simply disappears.

To crop a photo in Paint Shop Pro, follow these steps:

1. **Open Paint Shop Pro, and then open the image you want to crop.**

2. **If your image needs to fit fixed dimensions, calculate its aspect ratio.**

   Divide the width of the image by the height. Landscape-mode images (wider than they are tall) have an aspect ratio less than 1.0; square images exactly 1.0; portrait-mode images greater than 1.0.

3. **Select the Crop tool — the thing that looks like a DNA strand, the fourth tool down in the tool palette — by clicking it.**

   The Crop tool is highlighted.

4. **Click and drag across the area of interest to select the area to crop.**

   A box appears around the selected area. Don't worry about being exact just yet — simply select the area of interest.

5. **Fine-tune the cropping selection by moving the mouse to any side or corner of the cropping selection rectangle until it turns into a double-headed arrow, and then clicking and dragging that side or corner to move it in or out.**

   Watch the aspect ratio and image size as they display down at the bottom-left corner of the screen, as shown in Figure 9-3.

   Make sure to keep an eye on the size of your crop — don't crop the image too small.

6. **To complete the crop, double-click inside the cropping selection or click the "Crop Image" button in the Tool Options palette.**

   The rest of the image disappears and only the cropped part remains.

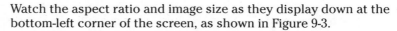

Figure 9-3:
Paint Shop
Pro shows
you the
aspect ratio
as you work
(it's 0.600 in
this image).

Cropping photos in Photoshop

As in Paint Shop Pro, save the original image before you begin; cropping discards the unselected portions of the image, and you need the uncropped image so you can recover from mistakes or changes in plan.

Follow these steps to crop an image in Photoshop or Photoshop Elements:

1. **Open Photoshop, and then open the image you want to crop.**

   For an image that needs to fit fixed dimensions, you can use either of two approaches: Either calculate the aspect ratio of the image, or identify the longer dimension — horizontal or vertical. (You need to do additional calculating if you choose the aspect ratio approach.) To calculate the aspect ratio, divide the width of the image by the height. The aspect ratio is greater than 1.0 for wide, landscape-mode images; exactly 1.0 for square images; and less than 1.0 for portrait-mode images.

2. **Open the Info window by choosing Window➪Info. If the Info window is already present, drag the Info tab away from the docking area so it will stay open. If the readout is not in pixels, click More and choose Palette Options from the submenu that appears; change the Mouse Coordinates Ruler Units to pixels.**

3. Select the Crop tool, which looks like a strand of DNA (as it does in most graphics programs), by clicking it.

The Crop tool is highlighted.

4. Click and drag the mouse to select the approximate area to crop.

A box appears around the selected area.

5. Fine-tune the cropping selection by dragging the handles around the cropping area.

Either crop the exact size you need, crop an area larger than you need with the exact aspect ratio (you may need to use a calculator for this as you work), or crop a square whose width and height are both at least as large as the smallest dimension of the area you need. Watch the image size, as shown in Figure 9-4.

6. To complete the crop, double-click inside the cropping selection or click the check mark in the Crop Tool options horizontal menu bar.

The rest of the image disappears, leaving only the cropped part of the image.

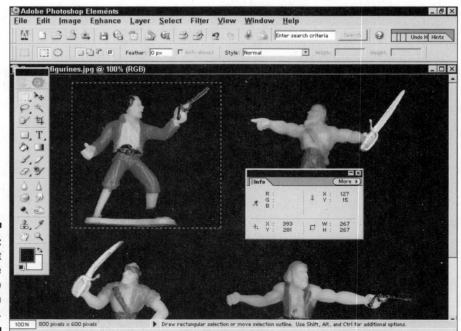

Figure 9-4:
The aspect ratio can be harder to get in Photoshop.

Color balance and saturation

Color is a very complicated phenomenon, the result of numerous interactions between the energy levels and numbers of photons reaching your eyes, processing in your eyes and brain, and interactions with memories from early childhood on. The study of color is far from an exact science; for example, brown, one of the most common colors perceived in nature, doesn't map exactly to the color scale but seems to be constructed somewhat by the brain from a combination of color, texture, and contextual information.

Grayscale images can be very interesting and evocative while also allowing for large images with small file sizes.

Photographs lack the wide range of depth and contextual cues that we find in the real world. If you consider the steps involved in capturing an image and bringing it onto your computer screen, it's somewhat of a miracle that it's recognizable, let alone that the colors are often pretty close to what they should be to mimic a natural scene. By using a few tricks in a good bitmap-editing program, you can remove effects that look unreal on-screen and bring the appearance of the image even closer to the original scene.

Color balance is one of the adjustments that can remove unreal-looking effects. Natural light tends to be cool (to have a lot of blue); early morning light and indoor light tends to be warm (to have more red). An image on the computer screen often looks odd because the various capture and conversion steps have left the color balance looking inappropriate compared to our expectations. The color balance adjustment lets you manually shift the color balance to make the image appear more real.

You can adjust color balance before you get an image on your computer by the use of specific types of film that are warmer or cooler, by adjustments by a photo processing technician using chemicals or digital equipment, by automatic or manual corrections in a scanner, by software in a digital camera, or by adjustments performed in software by someone who had the file before you did. Don't assume that knowing where and how a photo is taken is an infallible guide to knowing how to adjust it — develop an eye for this and trust your judgment.

Color balance also allows you to remove an overall color cast that's part of an image, for example, the yellowish or brownish cast that appears on a photographic print as it gets old. However, you have to be careful about removing the color cast on an image, because in doing so, the program may actually remove information. This is not likely to cause a noticeable problem by itself, but in combination with additional processing steps and compression may degrade the image in ways that you can't easily recover from.

Saturation enhancement is a similar technique to color balance adjustment. It has the effect of increasing the saturation or amount of color in a picture. Not all pictures need it, but pictures that are washed out can often benefit from it. Be careful, though — saturation enhancement can sweeten an image with color but make it appear unnatural rather than more real.

No correct setting exists for color balance or for determining when you should remove a color cast from an image. Similarly, the use of saturation enhancement is a matter of using a critical eye to make the image look more natural to you. Most of us have a good enough eye to make a badly balanced or washed-out image look better. You can use color balance, saturation enhancement, and other steps to make an image truly interesting and evocative. Just be ready to undo your changes quickly if your first few attempts make the image look worse.

Don't spend a long time fiddling with color adjustments and saturation enhancements to get the color balance just so — excessive fine-tuning will be quickly undone as others view your Web pages on monitors and in lighting much different from your own. Try to find a happy medium that looks great on good equipment and not too bad on other equipment. (If you're concerned about getting this right, you need to view your work on at least a couple of different traditional monitors, a couple of different laptops, and at least one Mac as well as several PCs.) Also consider that users work in a variety of different kinds of light, from bright daylight to complete darkness. This affects glare and how the user sees the image on the screen in contrast to the background around it.

Photoshop and Photoshop Elements have settings that allow you to view your work in a couple of different simulated environments, which is a good start toward addressing this problem. However, the problem will only be truly solved with much higher technical standards for monitors, followed by the passage of a decade or so to allow all previous monitors to get thrown out. Even then, users working in different lighting environments will see colors somewhat differently.

Adjusting color balance and saturation in Paint Shop Pro

Consider saving a copy of your image under another name before you begin to change the color balance. Then you can use the Auto Proof feature to use the whole image as a preview.

To adjust color balance and saturation in Paint Shop Pro, follow these steps:

1. **Open Paint Shop Pro, and then open the image you want to adjust.**

2. **Choose View⇨Normal Viewing to make the image accurate in size.**

   Some of the changes caused by adjusting the color balance are subtle and require you to see the image as accurately as possible.

3. **Choose Effects⇨Enhance Photo⇨Automatic Color Balance.**

   The Automatic Color Balance dialog box appears, as shown in Figure 9-5.

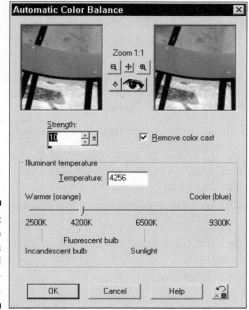

Figure 9-5:
Paint Shop
Pro does
several
things auto-
magically.

4. Experiment with the Temperature slider by dragging the slider to the appropriate setting; then adjust the Strength setting to modify the degree of change.

A typical indoor shot is 2500K, a shot taken under fluorescent lights is 4200K, and sunlight (from dimmer to brighter) is 6500K to 9300K.

You have to carefully select the area to zoom in on in the Preview box to see where the greatest changes are taking place. To apply the current settings to the whole image, click the Proof tool (the eye icon). To have settings applied to the whole image immediately as you change them, click the Auto Proof button (the down arrow next to the eye icon).

Seeing subtle changes in color balance in the little preview window in the Automatic Color Box dialog box is difficult. We suggest that you save a copy of your file under another name, keep both the original and the copy open, and run the Automatic Color Balance dialog box with the Auto Proof button on in one of them so that you can compare the images as an interactive preview.

5. If a color cast (an overall tint) remains over the image after you've found the appropriate Automatic Color Balance settings, click in the Remove color cast check box to set it.

Any color cast that the software can detect is removed from the image.

6. Click OK to complete the changes.

The changes are applied to the image, hopefully improving it.

7. **If colors are still washed out, use the Automatic Saturation Enhancement tool to make them stronger by choosing Effects⇨Enhance Photo⇨Automatic Saturation Enhancement.**

   The Automatic Saturation Enhancement dialog box appears.

8. **Change the Bias setting to let the software know whether the original image is Less colorful, Normal, or More colorful; change the Strength setting to make the enhancement Weak, Normal, or Strong.**

   Adjust these settings to bring the desired effect into your image. The preview window updates to show the results of your changes. As with the Automatic Color Balance dialog box, consider using the Proof or Auto Proof button to monitor your changes on the whole image, and consider keeping before and after copies of the image open to compare them as you go.

9. **If the image has large areas of skin tones, check the Skintones Present check box.**

   Paint Shop Pro moderates its color enhancements to prevent people from looking like they used too much self-tanning lotion.

10. **Click OK to complete the changes.**

    The saturation changes are applied to the image.

Both the Automatic Color Balance and the Automatic Saturation Enhancement dialog boxes have Revert buttons that return their settings to the original values. Be ready to use the Revert button freely.

Adjusting color balance and saturation in Photoshop Elements

You don't necessarily need to save a copy of your image before experimenting with its color balance and saturation in Photoshop Elements or Photoshop. (We describe the process in detail for Photoshop Elements here.) Photoshop Elements continually updates the main image with the changes you make in dialog boxes, so if you can see the main image and the dialog box on-screen at the same time, you have an ongoing preview of the changes you're making.

Modifying color balance and saturation in Photoshop Elements is a more technical process than in Paint Shop Pro. You have more control, but at the cost of more complexity. Be prepared to experiment in order to get the results you want in Photoshop Elements.

However, Photoshop Elements does offer quick fixes, which we demonstrate here. Follow these steps to adjust color balance and saturation in Photoshop Elements:

1. **Open Photoshop Elements, and then open the image you want to adjust.**

2. **Choose Enhance⇨Quick Fix.**

   The Quick Fix dialog box appears, as shown in Figure 9-6.

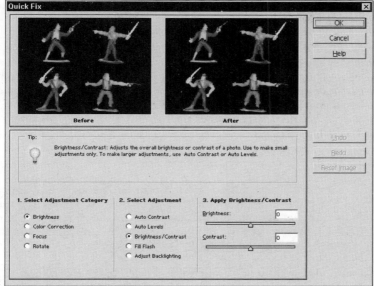

Figure 9-6:
Photoshop
Elements
offers quick
fixes — and
lots of
power too.

3. **In Category 1, select the Color Correction option (the other options update); then select the Auto Color option in Category 2 and click the Apply button to apply the fix.**

   The preview image is updated with the change.

4. **In Category 2, select the Hue/Saturation option; Category 3 updates to show the Hue, Saturation, and Lightness.**

5. **Adjust the hue (or color), the saturation (or intensity), and lightness (or brightness) in turn.**

   Continue experimenting until you have the result you want. Keep an eye on the main window, if screen size allows, to see the effects of the changes on the main image.

6. **When you have the image the way you want it, click OK.**

   The image is updated with the changes you made.

Enhancing contrast

If you're old enough, you may remember that many photographers — even amateurs — used to carry around light meters in order to adjust their cameras correctly. Now the light meter is the domain of the pro, but the concern about light remains. Photoshop and similar programs are a boon to photographers and people who handle photographs because a good bitmap-editing program can quickly and significantly enhance the contrast in a photo, which is much of what the pursuit of light is all about.

The problem with using a computer program to enhance contrast is that in amplifying the contrast between shades from low to high, subtle shadings are lost. A 35mm slide of an image that has been "Photoshopped" might lack important details, compared to a slide of an image that was adequately lit from the beginning. However, this is trading a major problem for a minor one, especially when the display medium is the computer screen — lower in resolution, and less subtle in brightness gradations, than a 35mm slide. Just realize that some tradeoffs are involved even when using a great tool like contrast enhancement.

If you're using a digital camera, it's important to avoid "white hotspots" — areas in the photo that are so bright that no contrast remains in the image. When using a digital camera, you may want to "shoot dark" — underexposing the film — if there's very bright light, as from the sun. You would then correct the underexposure in your graphics-editing program.

The methods for adjusting contrast described in the following sections only represent the quickest and most powerful of the different techniques for tackling this problem available in any good bitmap editor. If you are intending to spend much time preparing photos for Web use, plan to also spend some time reading the Help files and printed documentation for your chosen program to get a good grasp on all the techniques available.

Adjusting contrast in Paint Shop Pro

Follow these steps to adjust contrast in Paint Shop Pro:

1. **Open Paint Shop Pro, and then open the image you want to adjust.**

2. **Choose Effects⇨Enhance Photo⇨Automatic Contrast Enhancement.**

   The Automatic Contrast Enhancement dialog box appears.

3. **Set the Bias, or direction, of the enhancement.**

   Set Bias to Lighter for a dark image, Neutral for an intermediate image, and Darker for a lighter image. In other words, bias the enhancement away from the underlying image.

   The preview image changes to reflect the setting you choose.

   As with color settings, use the Proof or Auto Proof button to apply changes to the whole image as you work. Consider having before and after copies of the image open to afford an ongoing comparison between the enhanced and unenhanced images.

4. **Set the Strength, or intensity, of the enhancement; use the Normal setting for normal enhancement or the Mild setting for less enhancement.**

   Again, the preview image changes to reflect the setting you choose. Experiment with these settings to see which one better suits your needs.

Resizing the image may increase the apparent contrast, while converting it to JPEG may lessen it. For images whose appearance is critical, be prepared to cycle through the processing and conversion steps several times to get the final result you want.

5. **Set the Appearance of the image (actually like another level of enhancement) to Flat, Natural, or Bold.**

   Use the preview to experiment with all three settings to help choose the one you need.

6. **Click OK to complete the changes.**

   The changes are applied to the image.

Consider saving a couple of different versions of the image with various contrast settings, so that you have some options when it's time to resize and compress the image.

Adjusting contrast in Photoshop Elements

To modify contrast in Photoshop Elements, follow these steps:

1. **Open Photoshop Elements, and then open the image you want to adjust.**

2. **Choose Enhance⇔Quick Fix.**

   The Quick Fix dialog box appears.

3. **In Category 1, select the Brightness option (the other options update); then select the Auto Contrast option in Category 2.**

4. **Click the Apply button to apply the fix.**

   The preview image and the actual image in the main window are updated with the change.

5. **To fine-tune contrast adjustments, change the selection in Category 2 to Brightness/Contrast; Category 3 updates to show the Brightness and Contrast adjustment sliders.**

6. **Adjust the brightness and contrast in turn to get the effect you're looking for.**

   Again, keep an eye on the main window, if screen size allows, to see the effects of the changes on the main image.

7. **When you have the image the way you want it, click OK.**

   The image is updated with the changes you made.

Sharpening an image

Sharpening — and, oddly, unsharpening — an image may make the difference in making the image recognizable after reduction in size and compression.

Sharpening is basically an edge enhancement effect. When applied to text or large blocks of color, it makes things that stand out a little bit into things that stand out a lot. However, true photographic images are full of different colors, and therefore full of edges. Sharpening affects photographs in ways you may not expect until you gain considerable experience.

Sharpening is an important step in salvaging images that will be downsized and compressed because it increases, in a somewhat harsh way, the contrast within the image. It also battles the tendency of JPEG compression to blur an image. At the end of the day, sharpening may make it possible to compress an image, for example, of a person down to the point where he or she is still recognizable — even if the person involved is tempted to sue for your having made them look so ugly.

Sharpening can also be used more gently to improve images. It's a very powerful tool and one that you should use carefully on any image that needs to retain a natural appearance. Again, experimentation is the key.

In the examples shown here for Paint Shop Pro, we demonstrate the use of the Unsharp Mask filter, a powerful tool with several options. You should also experiment with the Sharpen filter, which is simpler and which may be sufficient much of the time.

When you're working on an image that's already been JPEG-compressed, sharpening it may make the artifacts that JPEG compression leaves in an image worse. Always keep your eyes open when modifying an image to make sure that you are in fact improving it.

Sharpening an image in Paint Shop Pro

Follow these steps to sharpen an image in Paint Shop Pro:

1. **Open Paint Shop Pro, and then open the image you want to sharpen.**

2. **Choose Effects⇨Sharpen⇨Unsharp Mask.**

   The Unsharp Mask dialog box appears, as shown in Figure 9-7.

3. **Set the Radius, or the area around an edge that's affected.**

   Set the Radius to a larger value to affect more pixels or to a smaller value to affect only those pixels closest to an edge.

   The preview image changes to reflect the Radius setting you choose. Smaller values tend to work better for on-screen images.

   As with other adjustments, use the Proof or Auto Proof button to apply changes to the whole image as you work. Consider having before and after copies of the image open to afford an ongoing comparison between the enhanced and unenhanced images.

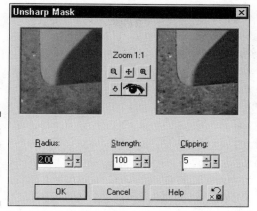

Figure 9-7:
Unsharp
Mask is a
powerful
tool.

4. **Set the Strength, or intensity, of the sharpening.**

   You can start at lower values and reapply the effect if a stronger
   sharpening is needed.

   You see the effect of the change in the preview image as you experiment
   with different values.

5. **Set the Clipping to specify how much contrast two pixels have to have
   before they're adjusted — the lower the Clipping value, the more
   pixels get sharpened.**

   Interactively use the preview to experiment with the three settings to
   help choose the combination you need.

6. **Click OK to complete the changes.**

   The changes will be applied to the image. Be sure to choose Edit⇨Undo
   or press Ctrl+Z immediately if you don't like the result!

Sharpening an image in Photoshop

To sharpen an image in Photoshop, use the Unsharp Mask filter as follows:

1. **Open Photoshop, and then open the image you want to sharpen.**

2. **Choose Filter⇨Sharpen⇨Unsharp Mask.**

   The Unsharp Mask dialog box appears, as shown in Figure 9-8.

3. **Set the Amount, or intensity, of the sharpening.**

   You see the effect of the change in the preview image as you experiment
   with different values.

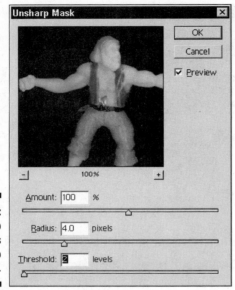

Figure 9-8:
Photoshop
offers
Unsharp
Mask tools.

4. **Set the Radius, or the area around each edge that's affected — a larger radius means more total pixels are affected.**

The preview image and the main image reflect the Radius setting as you change it. Smaller values tend to work better for on-screen images.

5. **Set the Threshold to specify how much contrast two pixels have to have before they're adjusted.**

The default value of 0 may be too low for most images on the Web.

Experiment with the three settings in turn, using the preview and, if you can see it, the image in the main window to verify the overall effect.

6. **Click OK to complete the changes.**

The changes are applied to the image. As always, choose Edit⇨Undo or press Ctlr+Z immediately if you want to try again.

Chapter 10

Resizing and Fixing Photos

. . . .

In This Chapter

▶ Downsizing a photo in Paint Shop Pro and Photoshop

▶ Editing a downsized photo in Paint Shop Pro and Photoshop

. . . .

*W*idespread use (and overuse) of the highest levels of JPEG compression has set an abysmally low standard for graphics on the Web. The human eye can recognize an image of a bald-headed basketball player even if it's JPEG-compressed to only a few hundred bytes of information. But after the hundredth such image you see, what's the point?

Small, highly compressed photos for illustration will always be with us on the Web. But as broadband becomes more common — for some audiences, even assumed — we see an opportunity for more effective use of images.

We advocate creating small images for use as story illustrations and thumbnails. But we also recommend that you take advantage of another strength of JPEG — its capability of creating large, stunning images with almost no visible compression artifacts, yet that are still roughly one-fourth or one-fifth of the file size of the original.

Mix and match small, highly compressed and larger, more attractive images in your Web pages. Don't put a 300K image on the home page and make dial-up modem users wait two minutes to click a link on your site — but don't try to sell someone a car by showing them a dinky, jaggedy 100 x 60 image of it either. Mix and match small and larger photos to accomplish your goals on the Web.

In this chapter, we illustrate our "how to compress" focus with both small images and much larger ones. Both are valid uses of JPEG!

Use WIDTH and HEIGHT attributes

We go into detail on this in Chapter 3, but always, always, always use the `WIDTH` and `HEIGHT` attributes in your `<IMG>` tag to specify the correct size of an image when creating a Web page. In nearly all cases, these attributes should reflect the actual size of the image in pixels after you're finished cropping and resizing it. (You might occasionally use the `WIDTH` and `HEIGHT` attributes to resize an image right on the Web page, but the results are usually poor.)

The `WIDTH` and `HEIGHT` attributes tell the Web browser the size of the image before it's downloaded. When these tags are present for every image used on a Web page, the Web browser can display the text and links quickly, setting aside accurately sized areas for graphics that will download more slowly. Users — especially dial-up modem users — can instantly size up the page's content before waiting for images to appear. They can decide to surf away without waiting or read the text while the images gradually appear.

Even with a fast connection, `WIDTH` and `HEIGHT` attributes are important. Without them, the browser tries to lay out the page, and then lurches alarmingly as the true size of each image becomes known. This is annoying, distracting, and disconcerting to the user, and makes you and your organization appear unprofessional.

Downsizing Photos

Downsizing an image means making it smaller in pixel area than it was before — taking a scanned image 600 pixels wide by 400 pixels tall, for example, and making it 125 x 100 pixels.

Considering just how big an image should be for your Web site is an important step. What happens all too often is that people look at a lot of big photographs to decide which image to use, choose the one that looks best at full size, then shrink and JPEG-compress it to the limits of recognition. In many cases, a different image would have borne up better under the twin pressures of downsizing and compression.

What you should do to achieve outstanding results is think simultaneously about what kind of image you want to use, how large a space you can afford to put it in, and what specific images — already existing, or yet to be created or captured — might best fill the bill. In this way, you use images to accomplish a goal, rather than just grabbing images and throwing them on the Web page.

Of course, artists, photojournalists, and advertisers have all discovered that great images impose their own demands. You may sometimes find yourself designing around a particularly evocative, interesting, or informative image. Fine — but almost no image that you shrink to 40 x 60 and JPEG-compress to within a pixel of its life is *great*. If you're going to use great images in your Web pages, let the user have the opportunity to see them in something close to their full glory.

In resizing photographs, you have these choices:

- **Make the image as small as possible while maintaining recognizability.** Generally, a 100 x 100 pixel image is pretty small. (A 100 x 100 pixel photo in a magazine would be less than ¼ inch-square.) This choice is defensible when using photos to illustrate a point that's made mainly with words, but it's an overused approach.

- **Make the image medium sized.** An image larger than 100 x 100 pixels is considered at least medium-sized because it stands out from all the little images on the Web. Mix in some medium-sized images on story or detail pages on your site, but not in main or navigational pages.

- **Offer only a large image.** You'll see relatively large images — more than 200 x 200 pixels or so — on more and more sites, and ads embedded in pages are now routinely this size. We believe that using images this large on pages where the main story is delivered by text is still unfair to enough users, stuck as they are with slow dial-up connections, to be avoided. It also imposes design challenges that are tough to meet on a typical Web page.

- **Offer both a small and a large image.** We believe that, in this increasingly broadband world, it's best to routinely use small images for spice and link them to large versions for users who want to see them. On product pages, or if you're practicing photojournalism or advertising, bag the little image and just use a big one. (You aren't going to sell many vacation condos with an 80 x 25 image of the view onto Palm Beach.)

Figure 10-1 shows small, medium, and large images to give you an idea of their relative size.

Follow the steps in the next two sections to resize images in Paint Shop Pro and Photoshop, respectively. But think about what you're trying to accomplish as you carry out the resizing operation. Consider routinely creating a thumbnail and a large version of each image.

Figure 10-1:
Small,
medium,
and large
images
have
dramatically
different
impact.

Why you need a big monitor — sometimes

You really need a big monitor to work effectively on images. Just juggling the palettes and toolbars in Paint Shop Pro, let alone Photoshop Elements or Photoshop, means you need at least 1024 x 768 resolution to work on images. Because you'll also often want to have a Web page open and visible for preview, reference, or research, 1280 x 1024 starts to look like a minimum size!

But such a high-resolution image can be misleading, especially when crammed into a medium-sized monitor. Everything becomes very small when viewed in real size. Pros often

have a second system with a medium-sized, medium-resolutions screen for previewing, such as a laptop.

If you can't afford the cost or the hassle of viewing your images on two computers, switch your monitor resolution frequently so you can get some idea of how your images and Web pages will look to others. You can drag a shortcut to the Display Properties dialog box (accessed from the Control Panel) onto your taskbar so it's always one click away. Now if someone can just tell us how to click it once for lower resolution, then again for higher resolution. . . .

Downsizing a photo in Paint Shop Pro

Use the Window➪Fit to Image command (Ctrl+W) to fit an image to a window in Paint Sh op Pro.

Follow these steps to downsize a photo in Paint Shop Pro:

1. **Open Paint Shop Pro, and then open the image.**

2. **Before starting, to have an unchanged version of the image open for comparison, choose Window➪Duplicate (Shift+D).**

   A copy of the image opens. Now you can resize the copy while keeping the original open for comparison.

3. **Choose Image➪Resize or press Shift+S.**

   The Resize dialog box appears.

4. **If the Pixel size radio button is not already selected, click it to select it.**

   The other options — Percentage of Original and Actual/Print Size — are more useful for print than for the Web. However, it's worth keeping an eye on them as they are updated along with the changes you make to the dimensions in pixels.

5. **Check that other options are at their default values, or change to these values if needed: Set Resize Type to Smart Size, check the Resize All Layers check box, and check the Maintain Aspect Ratio check box.**

6. **Change the width and/or height of the image, in pixels, to the value you need.**

   With the Maintain Aspect Ratio check box checked, changing the width causes the height to be changed proportionately, and vice versa.

7. **Click OK to complete the resizing.**

   Paint Shop Pro resizes the image. See Figure 10-2 for a before and after example that takes advantage of a copy of the image created with the New Window command, as described in Step 2.

8. **Inspect the image. If it isn't quite what you want, choose Edit➪Undo or press Ctrl+Z.**

   The image reverts to its previous size, and you can repeat the steps to make the image a different size.

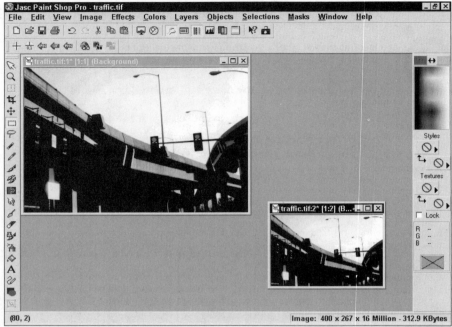

Figure 10-2:
You can use
Paint Shop
Pro to view
your image
before and
after
resizing.

Downsizing a photo in Photoshop Elements

These steps apply directly to Photoshop Elements, with specifics for Photoshop noted. Screen shots in this chapter are of Photoshop Elements.

The process of downsizing an image is noticeably more work in Photoshop Elements than in Paint Shop Pro. Follow these steps to downsize a photo in Photoshop Elements:

1. **Open Photoshop or Photoshop Elements, and then open the image you want to downsize.**

2. **To have an unchanged version of the image open for comparison, choose Select⇨All (Ctrl+A), choose Image⇨Duplicate Image (just "Duplicate" in Photoshop).**

   A copy of the image opens that you can resize while comparing it to the unchanged original.

3. **Choose Image⇨Resize⇨Image Size (Image Resize in Photoshop).**

   The Image Size dialog box appears, as shown in Figure 10-3.

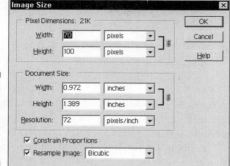

Figure 10-3:
Resizing an
image in
Photoshop
Elements.

The Image Size dialog box shows the file size of the image as the Pixel Dimensions of the image.

4. If the drop-down lists next to the Width and Height prompts under Pixel Dimensions are not already set to pixels, set them to pixels.

The alternative option, percent, is more useful for print than for the Web. You can keep an eye on the actual document size as you change the pixel dimensions, or vice versa.

5. Check that other options are at their default values, or change to those values if needed: Check the Constrain Proportions check box and the Resample Image check box; change the value of the Resample Image drop-down list to Bicubic.

Bicubic sampling gives the most accurate results.

6. Change the Width and/or Height prompts under Pixel Dimensions of the image, in pixels, to the value you need.

With the Constrain Proportions check box checked, changing either the width or height causes the other value to change proportionately.

7. Click OK to complete the resizing.

Photoshop or Photoshop Elements resizes the image.

8. Inspect the image. If it isn't quite what you want, choose Edit⇨Undo or press Ctrl+Z.

The image reverts to its previous size, ready to be changed to a different size.

Processing after Downsizing

Many photo-processing steps are best performed before downsizing the photo, and some are best done after. A few can even be used best after compression. How do you know which is which?

Most photo-processing steps are best performed before downsizing or compression because key processes in photo processing, such as adjusting color balance, enhancing contrast, and sharpening, take advantage of all the information in the photograph to produce the best results. These processes are best done before resizing, which removes information, or JPEG compression, which not only removes information but adds noise to the image.

Because these steps must take place before photo processing, they therefore dictate that other steps go with them as well. Rotating a photo into place, flipping its left-right orientation, and cropping it are all things you want to do before turning loose the little pieces of software code that perform functions such as adjusting color balance, where you're previewing the look of the image interactively as you're working.

Some steps are best taken, however, after downsizing but before compression. These are steps in which you're removing specific defects from the photo. They work better on the downsized image because you don't need to remove defects (or parts of defects) that go away anyway in the downsizing process. But you want to use the uncompressed image so there's enough information in the photograph for the defect to be repaired smoothly. Sometimes, if you try to perform these processes after compression, you end up trying to fine-tune individual pixels — and unless you're a talented artist who likes trying to work around compression artifacts, hand-editing very many individual pixels is not likely to give you good results.

Among the steps that you can best take after downsizing but before compression are

- ✔ **Red-eye removal.** If *red-eye* (or the sometime animal equivalent, *green-eye*) — reflections off the retina caused by a photo flash — are present in your image, now's the time to remove them.

- ✔ **Scratch removal.** Actual scratches in an image, dust that's brought in during scanning, or highlights or lowlights caused by reflections or shadows are all "scratches" that you can remove if they don't disappear in downsizing the image.

- ✔ **Expunging people and objects.** People and objects in your image may be positively unwanted — such as a Coke sign in the background of a Pepsi ad — or simply distracting from an image you want to focus on. Software makes it easy to remove them at this stage (though filling in the resulting blank can be much harder).

✔ **Blurring the image.** Some graphics pros blur images before compression because doing so makes the image compress better. Others view this as an unneeded removal of information before letting the JPEG compression algorithm do its stuff. It's up to you to try it and see what you think of the end result.

✔ **Other steps.** Paint Shop Pro has many tools for image processing, and Photoshop and Photoshop Elements have many, many more. You can use almost any of them at this point. Feel free to experiment, time budget allowing.

Processing steps taken after downsizing but before compression are reactive — you're trying to fix problems that you see in the image. So there's no fixed list of things you have to do. As you gain experience, you'll know what to look for in photos of certain types and from specific sources.

In the specific steps in the next two sections, we tour the major tools within Paint Shop Pro or the two flavors of Photoshop. We give you more of a guided tour than a recipe telling you exactly what to do, because exactly what to do varies so much for each image. Try following the steps as is for a few images you have handy, and then start experimenting.

There are many other tools for processing JPEGs besides the ones we focus on in this book, of course. After you master the tools in Paint Shop Pro, Photoshop Elements, Photoshop, or some other program, you may want to consider smaller, more specialized tools as well. One such tool we like is Boxtop Software's ProJPEG tool, which produces extra-small files. To find out more about ProJPEG and other tools from Boxtop Software, visit:

`www.boxtopsoft.com`

Post-downsizing editing in Paint Shop Pro

Paint Shop Pro makes it easy to use many of the most important effects on your image. Follow these steps to remove red-eye from your subject in a photo:

1. **Open Paint Shop Pro, and then open the image.**

2. **Choose Effects⇨Enhance Photo⇨Red-eye Removal.**

   The Red-eye Removal dialog box appears.

3. **Use the pan and zoom controls in the right-hand image in the dialog box to focus on one or two eyes that have the red-eye effect and need it removed.**

   If both eyes belonging to a given person are showing, put both eyes in the preview window so you can use the same color for both. If one of the person's eyes is out of view, focus on the remaining one.

4. **Choose Auto Human Eye or Auto Animal Eye from the Method drop-down list, and then, in the left-hand image, click in the center of the eye.**

   The tool automatically detects the eye's radius and selects an area around the eye's edge.

5. **Use the handles on the selected area to adjust the selection to include the colored part of the eye itself, but not the eyelid.**

   For human eyes, the shape is always circular; for animal eyes, you can drag it into an ellipse. Some of the colored part of the eye will not be included, but don't worry — the software will detect that as well.

6. **For the pupil, adjust the Pupil Lightness, Glint Lightness, and Glint Size options to remove any flash reflection and to make the pupil area appear normal. Check the Center Glint check box to move the glint to the pupil.**

   Watch the pupil area change as you adjust it. You may want to write down your adjustments to use as a starting point for the second eye.

7. **For the colored part of the eye, the iris, adjust the Feather, Blur, and Iris Size option to fit the eye in question. Choose the Hue (brown, blue, and so on) and Color (the specific shade of the chosen hue) options to fit the subject's actual eye color or the color you want to put there.**

   At any point you can click the Undo Eye button to reverse the changes to the currently selected eye.

   If you've done one eye and are working on another, don't use the main Undo function or you'll lose the work you've done on both eyes. Click the Undo Eye button instead.

8. **Click the Proof button to see the effects of your work in the main image.**

   (It's a bit of a waste to click the Auto Proof button and have the main image constantly updating as you make tiny little changes in glint size or some such. Use the Proof button instead.)

9. **Adjust the second eye if one is in the picture, and then click OK to complete the red-eye removal process.**

   The red-eye effect should be removed.

   Be careful — it's easy to overdo the red-eye removal process and make the eyes appear dull and lifeless.

10. **Inspect the image, and if it isn't quite what you want, choose Edit⇨Undo or press Ctrl+Z.**

    The eyes revert to their previous color and glintiness.

To remove any imperfections or scratches in an image by using Paint Shop Pro, follow these steps:

1. **With your image open in Paint Shop Pro, click the Scratch Removal tool.**

   The Scratch Removal tool is the 14th tool down in the tool palette and looks like a trowel.

2. **Zoom in closely on any highlights or scratches visible in the picture.**

3. **Click several pixels to the left of the scratch and drag the selection box over the scratch and a few pixels to the right, and then release the mouse button.**

   The scratch is blurred.

4. **Repeat the click-and-drag process to continue blurring the scratch until the scratch is gone.**

   Don't overdo scratch removal while zoomed-in; some variation is needed to keep the picture interesting.

You can also use the same editing session to remove unwanted people or objects from the image. This is too general a process for us to give specific instructions on, but be ready to invest time replacing removed objects and people with credible background areas.

Save a copy of your work before beginning the process of removing unwanted people or objects.

Post-downsizing editing in Photoshop Elements

Photoshop Elements takes a lower-key approach to red-eye removal than Photoshop. You use a brush to edit specific pixels instead of a dialog box with various settings and controls. It's a bit harder to quickly and completely remove any hint of red-eye or light reflection with the Photoshop Elements approach. But it's also much harder to make an error and leave your subjects with dull, lifeless eyes.

Photoshop Elements sticks with a tools-and-brushes approach to fixing your image. Follow these steps to get rid of red-eye in an image:

1. **Open Photoshop Elements, and then open the image.**

2. **Make a duplicate of the image so you can go back to an unchanged version easily in case the changes you make go awry.**

   See the earlier section, "Downsizing a photo in Photoshop Elements," to find out how to make a copy of an image.

3. **Pan and zoom to bring one person's or animal's eye or eyes into the image.**

   If both eyes belonging to a given person or animal are showing, try to keep both in view as you zoom in so you can make them look similar.

4. **Click the Red Eye Brush tool, the 6th tool down in the right-hand column of tools.**

   (The eye in the tool's icon turns red as you pass the mouse cursor over it.) The Options window updates with the available options for the Red Eye Brush tool.

5. **In the Options window, use the drop-down lists to choose a brush style and a brush size, in pixels.**

   Start by trying a brush width about the same width as the pupil of the eye.

6. **Choose the replacement color by double-clicking the Replacement color swatch to bring up the Color Picker, and then choose the color you want to use.**

   Alternatively, use the Eyedropper tool, with the color picker open, to pick a color from the current image.

   The Replacement color swatch updates with the new color.

7. **Choose the color to get rid of — usually a shade of red (for red-eye in people or animals) or green (for green-eye in animals).**

   You can specify this by double-clicking the color swatch to bring up Color Picker or by choosing First Click from the drop-down list. If you choose First Sampling, you can quickly clean up a large red-eye effect.

8. **Click the pixel to be changed.**

   If you chose First Sampling, all pixels of that color within the Size radius of the brush change to the replacement color. Click additional pixels to change them as well.

   The red-eye area is gradually replaced with the chosen eye-color.

9. **Repeat Step 8 to replace white glinting areas of the eye with a dark pupil color and to soften the restored eye color with nearby shades for a more subtle effect.**

   If your changes get out of hand, choose Edit⇨Undo or press Ctrl+Z as many times as needed to remove the changes and start over. If you can't find the point you started from, revert to the copy of the image you made, make another copy, and start over.

10. **Zoom out to see the effects of your work in the main image, and if necessary, zoom in and make more changes, undo the last few changes, or revert to the saved image as needed to complete the job.**

11. **Adjust the second eye, if one is in the picture, in a similar way to the first eye.**

To remove imperfections or scratches in your image, follow these steps:

1. **Open the image in Photoshop, and then click the Blur tool.**

   The Blur tool is the teardrop shape; in the tool palette, the eighth tool down and on the left.

2. **Zoom in fairly closely on any highlights or scratches visible in the picture.**

   As with the Red Eye brush, change the brush shape or size as needed. A size near the width of the fault is a good setting to start with. Adjust the Mode — Normal, Darken, Lighten, Hue, Saturation, Color, or Luminosity — to specify which characteristics will be used and in which direction. And adjust the Strength — a lower strength is fine, because you can just keep running the brush over the fault until it's softened sufficiently.

3. **Drag the Blur tool over the faulty area.**

   The scratch blurs.

4. **Blur throughout the picture to remove problems.**

As with Paint Shop Pro, you can remove unwanted people and objects in the same editing session. In either Photoshop or Photoshop Elements, you can use the Blur tool to help create background to replace the areas you clear.

In Photoshop, but not in Photoshop Elements, you find a tool called the Healing brush. This is a more precise tool than the Blur brush for fixing many problems in photos. If you have Photoshop, experiment with the Healing brush to find which problems you prefer to use it for.

Chapter 11

Compressing and Post-Producing Photos

- -

- -

Compressing photos appropriately using JPEG is an art that too few have mastered. Squeezing them to within a few pixels of recognizability is common enough — actually choosing appropriate tradeoffs between what you're trying to accomplish with a given photo, image size, file size, and image quality is an art that can't yet be referred to as lost, because there are very few instances in which it has yet been found.

In this chapter, we dive straight into the mechanics of compressing photos, and then show you some steps post-compression that can make your images more effective. We then give you some of our thoughts, based on long experience, about how to do this work efficiently and well for moderately large numbers of photos. And we finish by exploring how to be creative, or even artistic, with images.

Before you plunge into the arcana of compression, make sure that the image you're about to compress is appropriate for the particular Web page you plan to place it in. Only when you have the right image should you be worrying about whether Medium or High JPEG compression will better do the job in this particular case.

Actually compressing a photo with JPEG to a known degree of compression is pretty easy. Understanding your goals and your audience and training your eye to find the right degree of compression for your purpose is pretty hard. And setting up a process that allows you to see how the compressed photograph looks on different Web browsers, on different PCs, and in various lighting conditions is even tougher. (Though it's a bit easier with Photoshop than with other programs.)

Choosing good photos

In a sense, you're always choosing photos, whether you take them yourself, assign a photographer, or pick a stock image. Images are generated and experienced constantly — some already captured on film, others already stored in a computer, but most happening *right now* in the real world and in danger of being lost forever. We acknowledge, though, that choosing a yet-to-be-captured photo of a whale with a cowboy on its back is going to be a bit more work than choosing a head shot of your company's CEO. (Unless he or she is also that cowboy or cowgirl.)

But before staging or obtaining the photo, you need to figure out what the *right* image for the particular purpose is. For instance, say that one of the authors of this book, Peter Frazier, is going to have a photo taken for publicity purposes. He needs to decide whether to look more formal (therefore authoritative) or more casual (therefore approachable), and whether the photo should be shot in a studio, in an office, or outdoors. (Probably one of the first two, though Peter is outdoors a lot.) Only after these decisions are made should he take stock (so to speak) of what photos he has on hand or whether he should get in touch with a photographer. (The world's biggest fool is the person who has himself for a lawyer, but the one who has himself for a photographer may rank a close second.)

Compressing Photos with JPEG

Paint Shop Pro offers good facilities for compressing photos with JPEG and previewing them; Photoshop Elements and Photoshop offer great facilities.

Previewing images is a very important part of the Web publishing process — you want to make sure the image that looks sharp on your Mac doesn't look muddy on your PC, or the image that has sufficient contrast on your PC doesn't look garish on a Mac. So in the following sections, we show you how to preview images at different compression levels using Paint Shop Pro and Photoshop.

You may have noticed that many of the steps for completing certain effects in Paint Shop Pro versus Photoshop (or Photoshop Elements) are very similar, and that in some cases Paint Shop Pro makes steps a little clearer or easier. However, Photoshop makes previewing the effects of JPEG compression on your image much easier than Paint Shop Pro does.

The easiest way for a Paint Shop Pro user who wants to preview how the images created on their PC would look on a Mac might be simply to get a

Mac and try it. Photoshop, however, runs on both PCs and Macs, and on each platform, it offers a preview of what an image will look like on the other. We show you how to use the previews and more in this chapter.

In many cases, you can do simple JPEG compression with Microsoft Paint, a free program found on all Windows PCs. See Chapter 5 for details.

JPEG compression with Paint Shop Pro

Follow these steps to compress an image using JPEG in Paint Shop Pro:

1. **Open Paint Shop Pro and open the image you want to compress.**

   You can use a screen capture (press the PrtScrn key, as described in Chapter 5) or almost any kind of image; Paint Shop Pro opens just about anything. If you have a file format that Paint Shop Pro can't open, just get the image on-screen, do a screen capture, and then paste the image into Paint Shop Pro.

   Looking at the image, think carefully about how you'll use it and how much visible degradation of the image is acceptable. In some cases, you may want almost no visible side effects of compression. In other cases, you may have a general or specific file size or download time budget to consider.

2. **Click the Export JPEG button to begin the process of creating a JPEG-compressed version of your image.**

   The JPEG Optimizer dialog box appears, as shown in Figure 11-1. Inspect it carefully. The preview windows show the original, uncompressed image on the left and a preview of the compressed image on the right. Various tabs allow you to set the compression ratio, choose progressive JPEG format, or see estimates of the image's download times. You can also use a wizard to do compression, but the dialog box is easier and more powerful.

3. **Pan to an area of the image that's particularly sensitive to the results of compression, such as a person's face or other key area of detail, and vary the zoom to see the effects of compression from varying perspectives.**

   Frequently check the appearance of the image with the zoom set to 1:1 to give yourself the best idea of what the user will see.

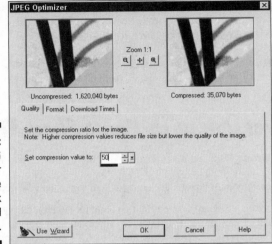

Figure 11-1:
The JPEG
Optimizer
can make
short work
of small
files.

4. **Vary the compression value by increments of 10 to see the effects of varying levels of compression on the image; click the Download Times tab to see the effects of various image sizes on download time.**

    (Focus on the 56 Kbps level, because it's the single most common download speed.) Trying all levels of compression is instructive, from slightly compressed (10) through very highly compressed (90).

    Note that even the lowest level of compression, 1, may compress an image by 10:1 or 20:1, while leaving almost no perceptible change in the image at 1:1 zoom. Consider using very light compression for large display versions of images.

    Paint Shop Pro and some other programs use lower numbers such as 10 or 20 for lower compression, higher quality; Photoshop and some other programs use lower numbers such as 10 or 20 for higher compression, lower quality. Be careful when talking to other graphics people — don't say *lower compression* or *higher compression,* say *lower quality* or *higher quality.*

5. **Set the compression value to a multiple of 10, click OK, export the image, and then open the exported image and compare it to the original at full size.**

    This step is time-consuming, but the preview windows in Paint Shop Pro are so small that it's hard to see the effects of various levels of compression for most images without looking at them full size. Repeat this step for at least a few versions of your image. Put the word *temp* in each filename so you know that these files can be discarded.

Consider writing down the quality value, file size, and download time at 56 Kbps and your impression of the image's appearance for various levels of JPEG compression in increments of 10. This gives you perspective on the process and helps keep you from wringing the last few tens of bytes out of the image when that comes at great cost to image quality.

6. **Identify the two increments of 10 for the compression value that bracket the quality you want, then start fine-tuning the compression value by increments of 1.**

    Check the quality of the image carefully. If the preview window is too small compared to the image you're creating, you may need to export the image a few times and check the appearance of the newly created file against the original to identify the exact level of compression that gives you the best appearance at the smallest reasonably achievable file size.

    Get the highest quality you can within your desired file size budget for the image and the page it's on, rather than the smallest file size you can achieve while keeping the image recognizable.

7. **Find the exact value you want, and then click OK. Save the exported file using a filename not containing *temp* so you know to keep it.**

    You should also test the image. You may want to view it on a Macintosh and in both Internet Explorer and Netscape browsers. This testing can be done virtually in Photoshop, as described in the next section. In Paint Shop Pro, you have to either go to the trouble to view your image on a different computer, or skip testing that you really should perform — not a very attractive choice.

It probably took you a while to carefully compress your JPEG file, but you'll get to where the cycle — assess, experiment, and export — happens very quickly. And your results will be far better than if you just stumbled through the process and guessed at what setting to use each time.

JPEG compression with Photoshop

Follow these steps to compress an image using JPEG in Photoshop:

1. **Open Photoshop and open the image you want to compress.**

    As in Paint Shop Pro, you can open almost any kind of image — or if you can't open the image in Photoshop, open it in another program, capture the image using the PrtScr key (described in Chapter 5), and then paste the image into Photoshop using the File⇨New from Clipboard command.

    Look at the image carefully and think about what you're using it for and how much you can allow it to degrade as a result of compression. Much of the file-size-reduction benefit of JPEG occurs before any noticeable degradation of the image occurs. You should also consider your file size or download time limitations.

2. **Choose File⇨Save For Web (Alt+Shift+Ctrl+S) to begin the process of saving the file in JPEG format.**

   (That mammoth four-key combination is surprisingly easy to hit when you get used to it.) The Save For Web dialog box appears, as shown in Figure 11-2. The uncompressed image appears on the left; the compressed image appears on the right. Each window shows the file size, and the compressed window shows an estimate of the download time at the connection speed you select. You can choose the compression settings a couple of different ways, and fine-tune JPEG compression from 100 (highest quality) to 0 (lowest quality).

   Pan to a high-impact area, such as a face, while you're experimenting with compression; use various levels of zoom, especially the 100 percent setting, to see the effects of compression in detail.

3. **Try the Low (that's low quality, numeric value 10), Medium (30), High (60), and Maximum (80) compression settings.**

   Monitor the file size and download time as you vary the quality. Note that even at the highest quality, 100, an image may be compressed by 80 percent with no perceptible change in the image. You can use high-quality settings for large versions of images.

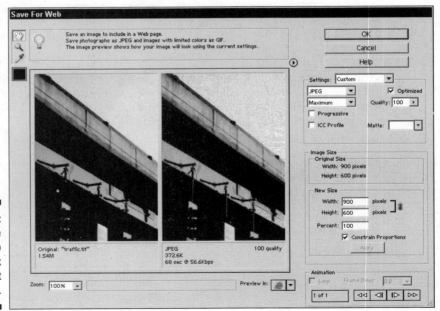

Figure 11-2:
The Save For Web dialog box packs a lot of punch.

If you see weird speckling or graininess in the compressed image, regardless of the compression level you're using, you need to turn off the Browser Dithering option in the Save to Web options menu. Click the right-pointing triangle at the upper-right corner of the right image to see this options menu and deselect the option.

As we mention in the previous section, Photoshop uses higher numbers and words such as Maximum for higher quality; Paint Shop Pro and some other programs use lower numbers such as 10 or 20 for lower compression, higher quality. Photoshop tends to set industry standards for graphics, but you should still make sure you and others are speaking the same lingo when you talk to them about compression.

4. **Though the preview windows in Photoshop are larger than in Paint Shop Pro, it still may be worth clicking OK to save the image, saving the file with *temp* or some such giveaway word in the filename, and then opening the new file to compare it at full-size to the original.**

5. **Identify the two named settings that bracket the level of quality you want, and then start fine-tuning the compression value by increments of 10, and finally by increments of 1.**

Usually, the Photoshop preview windows are large enough to allow you to get compression right the first time. However, you may want to export the image and check it against the original before making a final decision.

You can change the image size in the Save For Web dialog box by using the settings in the New Size area.

6. **To preview the image to see how it will look on the Web, click the triangle near the preview of the compressed image, as shown in Figure 11-3.**

You can preview the impact of browser dither, typical Macintosh colors, and typical Windows colors. *Browser dither* is the effect that occurs when a user's video system is only set to display 256 colors. It does bad things to your image, but users with displays limited to 256 colors, or set to 256 colors deliberately, will suffer from ugly images all the time. Standard Macintosh color tends to be brighter; standard Windows color tends to be darker. In the main image, make any adjustments you need to make sure your image is well-suited for your intended target platforms.

7. **Find the exact settings you want, and then click OK. Save the exported file using a filename that you'll recognize as your final version of the file.**

You'll get to where you can do these steps quickly by using the tools in the Save For Web dialog box that you've already tried, plus additional features as well.

You may want to try different tools to get specific effects. For instance, the worst quality setting in Paint Shop Pro is much lower-quality (and higher-compression) than the worst setting in Photoshop. The best setting in Paint Shop Pro is not as good as the best setting in Photoshop.

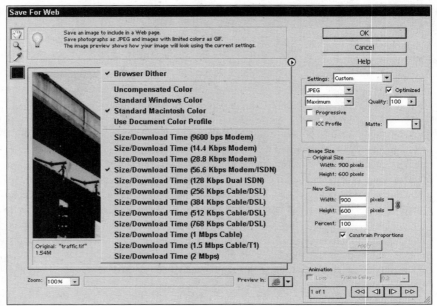

Figure 11-3:
Previewing
options in
Photoshop.

Post-Producing an Image

You can use many tricks on a compressed image to make it appear even better. For instance, you can apply filters to some or all of an image to smooth out jagged areas or to remove JPEG artifacts. Many of the things people talk about doing at this stage, however, should properly be done before you save the image as a JPEG. The correct order for using these tricks is described in Chapter 9. However, it may be worth using some of them a second time after the file has been compressed.

Two popular techniques for improving an image after compressing it with JPEG are sharpening the image and adding a black or other color border a few pixels wide around the image. Sharpening a heavily JPEG-compressed image does make it more vivid and recognizable; however, it also can uglify the image, because JPEG-induced noise in the image as well as valid edges can be among the things sharpened.

We recommend that you use sharpening on already-compressed images with care. For steps showing how to sharpen an image in Paint Shop Pro or Photoshop, see Chapter 9.

A step we can recommend with somewhat more enthusiasm is adding a border around an image. Painters have framed paintings for years to set them off from their surroundings. A thin border around an image can have a similar effect and improve the recognizability of the image without damaging the image itself. We show you how to add a border to the image itself in the following sections.

Whatever else you do, we recommend that you develop a standard procedure for processing photographs, especially if you handle several different types of images or work in a large production environment. The informal, "each one teach one," approach breaks down when there are many complicated possibilities and a lot of work to do. Instead, you should work with others in your organization to develop a standard approach and follow it.

Post-producing in Paint Shop Pro

Paint Shop Pro supports post-production steps, such as adding a border and cleaning up any problems that either remain in the image or that are induced by the compression process itself. It also has some support for previewing the image. Follow these steps to add a border around your image:

1. **Open Paint Shop Pro and open the JPEG image.**

2. **Make the current background color black (or whatever color you want the border to be) by clicking the rightmost of the two rectangles at the top of the Color Palette.**

   The Color dialog box appears.

3. **Click the upper-right square in the Basic colors block to choose true black as the background color.**

   The background color rectangle changes color to black. Also, the Styles display in the Color Palette updates to show true black as the current color.

You can do this more quickly without opening a dialog box. In the Color Palette area, under Styles, click the lower of the two rectangles. The cursor changes to an eyedropper. Carefully move the point of the eyedropper over the colored area into the upper left-hand corner. Keep adjusting the position of the eyedropper until the RGB reading at the bottom of the Color Palette shows R 0, G 0, B 0. This is true black. Click to select true black as the current background color.

4. **Choose Image⇨Add Borders.**

   The Add Borders dialog box appears, as shown in Figure 11-4.

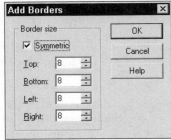

Figure 11-4:
Adding
borders in
Paint Shop
Pro is easy.

5. **In the Add Borders dialog box, leave the Symmetric check box checked so that all the borders stay the same, and then enter 2 as the width (in pixels) of the Top border.**

   All the other borders — Bottom, Left, and Right — are updated to match.

6. **Click OK.**

   A two-pixel wide black border is added around the image, making the image size larger. You can edit the border size while the image is open in Paint Shop Pro, but when you save and close the image, the border is made a permanent part of the image. If you want to get rid of it later, use Image⇨Canvas Size to crop out the border easily.

   You can also add a border simply by drawing a rectangle around the outside edge of the image. This doesn't change the image's size, but it destroys the original data on the outside edge of the image.

7. **Save a copy of the image for safekeeping.**

   You may now want to take additional processing steps on the image, especially to fix any eye-catching minor problems. Over time, you'll discover the techniques you need to fix any specific errors that tend to crop up — no pun intended — in your images.

Post-producing in Photoshop

Photoshop doesn't have a specific border tool like Paint Shop Pro does. However, Photoshop has extensive built-in support for previewing the image. Follow these steps to add a border to an image:

1. **Open Photoshop and open the JPEG file.**

2. **Make the current background color black by clicking the color rectangle in the upper right of the rectangle; then click black in the Color Picker or enter 0,0,0 as either the HSB values or the RGB values, and click OK.**

   The color rectangle changes to black.

3. **Choose Image⇨Resize⇨Canvas Size (in Photoshop Elements) or Image⇨Resize Canvas (in Photoshop).**

   A dialog box appears.

4. **Add 4 to the numbers in the Width and Height text boxes to get a border of 2 pixels on all sides of the image.**

   For a different border width, enter two times the border size you want for the height and for the width as well.

5. **Click OK.**

   The image is saved with a border, making it appear sharper when saved on a Web page.

6. **You may now want to take additional processing steps on the image, especially if a few pixels catch the eye in a troublesome way.**

7. **Save a copy of the image for safekeeping, then experiment with various effects.**

   Over time, you'll figure out techniques you need to fix any specific errors that tend to crop up in your images.

Being creative

You can do a wide range of other things to be creative with your JPEG images. One technology that allows you to create fascinating effects with images is Apple's QuickTime VR, which allows you to create either a rotatable object from photographs taken around a person or thing, or an immersive panorama from landscape or interior shots stitched together into a seamless whole. See the Apple QuickTime Web site for details:

    www.apple.com/quicktime

You can also create artistic and innovative special effects with either Paint Shop Pro or, especially, Photoshop. After you master the basics of these programs, you can go on and perform endless hours of experiments. Photoshop is the king of this kind of experimentation, more than Photoshop Elements or Paint Shop Pro. Just for one example, if you have access to the full Photoshop, try the Variations option of the Enhance menu. It's a very cool feature.

Part IV
Using GIF in Your Web Site

The 5th Wave   By Rich Tennant

THE GLACIER MOVEMENT PROJECT
UPDATE THEIR WEBSITE

Camera ready? Wait a minute, hold it. Ready? Wait for the action... steady...steady... not yet...eeeasy. Hold it. Okay, stay focused. Ready? Not yet... steeeady...eeeasy...

In this part . . .

In this part, we tell you just what's right — and wrong — with the way most people use GIFs. We also show you how to prepare GIF files and how and when to use animated GIFs without wasting your, or your users', time.

Chapter 12

Using GIF Images in Your Web Site

· ·

· ·

*I*n this chapter, we describe the major areas of interest with GIFs, and then give big examples of how to use Paint Shop Pro or Photoshop to handle GIF creation, color palette selection, transparency, and interlacing in a single operation — the way you would generally work in creating GIFs for online use. It's a lot to absorb, but taking in all the information together will help you creatively use the tradeoffs among different GIF capabilities, and between GIF and JPEG, to get the effect you want.

As we mention earlier in the book, the best thing about GIF is that it's generally lossless — it preserves all the information in the file. However, unfortunately, you can easily lose information in GIF images, as described in the sidebar later in this chapter, "How to lose information in GIF without really trying."

Painting from a Limited Palette

GIF identifies patterns in each scan line, or row of pixels, in an image. It saves the pattern as a short code. This makes the encoded file smaller than the original file. When a GIF image is displayed, the file is decoded, replacing the codes with the bit patterns.

The fewer colors there are in the original image, and the larger that areas of a single color are, the more likely that large patterns in the image can be stored in a short code. GIF can achieve very impressive compression ratios on simple graphics like a Stop sign, a smiley face, and so on. It also does a fantastic job of compressing text.

Unisys, a computer company, has a patent on the LZW (Lempel-Ziv-Welch) compression algorithm used to compress and decompress GIF files. The patent expired early in 2003, but one can't be certain that all controversy over the use of GIF will die down at that point. If you want to know more about the current status of the GIF patents, search online using a search engine such as Google (at www.google.com) using search terms such as "GIF patents." If you're more interested in how GIF actually works, visit the following site, which has an interactive demo:

```
http://www.cs.sfu.ca/cs/CC/365/li/squeeze/LZW.html
```

GIF depends on a graphic image having many areas of the same exact color in order to work well, so a file in which every pixel was a different color from the preceding pixel would not compress very well using GIF. Luckily, most graphics that people create have many areas of the same color fit — think of a simple image of a stoplight, or even a night-time image of a moonlit beach.

Where this simplicity breaks down is in shaded images and photographs. In a shaded image, a skilled graphics artist gets the computer to generate a range of tones, or shades, to mimic a 3-D lighting effect or to make an image more interesting. In a photo, of course, a camera captures an image with real-life 3-D lighting. It's this kind of lighting that produces the thousands or even millions of subtle shades that give the illusion of depth to an image — and that send typical Web graphics people running for the Save As JPEG command in their graphics programs.

So the first thing that a program does when it saves an image in GIF format is to reduce it to 256 colors, which can damage the appearance of a shaded image. Converting an image to the Web-safe color palette can damage the image as well.

Figure 12-1 shows an image before and after conversion to the GIF format and the Web-safe color palette. We've deliberately chosen an unsuitable image for our illustrations; the effect is usually more subtle.

The Web-safe color palette is 216 colors that are guaranteed to work as is on both Macs and Windows PCs running in the simplest, fastest, cheapest graphics mode, 256 colors. (Not all the colors overlap on both platforms, so only 216 are safe on both.) If you do all your Web graphics work in these 216 colors, you're guaranteed to avoid problems that occur if you try to display other colors on PCs and Macs that are running in 256-color mode.

The conflict here is between novice and more advanced graphics creators. To a novice, 216 colors sounds like a lot. And it's pretty easy to do a cartoonish-looking image in 216 colors. (Though trying to render Scooby-Doo exactly can be a bit tough.) But to a skilled graphics person, 216 colors are not nearly enough. The first thing an advanced user might note is that there are hardly any good grays in the Web-safe color palette — and grays are a nice thing to have if you're limited in all the other colors of the rainbow.

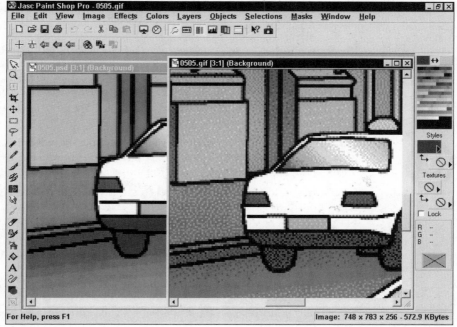

Figure 12-1:
Conversion
to GIF and
Web-safe
colors, as
shown on
the right,
can
oversimplify
an image.

A fixed set of 216 colors is also very limiting if you're trying to convert a shaded image or photograph to GIF format for easy transmission. The 216 colors you've got are unlikely to be the best 216 colors for mimicking the wider range of colors in the source image. Instead, banding and other problems that occur due to a lack of shades are going to be worse because the shades available are usually going to be the wrong ones.

The solution to this problem is to use an adaptive color palette. An adaptive palette is made up of custom-picked colors that best match what the artist was trying to do in creating the original image. (Though doing a 40 x 60 pixel image of Scooby may not quite make you an artist.) But there are two pieces of bad news here. The first is that the custom colors are going to get attached to the front of the GIF file (prepended, in techno-speak). Adding the adaptive palette makes the file as much as nearly eight hundred bytes larger. The second piece of bad news is that a Mac or PC that's in 256-color mode is going to laugh at your pathetic little list of adaptive colors and force the image onto the screen using the fixed set of colors it has handy to work with.

Here's a list summarizing the tradeoffs in dealing with the GIF format's color choices:

✔ **Photo or shaded image converted to GIF, adaptive palette:** Results may be pretty good, especially for a small photo (100 x 100 pixels or smaller). Definitely worth a try to see if you can save on file size and JPEG's slightly longer decompression time without too much loss in quality. The small number of users running at 256 colors will see an uglier version, though.

Photoshop and Photoshop Elements allow you to preview what an image looks like when it's forced to display in 256-color mode, allowing you to know in advance what you're forcing some of your users to look at.

✔ **Photo or shaded image converted to GIF, Web-safe palette:** Usually significantly worse results. Safe for everyone, but also ugly for everyone. Preview this to see if it saves on file size without making your close-up photo of yourself on vacation look like Scooby-Doo.

✔ **Non-shaded illustration converted to GIF, adaptive palette:** You probably don't have enough time on your hands to have used 256 colors or more without turning on your graphics program's shading feature anyway. So, when saving to GIF, your graphics program will construct a well-suited adaptive palette and attach it to the image, and your image will be displayed perfectly. (Except on limited-color computers, which will uglify it somewhat.)

✔ **Non-shaded illustration converted to GIF, Web-safe palette:** If you created your illustration using Web-safe colors, or a simple set of colors that happen to be close to them, it will be modified only a little bit or not at all. But if you used wildly different colors, switching to the Web-safe palette will make for a big change.

In any case, it's worth experimenting — especially within Photoshop or Photoshop Elements, which give you a chance to see the 256-color version from a preview within the program. You can trade off among the various options until you find the one that will render your image most faithfully for most or all of your users.

How to lose information in GIF without really trying

GIF is generally said to be a lossless compression technique, but it's still easy to lose information in GIF — in the actual file, or in the image that gets displayed — without meaning to. You can lose information in GIF in three ways:

✔ **Reduction to 256 colors.** GIF only supports 256 colors. As we describe in this chapter, if you save a file of more than 256 colors as a GIF, some of the colors will be thrown away. Whammo — you've just lost data.

✔ **Use of the Web-safe palette.** If you use the Web-safe palette when compressing an image into GIF format, rather than an adaptive palette, every color that isn't in the Web-safe palette will be translated into a color that is. Also, there are only 216 colors in the Web-safe palette, so if you have more than 216 colors, some of them will be lost.

✔ **Display on a 256-color system.** If you use an adaptive palette, then send your image to a computer system that can only display 256

fixed colors, many of your colors are likely to be changed at display time to colors that the receiving system can handle. You can avoid this by creating images using the Web-safe palette as your starting point.

You can minimize the effects of these problems with planning, care, thought, and by bailing out and switching to JPEG when it looks like GIF is going to be too hard on your image (pun intended). Just be aware that GIF is only loss-less when used carefully and appropriately.

Telling the Truth — Transparently

A particularly egregious untruth is called a transparent lie. But we'd be lying if we said that transparency isn't useful — or that it isn't, at first, confusing.

The basic idea of transparency is nice. You can take a solid background around an image and make it transparent. That is, whatever is behind the image (usually the background color of the Web page) shows through. That way, the central part of the image — the interesting part — appears to float on the Web page, instead of being isolated in a solid-colored rectangle.

You can create the same effect as a transparent GIF more easily just by making the background color around your image the same color as the Web page it rests on. However, in the early days of the Web, many users had early versions of Netscape, which had a default background color of gray, while others had Internet Explorer, which had the more sensible default background color of white. So making the background of a graphic right for one would get you in trouble on the other. A transparent background let the Web page's background color show through and therefore worked equally well on either, as well as on Web pages where the developer specified a different background color.

Using transparency is easier if you take all the background around the subject or core of your image and make it the same color. Use a background shade that doesn't appear anywhere in the subject. Making the background a single color also makes the image as a whole compress much better.

A problem with transparency is that it's very easy to accidentally make the background the same color as a color used in the core or subject area of the photo. Say your subject is a book cover with a black area that has white text on it, for instance, and you make the image's background black. Then you make black transparent to get rid of the background. The black area on the book cover goes transparent too, allowing the Web page it's displayed on to show through.

Figure 12-2 shows a book image without transparency and with the wrong color transparent.

If the Web page is white, you're going to end up with a book cover that has white text on a white background, making the text mostly disappear. Even when the effect is less disconcerting than that, having the Web page color poke through your image is not generally going to look very good.

The best way to avoid having transparency cause problems in the subject part of your images is to get in the habit of using some odd, non-Web-safe color for backgrounds, and also to get in the habit of checking that your background color isn't matched by any color in the subject. That way you'll avoid this problem.

What we can't help you with is the other problem: If you try to explain this to someone, the words "the transparency color" or similar phrasing are almost guaranteed to confuse them. After all, transparency isn't a color, now is it? But you, having read this thorough explanation and tried using transparency once or twice in Paint Shop Pro or Photoshop, will be able to explain it to them, rendering a valuable service to your listener in particular and to the cause of better understanding of graphics in general.

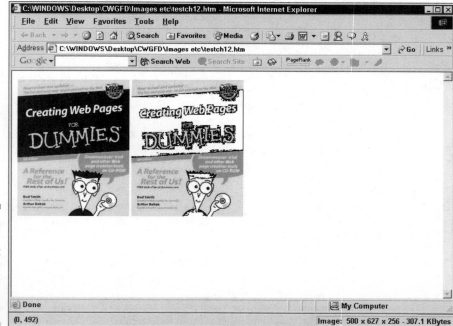

Figure 12-2:
Transparency is great when it's right — and scary when it's wrong.

TV and movie directors do something very much like transparency when creating special effects. The technique is called *bluescreening*. Two actors have a light saber fight, for instance, on a stage in front of a blue screen. (Nowadays, other colors are used as well, with green being a popular choice.) Special effects people then drop all the background color out of the image and drop in a computer-rendered image of, for instance, the hangar deck of the Death Star. Needless to say, the actors are costumed in clothes without any blue in them before taking their places in front of the blue screen! Otherwise, when blue was subtracted from the shot, part of their clothes would disappear as well.

Interlacing the Lacy Person's Way

As we described in Chapter 6, *interlacing* is the technical term for an impressive effect. Normally, when an image downloads, it appears from the top down, one line at a time. An image of a face that takes 20 seconds to download, for instance, might not be recognizable for 10–15 seconds, and will continue to look jarringly incomplete right up until the full download is completed at the 20-second mark.

With interlacing, a fuzzy version of the same image appears in 5 seconds. A slightly sharper one appears 5 seconds later, then a pretty good-looking one at 15 seconds, and a full-resolution image by the 20-second mark.

How is this done? Pretty simply.

With interlacing, the actual contents of the GIF file are rearranged. Normally, the file contains the first line of pixels, then the second, then the third, all the way down to the end of the file — just as you might expect. With interlacing, however, the file contains the first line of pixels, then the fifth line, then the ninth — every fourth line, all the way to the end of the file.

When the Web browser starts to display a GIF file, it looks for a flag at the beginning of the file to see if the image is interlaced. If the file is interlaced, the Web browser repeats the first line it sees four times, then repeats the second line four times, and so on, until a complete image with a lot of repeated lines has been displayed. After these interspersed lines are all displayed, the image appears as a fuzzy version of itself.

Then the whole process repeats with the third, seventh, eleventh, and additional lines, on through to the end of the file. Half the file has now been downloaded, but the image is far more than half-recognizable. It looks like a complete image that's slightly fuzzy.

Two more sets of lines follow, starting with the second, then the fourth line in the file. The image is finally complete. The file format is called interlacing because the sets of lines that appear are interspersed, or interlaced, with each other.

TV sets and older computer monitors, which have relatively slow-moving electron guns, also use interlacing to keep the display refreshed on an ongoing basis (though they use a pattern of every other line instead of every fourth line).

One of the beautiful things about interlacing is that an interlaced GIF doesn't need a separate command in the Web page to make it appear — the information that this is an interlaced image appears within the beginning of the GIF file. The browser simply looks at the file and displays it appropriately, as either a non-interlaced or an interlaced image. (Although you can imagine what it would look like if an interlaced file were accidentally displayed in non-interlaced mode! If you're really bored sometime, you can simulate what this would look like by moving lines of pixels around in your graphics program.)

Interlacing is really cool, and you should routinely use it. It will have almost no visible effect for users on fast connections, but it will make life noticeably better for users on slow modem connections. We show you how to turn interlacing on for GIF images created in Paint Shop Pro and Photoshop later in this chapter.

Is there any reason why one wouldn't use interlacing? There are actually three reasons, none of which is very strong:

- ✔ **File size.** An interlaced file is a bit larger than a non-interlaced file because of the extra information needed to communicate re-ordered information — somewhere around 10 percent. However, for a small image, the extra file size won't cause a noticeable impact on download time, and for a large image, the benefits of having the image interlaced are so great that it's worth the extra download time.

- ✔ **Moving image.** When an image downloads fairly quickly — neither instantly nor very slowly — interlacing can create an effect that's eye-catching in a somewhat disconcerting way. If the user isn't looking right at the image, it gives the impression of appearing as the initial set of lines is displayed, then shifting or snapping into place as the remaining information comes in. This can be a bit off-putting to the user, but is not sufficient reason to avoid interlacing (which still helps users on slow modems).

- ✔ **Small benefit.** Most GIF files used today are quite small, and even slow modems are quite a bit faster than when the Web first became popular. Back then, 14.4 Kbps and even 9600 bps modems were still in widespread use, running at about one-third the speed of the 33.6 Kpbs and 56 Kbps modems of today. Yet even as modems have sped up, Web designers have developed good habits in terms of getting the most out of small images rather than using large ones. When an image is less than 5K, and therefore downloads in 1–2 seconds over a typical modem, it might not make much difference to the user whether the image is interlaced or not.

You shouldn't interlace animated GIF images, as we describe in the next chapter. Also, test files with text in them before committing one way or another on interlacing; they may look odd during the download process.

Using GIF for JPEG-compressed Files

GIF and JPEG work very, very differently. One of them preserves all the info it can. The other one cheerfully messes up your image to make it compress better. One of them works best for illustrations drawn on the computer. The other shows its strengths on photographs and other shaded images.

But you can use them together in a clever way. The trick is to send a JPEG-compressed photo as a GIF file. To do this, you export an image in JPEG format, open the JPEG version of the image, and save it as a GIF for use in your Web page. This accomplishes a few things:

- ✔ **Making the image smaller.** JPEG generates a whole bunch of new colors as it compresses an image. GIF reduces the color count to 256 colors — 216 if you use the Web-safe palette — and stores each color as a 1-byte number. This can save a noticeable amount of file space.

- ✔ **Improving the image (sometimes).** The extra colors that JPEG generates can appear as noise, especially when an area of an image is supposed to be all one color (which gets traduced by JPEG into several shades). Forcing the image to 256 colors by converting it to GIF can help improve some images, and doesn't hurt some others, especially little ones.

- ✔ **Making the image display faster.** The browser decodes GIF faster than JPEG, so after the image downloads, a GIF image appears on-screen a bit faster than a JPEG image.

- ✔ **Making the image interlaced for more users.** Interlaced GIFs have been around for a long time, but widespread support for interlaced JPEGs is only a few years old. If you interlace a GIF image, more users will get the benefit of interlacing than if you interlace a JPEG.

- ✔ **Using transparency.** While you can make a JPEG interlaced, you can't make its background transparent. What better way to improve the user's ability to focus on the foreground of an image than to remove the background entirely through GIF's transparency feature?

You should routinely try saving your JPEG image as a GIF, especially for smaller images. If it makes the file smaller, even a little bit, without visibly harming the image, then use the GIF version — the download time that the user saves will be multiplied by the effect of faster rendering after the image reaches the user's computer.

Using GIF Features in Paint Shop Pro

This example shows you how to use all the GIF features in Paint Shop Pro. Although you can do many things to prepare a file to be GIF-compressed, such as reducing the number of colors in it, removing unneeded parts of the image, and making the background all one color, the core parts of the process are fairly simple.

Follow these steps to use Paint Shop Pro's GIF-related features.

1. **Open Paint Shop Pro, and open an image that you want to compress in GIF using Paint Shop Pro.**

   In this example, we use a screenshot from Paint Shop Pro itself — one that includes a photo — to demonstrate both strengths and weakness of GIF.

2. **Before you begin, you can select an area to protect from transparency.**

   If you want everything outside a certain area to be made transparent, select that area. (Shift+click to create a compound selection with multiple areas.) You can also prepare the image for transparency by editing the background to make it all one color. Make sure to choose a color that's not in the other part of the image.

   If you're going to use this option, make your selection accurate down to the pixel — otherwise the end result is likely to look odd.

3. **Click the Export GIF arrow.**

   The GIF Optimizer dialog box appears, displaying preview windows showing both the uncompressed and compressed versions of the image.

4. **If it's not already selected, click the Transparency tab.**

   The Transparency tab appears, as shown in Figure 12-3.

5. **Choose the transparency option you want: None, Existing Image or Layer Transparency, Inside the Current Selection, Outside the Current Selection, or Areas That Match This Color and Tolerance.**

   The choices are very different; some require preparation before you open the GIF Optimizer window, others don't. The next step tells how to use the most popular option.

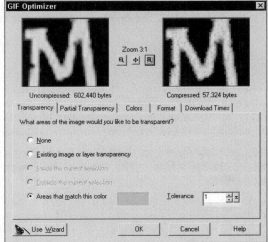

Figure 12-3:
Make your
intentions
transparent
in the GIF
Optimizer
dialog box.

6. **To use the Areas That Match This Color option, click the radio button.**

    Move the dialog box out of the way so you can see the part of the image that contains the color you want to make transparent. Move the cursor out of the dialog box — it changes into a medicine dropper — and click an area with the color you want. Then use the Tolerance setting or slider to set a range of shades that will and won't be made transparent.

    Watch the preview window to see how much of the image is affected by your choice of a Tolerance setting.

    Unfortunately, you can't use the Outside the Current Selection option to protect part of the image while using the matching option to make certain colors transparent. Also unfortunately, the medicine dropper doesn't appear in the preview window, which would be a useful capability.

    The Tolerance setting can save you from a fair amount of work that you might otherwise have to do to make a dark background, for example, into one specific shade of in order to drop it out using the matching option. However, it also makes it much easier to render transparent parts of the image that you want to keep. Use this option with caution.

7. **Click the Partial Transparency tab (even if you don't know or care about partial transparency).**

    The Partial Transparency area appears.

8. **Click the color swatch next to the prompt Yes, Blend with the Background Color, and then click the color swatch to choose a background color.**

   The Color dialog box appears.

   You need to choose the background color so your GIF image will display with the correct color in the areas you've made transparent. This allows you to see what the image will look like to your users before you put it on the Web page, and to see if the background color will bleed through any parts of your image that have been rendered transparent unintentionally.

9. **In the Color dialog box, either select the color that you're using for your background, or choose white — the color in the lower-right corner of the Basic colors.**

   White is the default background color for Web pages, so you should select it unless you're sure you'll be using a different background color.

10. **Click the Colors tab.**

    The Colors tab appears.

11. **Answer the questions for the following options: How Many Colors Do You Want (3 to 256), How Much Dithering Do You Want (0 to 100%), and What Method of Color Selection Do You Want to Use — Existing Palette (if you have one), Standard/Web-safe, Optimized Median Cut, and Optimized Octree.**

    In most cases, you want to use either the Web-safe option, which makes your image predictable across a wide range of systems and monitors, or the Octree option, which creates the most attractive image.

12. **Check the Include Windows' Colors check box so you keep the standard 16 Windows colors in the palette.**

13. **Click the Format tab and select the Interlaced option, unless you have a particular reason for the image to be non-interlaced.**

    The Format tab appears. Neither option changes the preview.

14. **To see predicted download times, click the Download Times tab.**

    The download times information appears. Concentrate on the 56 Kbps option as representing the user experience for a plurality of your likely users. If the transfer time is greater than 10 seconds for this image, or if it will be on a page with graphical navigation or several other images, consider taking strong steps to make the image's file size smaller, including making the display size of the image smaller or eliminating extra details from the image.

15. **Click OK to save changes to the image.**

    The Save Copy As dialog box appears. Navigate to the folder where you want to save the image and then click the Save button.

After you save the GIF, open the image and inspect it carefully, looking for any problems. Consider further changes if the image is too large for the Web page it's going into.

Using GIF Features in Photoshop

As with the previous example for Paint Shop Pro, this example is a quick tour of all the major GIF options in Photoshop and Photoshop Elements, except for those relating to animation. You can do many things to prepare an image for GIF compression in Photoshop, such as cropping the image, simplifying the background, and more. However, when you're ready to compress the image in GIF format, the process is fairly simple.

Photoshop and Photoshop Elements have a unified interface for saving files as GIF or JPEG. This makes it easy to consider both formats in turn, switching the preview and getting a file size estimate for easy format.

Follow these steps to save a file in GIF format in Photoshop Elements:

1. **Open Photoshop Elements, and then open an image that you want to save as a GIF file.**

   In this example, we use a screenshot from the opening screens of Photoshop Elements itself.

2. **Before you begin, make the background area that you want to make transparent one solid color.**

   Choose a color that does not appear elsewhere in the image. Some options in the Photoshop Elements' Save For Web dialog box might allow you to make the background, and nothing else, transparent. However, until you master those options, it's easier to simply force everything that you want to make transparent to be a single color so you can explicitly make those areas, and only those areas, transparent.

   If you're going to use transparency, specify the area to make transparent right down to the pixel, or the result will look odd.

3. **Choose File⇨Save For Web (Alt+Shift+Ctrl+S) to begin the process of saving the file in GIF format.**

   The Save For Web dialog box appears. Arrange the preview so you have Original and Preview views next to each other.

4. **From the drop-down list, choose GIF as the format.**

5. **Choose the color scheme.**

   You can choose Web to choose only Web-safe colors or Perceptual, Selective, or Adaptive as other options.

   The Preview image updates to reflect your choices.

6. **Use the Colors menu to choose the maximum number of colors in the color table.**

   We suggest you choose Auto in most cases, so the color table includes all the colors in the optimized image and no more.

7. **Check the Transparency check box if you want to make part of the image transparent.**

   The Color Table area of the dialog box displays any transparent colors with a line through them.

8. **Select colors to make transparent.**

   You can select a color by using the Eyedropper tool to select it in the preview pane, or by clicking the color directly in the Color Table. To add colors, hold down the Shift key while selecting them.

   The Color Table is updated to reflect the selected colors.

9. **Click the Map Transparency button in the Color Table palette.**

   The selected colors are marked with a Transparency Grid to indicate that they have been locked as transparent colors. An example of a preview with some colors locked out as transparent is shown in Figure 12-4. The Map Transparency button is the small button with a checkerboard pattern next to the number 256.

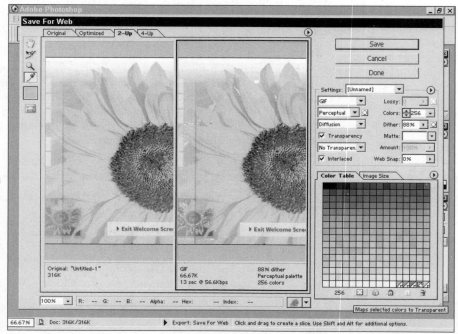

Figure 12-4: "Transparentize" several colors at once in the Save For Web dialog box.

10. **Check the Interlaced check box unless you have a specific reason for the image to be non-interlaced.**

    Interlacing adds somewhat to the file size — you can see how much in the preview window by watching the file size change as you check and uncheck the Interlaced check box.

11. **Click the Save button to save changes to the image.**

    The Save Optimized As dialog box appears; use it to navigate to the folder you want to save the image in and save it.

Open the image you just saved and inspect it for any problems. Make further changes if needed to reduce the file size, including reducing the image size if needed.

Chapter 13

Using GIF Animation

You have to think carefully about putting animation on your Web page. On the plus side, life moves and there's no reason the Web shouldn't. Movement grabs people's attention and communicates some things much more clearly than static content. On the minus side, some people are opposed to seeing any form of multimedia on Web pages. Given that the Web reminds many people of a hyperlinked magazine or newspaper — and images on printed pages don't move themselves around — you can see their point. Others aren't opposed to animation in principle, but tend to dislike most of the animations they do see.

Users are accustomed to animation being done in a high-quality way in other media such as TV and movies. Animated GIFs are lower-resolution and not as smooth. However, used with care, animation can help you make your point online — whether that involves entertainment, education, e-commerce, or even something not starting with an E.

In this chapter, we show you how to use the peanut butter and jelly sandwich of animation — GIF animation — a cheap, serviceable animation technique that gets the job done. We describe how to create GIF animations in Paint Shop Pro's animation package, Animation Shop 3, as well as in Photoshop, which supports animations directly.

Then we give a brief introduction to Macromedia Flash, the champagne and caviar approach to making things move. By reading this chapter, you'll know how to use GIF animation when you need it — and when to install that trial copy of the Macromedia Flash authoring tool on this book's CD-ROM and get cracking.

Introducing GIF Animation

Most GIF animation is simple flip-book animation — show an image; completely replace it with another image; completely replace it with a third image, and so on. Given that it takes time for each image to download across the Internet, the effect can be slow and somewhat jerky, but effective.

GIF animation is based on a feature of the GIF 89a format that allows several GIF images and simple timing information to be placed in a GIF file. GIF animation and transparency, another GIF 89a feature, became so popular that they led GIF 89a to completely replace the earlier GIF 87 format for use on the Web.

GIF animations are, to a certain extent, an irresistible force — they just roll along, image, image, image, image, with no way for users to stop them short of clicking the Back button, clicking a link, or closing their browsers. So users don't have many options for controlling them. Still, you, as the one creating a GIF animation, have several options for controlling it, which are described in the sections on creating GIF animation, later in this chapter:

- **Frame delay.** You can specify the pause between frames to within a few hundredths of a second. However, because some Internet connections download graphics far faster than others, you don't really have a fine degree of control of the frame delay. However, if a GIF animation loops — that is, repeats — frame delay comes into play on the second and any subsequent repetitions.

- **Looping.** This is an important option because setting it to the wrong value can drive your users loopy. (Sorry, bad pun.) We suggest you consider looping two to four times through most animations, with a message directing users to click the Reload or Refresh button on their browser to see the animation again. If most animations worked this way, users would like them more.

- **Interlacing.** You can interlace images, but because the file is an animation, having the images progressively sharpen could be disconcerting. We suggest leaving interlacing off.

- **Dithering.** You can tell the browser to use patterns when it doesn't have a color it needs. You should leave it off, as it can cause the file size to grow.

- **Background color.** This option only sets the background color used for your image when you're in the authoring tool — the background color that shows through transparent parts of the image in the browser will be the Web page's background color or background image. So set the background color as closely as you can to the background color or image in the Web page that will contain the animated GIF.

- ✔ **Transparency.** You can leave parts of a frame transparent so that the relevant parts of the previous frame (or the browser background) can show through. However, this effect can be buggy in older browsers as well as in authoring packages.

  Create GIFs without transparency first. Get the look and feel the way you want it. Then consider using transparency in optimizing your GIFs.

- ✔ **Depth.** The color depth of the palette used for the GIF file. You should leave this set to 8 bits until you start doing a lot of optimization work on your GIF animations.

- ✔ **Disposal.** Normally, a frame disappears when a new one comes in. You can, subject to browser authoring tool support, have it hang around or do other tricks. Again, save this option for optimization steps after the GIF looks and works the way you want it to.

- ✔ **Palette options.** You can use a global palette for the entire animation or separate palettes for parts of the animation, even for each frame. We suggest that you stick to one palette for the whole thing.

We recommend that you initially create and test your GIF animation using only the frame delay and looping options, experimenting with the images themselves and their timing until you create the animation that works the way you want. Only then should you consider optimizing the image by using interlacing, dithering, and other options.

Using GIF Animation Appropriately

GIF animation was discovered by an alert Web designer shortly after GIF 89a was released. Other Web designers were surprised and delighted to learn about this new feature, which was the first and only tool for adding animation to Web pages without plug-ins, add-ons, or updated browsers. It was like adding a third dimension to text and graphics, the other media available on the Web.

Yet today, the uses that are most often made of GIF animation are somewhat disappointing. Most Web sites don't use animated GIFs at all except in banner ads or JavaScript pop-up ads, which users generally dislike. Apparently, Web advertising hasn't yet reached the advanced status of Super Bowl ads, which are sometimes more popular than the game itself.

Why users don't like GIF animation

The reason users don't like GIF animation is that it's distracting. We agree. Both of us are Web professionals and we usually work with several windows open at once. Not only do we dislike animations on Web pages that we're trying to study or read, we don't like them in background windows, either. We waste several minutes every day doing window management to try to get animations out of the way so we can concentrate.

People also dislike GIF animations because they're low quality. The format, used without optimization, tends to display frames slowly, making the animation look clunky. (Ten frames per second is the minimum needed for motion to appear smooth; GIF animations are lucky to achieve one frame per second the first time through.)

GIF animations also are frequently used for advertising. So not only is the animation on a Web page distracting, it's most often used for something that's trying to pull the user away from what they came to the Web page for. If an up-to-date browser appeared tomorrow with the option to turn off animations, many users would take advantage of it.

These negative factors have a cumulative effect. Users get so accustomed to finding animations annoying that they tend to do so even when that reaction isn't justified. You have to swim upstream quite a bit to overcome this built-in negative user reaction to GIF animations.

Making GIF animation better

You can do a few things, at this late date in the life of GIF animation on the Web, to make your animations useful, interesting, attractive, and fun — a benefit to users rather than a distraction:

- **Give users control.** Users love the Web because it gives them control. GIF animations take control away from users. You can give users back control by letting them know that an animation will be on an upcoming page and by only playing the animation once or twice before stopping it.

- **Use high-quality graphics.** It's not true that if you build it, they will come; but it is true that if you make it look good, users are more likely to look at it. Seeing high-quality images will also break users' expectations of GIF animations and cause them to give yours a second chance.

- **Make a point.** Even animating your company logo occasionally can serve a purpose, and explanatory graphics, such as the one we use as an example later in this chapter, can actually be interesting and valuable.

- ✔ **Test usefulness and usability.** Test your animations on real users to see if they're used and appreciated, and to make sure they don't detract from the rest of the Web page or Web site they're on.

- ✔ **Optimize, optimize, optimize.** We recommend that you not optimize file size when you first experiment with GIF animation — concentrate on creating high-quality images that have a point to them instead. But then use all the tricks you can to make your high-quality, useful GIF animations run fast and smoothly on your users' browsers. You'll have your users clicking the Reload or Refresh button to see your animations again in no time!

Creating GIF Animation in Paint Shop Pro and Animation Shop

Recent editions of Paint Shop Pro come with a free companion program called Animation Shop. This program is just for creating GIF animations. You use Paint Shop Pro to create the GIF files and Animation Shop to combine them into a single animated GIF file. Figure 13-1 shows a screen image from Animation Shop.

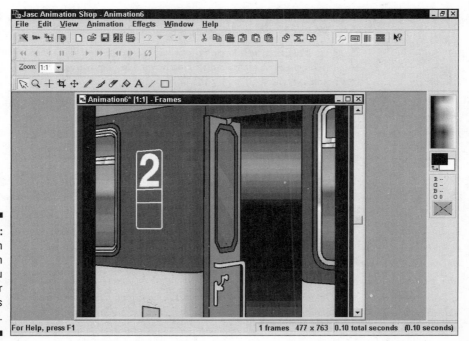

Figure 13-1: Animation Shop can help you get your animations on track.

You can create files to use in an animation and combine the files in many ways. We show you one simple way to get you started. Follow these steps to create a simple GIF animation:

1. **Open Paint Shop Pro and open the GIF image, if any, that you want to use as the starting point for your animation.**

2. **Modify your existing file or create a new GIF file that will serve as the base for your animation.**

   Take your time with this image. If you do it well, it will serve as a solid base for the rest of the animation sequence.

3. **Starting with your first file, create additional GIF files that will serve as the base for your animation.**

   Save the GIF files with names that indicate the order you want to use them in — for example, `train1.gif`, `train2.gif`, `train3.gif`, and so on. Also make sure that all the images share the same dimensions. Otherwise, managing them simply becomes too complicated, even if you use transparency to drop out the background and try to make the file size differences less obvious.

   Don't do anything complicated at this point — you'll want to cycle through the steps a number of times, checking your progress, to make it easier to experiment and recover from mistakes. If you want to make a long animation, start by creating the first 3 or 4 images.

4. **When you finish, if your system has limited capability, close Paint Shop Pro; otherwise, leave it open.**

   Close any other open programs or documents at this point. Some computers become unstable when running two graphics programs at once, so you don't want to put your other work at risk.

5. **Start Animation Shop 3 and open the first image in the animated sequence.**

   The Animation Shop window appears.

6. **Choose File⇨Animation Wizard (Shift+A).**

   Finally, a wizard with some magic in it! The Animation Wizard dialog box opens. The wizard asks you if you want to use the current image for the size of the animation, or a size that you enter.

7. **Choose the first option, Same Size As the First Image Frame, and then click Next.**

   The wizard asks you what default canvas color to use.

8. **Choose Opaque for the canvas color and click the color swatch to choose a color (use a contrasting color to the Web page background to make the image stand out, or the same color if you want it to seem part of the page), and then click Next.**

   The animation wizard asks you where to put differently shaped source images and how to fill empty parts of the frame.

9. **You can ignore these questions for now, because we're keeping it simple. Click Next.**

   The Animation Wizard asks if you want the animation looped and for how long.

10. **Click the radio button for the Yes, Repeat the Animation Indefinitely option to make the animation repeat during testing.**

   (You can always click the Stop button in your browser to stop it.)

11. **Enter a large value in the How Long Do You Want Each Frame To Be Displayed (In 1/100th of a Second)? text box; 10, or one-tenth of a second, might be a good choice. Click Next.**

   The Animation Wizard asks you to add the images to be used in the animation.

12. **Click the Add button and use the Open dialog box to select the first file.**

   Repeat this step for additional files in the animation. Use the Move Up and Move Down buttons to reorder the files. When the files you want to begin with are in the list and in the correct order, click Next.

   The Animation Wizard displays the Finish button. Click the Finish button, and the animation appears in a new window in Animation Shop.

13. **Choose View⇨Animation to turn on the control buttons for the animation and start the sequence playing.**

   Click the Pause button in the upper-left corner of the window to pause the animation, and the Play button to play the animation. Use other buttons to pause, rewind, fast forward, and so on.

   Be careful — the Slow Forward button is right next to the Play button. Be sure to click the Play button and not the Slow Forward button, or your carefully constructed animation will play slooooowly.

   Write down your observations about what needs to be changed — believe us, you'll forget things that need to be fixed if you don't write them down.

14. **Choose File⇨Save As.**

   The Save As dialog box appears.

15. **Change the filename to indicate that the file is an animation — add "anim8" to the filename, or something similar. Navigate to the folder you want to save the file in and click the Save button.**

    The Animation Quality Versus Output Size dialog box appears.

16. **Use the slider to choose the top option, Better Image Quality.**

    Animation Shop will optimize the file, reducing its size without noticeably changing the look of the animation.

17. **Click Next.**

    The Optimization Progress dialog box appears and you see Animation Shop optimizing the file.

18. **Click Next again.**

    The Optimization Preview appears, which is a bit silly for larger images because the small preview doesn't give you a good sense of the results.

19. **The Optimization Results appear.**

    The results compare the current and optimized files.

20. **Click Finish.**

    The file is (finally!) saved to disk. Time to start over!

Now that you can view your animation, you're almost certain to have some ideas for extending or changing it. Also, you probably didn't get everything right the first time. Take a minute to catch your breath, and then start over.

Creating GIF Animation in Photoshop Elements

Now that the Image Ready Web editing program has been incorporated into Photoshop and Photoshop Elements, the two programs have the built-in capability of saving a file as an animated GIF, which is a big advantage. You can seamlessly move back and forth between editing your images and modifying the way they play back in the animated GIF file.

As with Paint Shop Pro and Animation Shop, you'll find that in Photoshop, you have innumerable ways to create GIF files for use in animation and to combine them into an animated GIF image. The following steps are one path through the maze using Photoshop Elements:

1. **Open Photoshop Elements and open any GIF image you want to use as the starting point for your animation.**

2. **Modify the existing file, or create a new GIF file that will serve as the base for your animation, and then choose Image⇨Mode and select RGB Color as the mode.**

   Make this image the best it can be so you can easily use it as a base for the rest of the animation sequence.

3. **Create additional images for the sequence as GIF files, then open the GIF images as separate windows in Photoshop Elements.**

   Unless you're an expert in working with layers, keep each different image in a separate file until you have them all the way you want them.

4. **Add each image in turn as an additional layer on top of the first image by selecting the first image and then choosing Layer⇨New⇨Layer (Shift+Ctrl+N) to add a layer to the image.**

   Repeat until the image has as many layers as the number of frames you want in your animation.

5. **Choose Window⇨Layers to open the Layers window, as shown in Figure 13-2. Then choose each layer in turn and copy and paste an image onto it. When you're done, choose File⇨Save to the file in Photoshop format for later editing if needed.**

   You'll build up a multi-layered image.

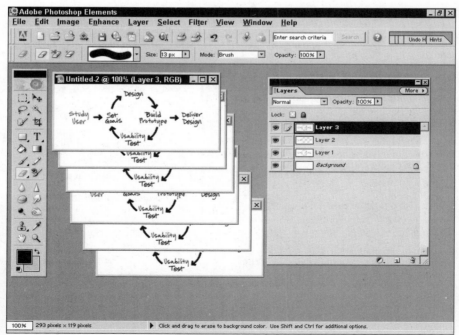

Figure 13-2:
Take a layered approach to images in Photoshop Elements.

6. **Choose File⇨Save For Web (Alt+Shift+Ctrl+S).**

   The Save For Web dialog box (the same one used to create JPEG images and non-animated GIFs) opens.

7. **Click the Animate check box.**

   The Animation options at the bottom of the dialog box no longer appear grayed out.

8. **Use the drop-down list to choose the frame delay.**

9. **Check the Loop check box to have the animation loop, or leave it cleared to have the animation only play once.**

   Photoshop Elements doesn't allow you to set a limit to the number of times the animation loops.

10. **Click the OK button.**

    The Save Optimized As dialog box appears.

11. **Navigate to the folder you want to save the file in and click the Save button.**

    You return to Photoshop Elements.

12. **Open your animation from within a browser window to preview it.**

Optimizing animations

The basic problem with the download speed of GIF animations is simple: Each frame is a separate image, so the more frames you use, the larger the animation is. A 30K GIF might cause a user a 10-second wait; an animation with 12 frames of 30K each will cause a 2-minute wait. That's a huge difference in the user experience. So naturally, you want to reduce the file size of the animation.

Many people start optimizing GIF animations the wrong way, though, using transparency and other tricks when simpler methods yield better results that are also more consistent in different browsers. Here are the steps we suggest you follow for optimizing animations:

1. **Make the original image smaller.**

   Use every trick you've got on the starting image of an animation: Make the image size smaller, simplify the background so it compresses better, compress the file with JPEG before exporting it as a GIF. Every hundred bytes you save may be worth 1K in the final file size, so have at it.

2. **Reduce the number of frames.**

   The file size of a GIF animation is the product of the average file size times the number of frames, so cutting the number of frames quickly reduces the overall file size. So reduce your animation to a few frames.

3. Keep colors consistent and use a small palette.

If you keep colors consistent between frames, you can use a smaller palette for the animation, saving some space. (Note that you only save this space once for the whole file, not for each frame.)

4. Try transparency and adjusting disposal options.

If you keep previous frames around and use transparency, you may be able to save space in the file. However, you fight for every byte when using this approach, and you're very likely to have the wrong thing show through at the wrong time. Also, expect complaints from users of older browsers who don't see it the way you intended it. Use these tricks — which many people dive right into — as your last resort.

Introducing Macromedia Flash

Flash animation is a multimedia technology from Macromedia. In some ways, a Flash animation is like a QuickTime or Real format movie that plays in your Web page, but with smaller file sizes. However, Flash movies are better integrated with Web pages than that, and can actually be combined with HTML to create interesting effects.

One of the most irritating things about the Web, to people who want to liven up Web pages, is that it doesn't support vector graphics. Vector graphics are graphics that are defined by computer commands, such as "draw a thin red line from point 0,0 to point 10,10." The nice thing about vector graphics is that they can have much smaller file sizes than bitmap graphics — the kind of graphics encoded in GIF and JPEG files. They also can be scaled to larger or smaller sizes smoothly.

Macromedia Flash is, at heart, a program that enables you to get animated vector graphics into Web pages, allowing for small graphics files that make a big difference in the appearance and activity level of a Web page. Flash animations are much smoother in appearance than GIF animations.

Unfortunately, viewing a Flash movie requires a separate player, and many users don't have it — or they have an older version that doesn't support all the latest and greatest features. If you use Flash movies on your Web site, some of your users will be irritated at having to get the player — and others won't bother, and will miss out on whatever Flash content you put on your site.

Flash content can be used with the Web in three ways:

- ✔ **Playing an animation in a window.** Flash movies can be placed in a window, just like a QuickTime movie, except with graphics instead of images and with smaller file sizes. Many companies use Flash animations in this way to create animated trailers on the home page of their Web sites or to create animated banner ads.

- ✔ **Playing an animation directly in a Web page.** You can use Macromedia Flash to actually animate images over a Web page, as if on a separate layer over the page. This might be disconcerting to see at first, but the effect can be interesting.

- ✔ **Using a Flash application instead of a Web page.** There's a subtle but important difference here; Macromedia Flash can be used to create what are basically application software screens for users to interact with instead of Web pages.

Flash movies can be displayed in a window in a Web page, on top of a Web page, or instead of a Web page, but Flash animation is not really a Web technology — more a hitchhiker on Web sites. (The same is true of any animation, video, or sound technology, because support for these file types isn't built into the HTML specification and into browsers as it is for text and graphics.) Using Flash animation may also be unfamiliar to users compared to sound and video clips. As such, many Web authors reject its use out of hand.

However, the world is changing. More users are getting fast Internet connections, and they expect more out of Web sites. And many users are action- and entertainment-oriented; static Web pages are just not very interesting to them. Flash animation is perfect for sites that need to reach these kinds of users.

The most recent tool for creating Flash content is called Macromedia Flash MX. Macromedia Flash MX is a powerful tool, but it's not for the fainthearted. You may want to install the trial version on the *Creating Web Graphics For Dummies* CD-ROM and experiment with it.

We cautiously recommend that, after you master the graphics basics in this book, you learn enough about Macromedia Flash to have a feel for what it can and can't do. Then, keep your eyes open for opportunities to use Flash animation where it makes sense. *Macromedia Flash MX For Dummies,* by Gurdy Leete and Ellen Finkelstein (published by Wiley Publishing, Inc.), describes how to create Flash content. It's up to you to use it in a way that adds value for your users.

Chapter 14

Creating and Obtaining Images

. . . .

. . . .

*I*f you're a natural artist, you may already have hundreds of images on paper, canvas, sculpted into clay or stone, or even on your computer and ready for use on the Web. Or you may not be an artist, but you know how to use imagery to communicate. You may be good at sketching ideas or you may be the office expert on PowerPoint. Like an artist, you have work lying around, ready to be put on the Web.

This is the chapter for you, even if you know what you like in terms of Web graphics but the idea of staring at a blank canvas or screen and creating new images doesn't inspire you, it makes you perspire.

In this chapter, we show you how to create images and give you a few ideas for how to make sure your images look good. We also describe the mechanics of using Paint Shop Pro or Photoshop to implement your ideas. (Converting your image to a JPEG file is covered in Chapters 5 and 11, and converting images to GIF files is covered in Chapters 6 and 12.)

A few tips in a Web-oriented book won't turn your artistic or graphics skills from imperceptible to impressive overnight, so in this chapter, we also tell you where to find images you can download for free or for a fee. Check out Chapters 15 and 17 for more information about how to hire a professional and where to find resources to hone your creative skills.

Creating Images

Images for Web pages need to be simple. Simple, simple, simple. They need to convey a single point or emotion clearly. Why? The most important reasons are the following:

Panic early

It takes real skill to create an attractively designed Web site or an illustration that makes a point clearly. If you need professional-quality graphics work in a hurry, you may find that the best choice is to hire a professional. It's very unlikely that books, videos, Web sites, or even advice from a talented friend are going to enable you able to create top-quality work quickly and consistently.

The availability of tools like Photoshop and Illustrator allow people who can't draw a straight line to, well, draw a straight line. And the low resolution of Web images can obscure some of the finer points of expert versus amateur work. However, talented amateurs do, by definition,

have talent. Unless you have some indication that you're one of these people and you're ready to invest the time to take a professional class, it's not fair to you or your future Web site visitors to saddle yourself with the task of quickly creating a large quantity of top-quality work.

Use the information in this book for its intended "how to" purpose, but realize that if you have tough design or artistic tasks in front of you, you'll probably need to spend time, money, or both to get them done well. Honestly evaluate what you have to do and the time and money you have available to do it early in the process so that you can set your goals appropriately and then succeed in meeting them.

✔ **People view Web pages on low-resolution screens.** Fine detail and complexity disappear in the move from the 1200 dpi and more available on a book or magazine page to the 100 dpi or less that are available on a typical computer screen. The subtle edges or shading that looked so cool in print are likely to look like an errant pixel or three on-screen.

✔ **People view Web pages quickly.** People are usually task-oriented when they use the Web. Because reading and seeing images are harder tasks to do on-screen than on a printed page, and because the Back button and a million other sites are always just a click away, everything on the Web happens fast. Even if you could create an image that was visually or conceptually complex on-screen, people usually would not take the time to absorb it.

✔ **Site designs are still in their infancy.** Guiding people through the many possibilities of a Web site is difficult, and the kind of site designs that would cause people to slow down and carefully consider complex ideas aren't yet much in evidence. A well-executed, complex graphic presented on the Web is likely to be a bit of a diamond in the rough — beautiful, but unlikely to be appreciated fully.

What works on the Web is simple, powerful images that make a point quickly and then let users get on to the next thing they're doing. In this chapter, we show you how to create a simple informational graphic in both Paint Shop Pro and Photoshop.

Don't be afraid to use other programs as a source for graphics. For example, you can easily build a nice-looking chart in Excel or a table in Word, then use a screen capture (as described in Chapter 4) to bring the image into Paint Shop Pro or Photoshop and make it a GIF.

Sketching an effective graphic

Suppose that you need to create a graphic to accompany a story on the Web about a local charity whose donations have dwindled but recently recovered.

You want to create a graphic that both shows the details — total funds donated — and at the same time gets across the main idea of the story: Things have been tough, but are now on track to get better.

Studies, such as those at usability pro Jakob Nielsen's Web site (www.useit.com), show that people who read online will read a headline, read or scan any bulleted points or bolded words, read an illustration's caption, look at the illustration itself, read the text of any hyperlinks, and then leave the page. So it's very important that the illustration make its point clearly.

The sketch in Figure 14-1 serves as the basis of Web-ready graphics we'll create in Paint Shot Pro and Photoshop.

While not Web-ready itself, the sketch gives us something to look at — and talk about with others — before plunging into the details of creating a Web-ready image.

A fun way to use Photoshop to make a photo into an image is by using the Impressionist Brush tool to paint over a normal photo — that you have the rights to, of course — and turn it into a painting. You can also perform a similar trick in Paint Shop Pro.

Creating a graphic in Paint Shop Pro

Using a computer program, such as Paint Shop Pro, to create an image isn't as intuitive as drawing with a pencil and paper; you have to think much more while sketching in a computer program. When you've become familiar with a particular program, the process of creating an image will get easier. People who have a lot of experience with a particular program can work nearly as effortlessly in that program as they work on paper.

Follow these steps to create a Paint Shop Pro image like the one shown in Figure 14-1.

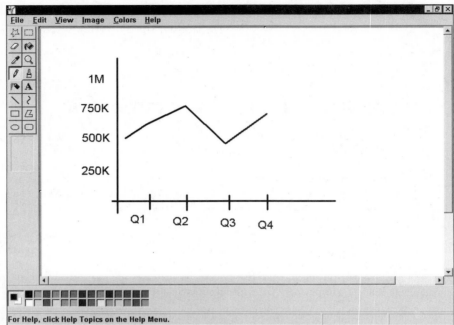

Figure 14-1:
A quick
sketch in
Windows
Paint.

1. **Open Paint Shop Pro.**

2. **Choose File⇨New (Ctrl+N) to open a new window.**

   The New Image dialog box appears, as shown in Figure 14-2.

3. **Set the Width and Height to 200 x 200 pixels. Set Resolution to 96 pixels/inch. Under Image characteristics, set the Background color to White, and set the Image type to 256 colors (8 bit).**

   You get a fairly large image (by Web standards) that will display at actual size on a typical Windows system setup. The image will be somewhat oversized on a Mac, but you can always reduce it. Using 256 colors as the image type allows you to use spot color for highlights if needed, while still making it easy to compress the image in GIF format, with its 256-color limit.

4. **Click OK to set up the image.**

   A small window, about 2 inches square, opens in Paint Shop Pro.

   The foreground color — the color that Paint Shop Pro "draws" in — could be just about anything at this point, including white. Drawing in white on the white background you chose in Step 3 leads to some rather uninteresting results!

Using real illustration packages

In this chapter, we create images directly in Windows Paint, Paint Shop Pro, and Photoshop. These tools are good for creating and modifying simple images that will go straight to the Web. However, if you're creating images that may also be used in print, or if you need to work through complex versions of an image before reducing it to a simplified Web version, you may find that other programs are better suited to the task.

Pencil and paper are still the best mechanisms for conceptual sketches in the early stage of creating an image. A few artists and illustrators are so skilled with the computer that they never let go of their mouse or stylus and drawing tablet — but for most of us, a pencil is a more natural and flexible tool for making quick sketches than a mouse or drawing tablet stylus.

To implement a complex drawing, the two top tools are Adobe Illustrator and Macromedia FreeHand. These tools are both so good for their purpose that you can use whichever you prefer without concern that you're missing much from the other. If you have a graphically skilled colleague or friend who prefers one of these tools, you might consider getting the same program in hopes of getting a little free instruction and support.

Both Illustrator and FreeHand allow you to save files in Web graphics formats, and both create images that you can convert to Paint Shop Pro or Photoshop formats easily. The things that you might have trouble converting, such as complex layered images and varying color spaces, are not usually concerns when the ultimate goal is a Web graphic anyway. If worse comes to worse, you can always scan an image in with a scanner or use a screen capture, as described in Chapter 4, to get an image into your tool of choice.

Feel free to start with a "real" graphics tool when you have "real" work to do — and to use Web-savvy tools, such as those described in this book, to create the Web-ready version of an image.

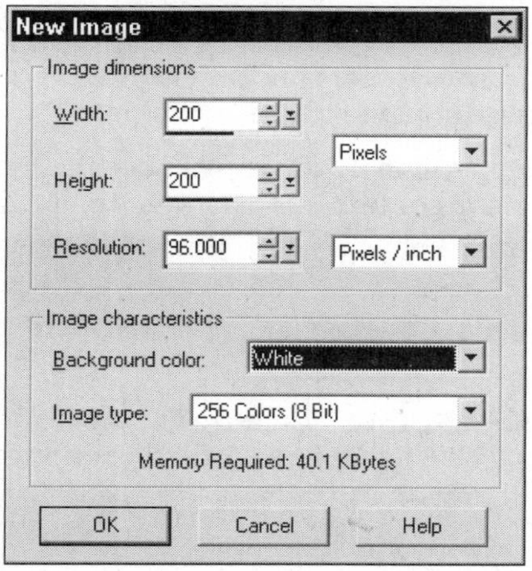

Figure 14-2:
Beginning an image in Paint Shop Pro.

5. **Click the box under the Styles menu, located at the right edge of the PSP window, to set the foreground color.**

   The Select Color from Palette dialog box appears.

6. **Click on a black square, and then click OK.**

   Check the RGB settings at the bottom to make sure they're 0, 0, 0 — that way you know you've chosen a true black and not a dark gray.

7. **If no rulers are displayed, choose View➪Rulers to display rulers.**

   Rulers, in pixels, display.

8. **Choose View➪Zoom In by 1 to zoom in and make your working area larger.**

   The apparent size of your working area doubles. Note that the pixel settings displayed on the rulers stay the same, but they will be more spread out.

9. **Click the Draw icon (the one that looks like a pencil drawing a squiggle, and appears near the bottom of the line of icons down the left side of the Paint Shop Pro window) to start drawing lines.**

   The Draw icon appears selected.

10. **Hold down the Shift key while drawing to draw straight lines. Draw the main gridlines and the indicators for quarters and donation amounts.**

    Use the Undo command (Ctrl+Z) to undo mistakes, and don't be afraid to experiment.

    Choose View➪Grid to turn on a visible grid. This gives you something to align your image with.

11. **Click the Text icon to create the labels for the gridlines, and then click the first spot where you want to enter text.**

    The Text Entry dialog box opens. In it, you can choose the font, size, color, and other characteristics of text that you want to use. We suggest that you begin with a sans serif font, such as Arial, at a modest size, such as 9 pt.

12. **Create the text that you need. Use the Object Selector tool to drag it into place.**

    If you're like us, you have to try several times to get the text correct and where you want it. You may also find yourself rotating or stretching text you intended to drag. With practice, of course, basic actions like this become second nature.

13. **Draw the curve that plots the donation amounts, which illustrates the point of the article.**

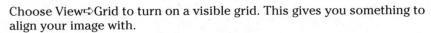

Again, you may find yourself experimenting quite a bit. We found it easier to draw each new segment from its end back toward its beginning rather than draw each segment from left to right. Or try drawing from left to right, but before beginning each new segment, press the Esc key. This removes the selection box around the segment you just finished so you can resume drawing the next segment without accidentally activating some arcane line changing function on the original segment.

14. Save the result in Paint Shop Pro format.

The image should look something like the one shown in Figure 14-3.

Always work on the image in Paint Shop Pro format to make changes, then save the finalized image as a GIF. This preserves specific details and editability much better than trying to make changes directly in the GIF image.

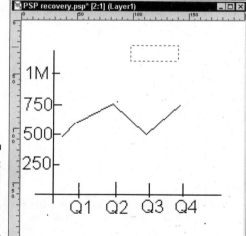

Figure 14-3:
The finished image in Paint Shop Pro.

15. Click the Export GIF arrow to save the image in GIF format.

If you need help with the details of how to save this image in GIF format, see Chapter 12.

Whew! That wasn't easy, no doubt, but you can begin to see what it takes to make a "simple" image. With practice, you can do simple things simply, and only complex graphics will require much effort.

Creating a graphic in Photoshop

As with using Paint Shop Pro, creating a simple graphic is a lot more work in Photoshop than it is on paper. As you gain experience, you'll be able to work more freely in Photoshop.

Follow these steps to create a Photoshop image like the one shown in Figure 14-1:

1. **Open Photoshop.**

2. **Choose File⇨New (Ctrl+N) to open a new window.**

   The New dialog box appears, as shown in Figure 14-4.

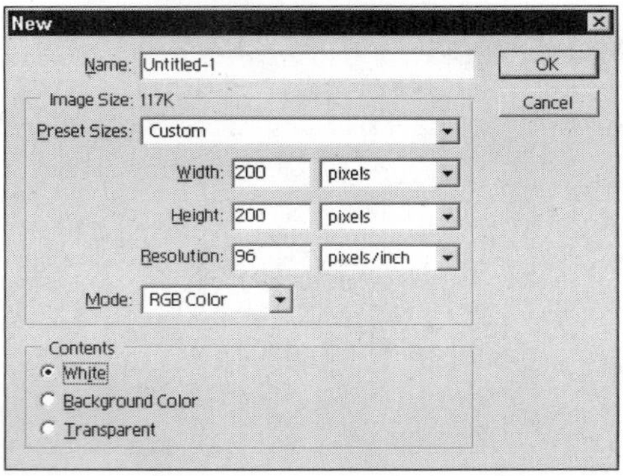

Figure 14-4:
Creating a new image in Photoshop.

3. **Set the Width and Height to 200 x 200 pixels. Set Resolution to 96 pixels/inch and Mode to RGB Color. Under Contents, choose White.**

   This image will be fairly large, by Web standards, and will display at actual size on a typical Windows system setup — a bit larger on a Mac.

4. **Click OK to set up the image.**

   A small window, about 2 inches square, opens in Photoshop.

5. **Click the Set foreground color box on the Tool Palette to set the foreground color.**

   The Color Picker dialog box appears.

6. **Click the Only Web Colors check box to reduce the color choices to those from the Web-safe color palette. Then set the foreground color to black (RGB 0,0,0). Click OK.**

7. **Click the Set background color box and follow the same steps to set the background color to white (RGB 255, 255, 255). Click OK.**

8. **If no rulers are displayed, choose View⇨Rulers (Ctrl+R) to display rulers.**

    Rulers, in pixels, display.

9. **Choose View⇨Zoom In (Ctrl++) to zoom in and make your working area larger.**

    The apparent size of the working area doubles, while pixel settings displayed on the rulers stay the same but appear spread out. You'll also need to drag on the lower-left corner of the window to expand it so you can see everything.

10. **Select the Line tool to start drawing lines.**

    You can find the Line tool by clicking and holding on the custom shape tool, which looks like a cartoon speech bubble. When you do so, an option menu appears; select Line from the option menu.

    The Line icon appears selected.

11. **After you begin drawing a line, press and hold down the Shift key to draw lines that are horizontal or vertical. Draw the main gridlines and the indicators for quarters and donation amounts.**

    Note that different objects tend to go on different layers; switch layers as needed to modify objects.

    Use the Undo (Ctrl+Z) and Step Backward (Ctrl+Alt+Z) commands to undo mistakes, and don't be afraid to experiment.

12. **Select the Horizontal Type tool to create the labels for the gridlines, then click the first spot where you want to enter text.**

    The Options window shows options for text. Use it to choose the font, size, color, and other characteristics for your text. We suggest that you begin with a sans serif font, such as Arial, at a modest size, such as 9 pt.

13. **Create the text that you need. Use the Move tool to drag it into place.**

    It may take you several tries to get text entered, sized, and located correctly. Your skills will improve with practice.

14. **Use the Line tool to plot the donation amounts, which illustrates the point of the article.**

15. **Save the image.**

    It should be something like the image in Figure 14-5.

    Always save Photoshop files in Photoshop format. Save versions of the image to GIF for use on the Web, but go back to the original Photoshop version to make changes. This makes editing much easier.

16. **Choose File⇨Save For Web (Alt+Shift+Ctrl+S) to create a GIF version of the image.**

    If you need help with the details of how to save this image in GIF format, see Chapter 12.

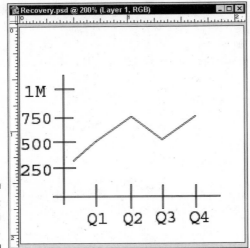

Figure 14-5:
The image in
Photoshop.

Creating an image in Photoshop is, at first, not easy. Dealing with layers and other complexities makes it much harder to use Photoshop than to do a sketch by hand. You'll find, though, that Photoshop is both simple and powerful when you become adept at using it.

Getting Images from Elsewhere

Finding free images for use on the Web is both very easy and very difficult. How can both be true? Whenever change occurs, some things get easier and some things get harder. The advent of the Web has created huge changes in the world of images.

In general, though, the advent of the Web has made life much more interesting and exciting both for creators of information — whose ranks have increased tremendously — and for consumers of information, who have access to a much wider variety of work than before.

One way to use the Web for creating images without infringing on someone's copyright is to use a search engine (such as Google) to find images. Gather images that might suit your purpose and use them as examples for discussion of what you do and don't want. You'll be amazed at the subtle factors you can identify in this way that make an image more suitable, or less suitable, for your purposes. Then use what you find out to help you go out and photograph or create an image that doesn't copy the original, yet exactly suits your needs.

If you create an image that looks like a copy of something that someone has rights to, you may get a strongly-worded letter from a lawyer — or a subpoena. So be careful to make sure your effort is truly original and independent of any specific source you considered in deciding what you wanted to create or capture yourself. To quote an old saying, "Copying from one source is plagiarism; copying from three sources is genius."

Getting images is easier — and harder

Here are the key factors that make finding free images for Web use easy:

- ✔ **Ease of searching for images.** You can easily search for images within a specific Web site or on the Web as a whole. Popular search engines, such as Google and AltaVista, have image search capability, and some large photo sites (such as those listed in the "Finding images on the Web" section, later in this chapter) allow you to enter very specific search parameters.

  Photos are great as references for illustrations. A great way to start a drawing of a crescent wrench is to use Google image search to pull up a dozen or so photos of crescent wrenches.

- ✔ **Low resolution requirements.** One of the chief difficulties in licensing images for use in print is the fact that high-resolution images are harder to find and cost more — much more for the very best. The low resolution requirements of the Web keep you out of the pricier precincts.

- ✔ **Proliferation of images.** The very popularity of the Web and of digital technologies associated with it has caused a huge explosion in the number of images being created and in their accessibility. Many more images are around to give you ideas, and quite a few of them are available for you to license.

The Web has led to the democratization of image markets just as it has opened up the ability to publish to and reach a wide audience using Web pages. But the growing accessibility of images has also led to problems — not new problems, but an intensification of problems that were present before the Web was around. These problems include

- ✔ **Unsuitability of images.** Finding the exact image you need is difficult. You might start out thinking that any image of a map of Nigeria will do — but then you find yourself getting very uptight about specifics of color and contrast, image size, text anti-aliasing, identification or non-identification of specific cities and natural features, and so on. People react to images in complex ways, so finding the right one for your needs is often surprisingly difficult.

- ✔ **Quality of images.** Nothing is more disappointing than finding an image that's right in every way, except that it's just not quite done well enough to suit your needs. The image might be too low in resolution, or be lit poorly, or use color combinations that aren't appropriate for Web display. As with suitability, quality requirements can get very detailed surprisingly quickly.

- ✔ **Rights, rights, rights.** Copyrights are a huge issue with digital images — so much so that many organizations restrict themselves to using well-known image banks plus images they create themselves. Accidentally violating some narrowly-drawn license agreement is easy, even for those of us with the best intentions. And you can't do much to stop people from suing you over a claim, whether accurate or not, that you infringed on their rights in using an image.

All of these concerns will arise when you consider using images from others. But developing familiarity with the sites, search engines, and contract terms of two or three image providers can greatly increase your ability to provide high-quality images on your Web site.

You'd be surprised how often the right source for an image for your site turns out to be you. Searching for the right image, with the proper rights, is so difficult and time-consuming that you may be just the person to create the image yourself.

Finding images on the Web

To find images on the Web to spark your imagination or to use as examples of an image you want to create, you can use a search engine such as Google or AltaVista. These search engines both have image search options that return pictures based on the words around them in Web pages. The image search options can be found on the home page of either Google or AltaVista, or you can go directly to them at the following URLs:

```
images.google.com
www.altavista.com/image
```

You can also use the regular text search in Google, AltaVista and so on to search for terms such as "public domain clip art." Such searches will lead you to many sources for images.

To find images that you can use directly, many different image banks are available. However, in the aftermath of the dot-com crash, the viability of some of these image banks may be questionable. Starting with larger and presumably better-backed image banks is probably safer. And because you need to review the contract of each image bank you use, it's probably best to start with the ones that have the most images.

Looking out for your rights

Carefully read the contract terms before licensing images for use on your Web site. You also need to save the terms you're agreeing to someplace, because the terms may change in the future; you're bound by the terms in force at the time you made the agreement, not by changes that may take place in the terms later on. Also, don't assume that the lack of a copyright notice means that images are freely available; they're protected by copyright unless there is specific notice otherwise.

The biggest restriction is for commercial versus non-commercial use of images. Many sites make images available freely for non-commercial use, but the definition of commercial use can be slippery. Read the contract you're subject to carefully for their definition, and follow it scrupulously. And don't assume that just because an image was usable for one purpose in your organization, that it will then be usable for some other purpose; the other purpose might not fit into the same contractual category.

Many image providers want royalties for views of their images beyond a fixed minimum number. Tracking views is a big administrative headache. (Even if the site you license from tracks usage for you, you'll also want to track usage so you aren't surprised by a big bill at the end of a month.) In fact, you may want to simply remove an image from a page after a certain period just to make sure that archival use of the page doesn't someday put you over the limit — and subject you to big bills or even litigation.

You may also see the term *royalty-free use*. That doesn't mean completely free use! It means that after you pay, you don't have additional payments for large numbers of views of the image. Though it can be expensive up front, this is a great way to pay for images because you don't have the burden of tracking page views for royalty purposes.

Consider having an attorney review any rights contracts you sign. You may be surprised to find that, for example, you have to take strong steps to prevent images you license from being illegally copied from your site. You also want to make sure that you are *indemnified* — protected from litigation — if the image you licensed was in fact not fully controlled by the people you licensed it from. (In image rights licensing, the buck does not stop with a given middleman unless that entity stipulates, in detail, that it does.) Lots to worry about — but often worth it, if you deal with reputable organizations and take some care up front.

Three of the largest and best-known photo image banks are Corbis, Getty, and PictureQuest. You can visit their Web sites at the following addresses:

```
www.corbis.com
www.gettyimages.com
www.picturequest.com
```

Figure 14-6 shows a close-up of the banner image for the Zanzara site, which was created as a collage of licensed images. The total cost was under $1,000 for images that are used as a theme for the entire site. However, it took experience to know where to look for the images, and skill to combine them artfully.

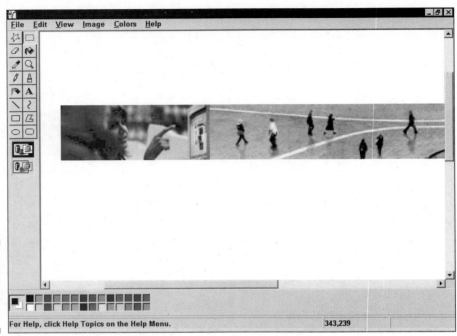

Figure 14-6:
Licensed
images from
the Zanzara
site.

For GIF images, a large number of providers exist, some of which also include photos and/or animated GIFs. Three of the best-known are ClipArt.com, Clipart-graphics.net, and DesignerFuel, at the following URLs:

```
www.clipart.com
www.clipart-graphics.net
www.designerfuel.com
```

Images and animations on CD-ROM

Many illustrators and computer artists have a few CD-ROMs of images on their bookshelves. The most useful of these packages gives you an "all you can eat" license — after you buy the CD-ROM, you can use the images on it freely.

You have so many choices of style, type, and terms in image CD-ROMs that it's hard for us to recommend any short list of options. We suggest you start by visiting a computer superstore to check out the options in person. Or search online for "image CD-ROM" or similar search terms. Buy a couple CD-ROMs that you like, then contact the makers of those packages for a catalog. And ask your friends — those who are into computer graphics are likely to have some favorites they can recommend.

Chapter 15

Laying Out Web Pages with Images

*H*ere's a riddle for you: What appears on every page of a Web site, but can't be seen on any page of a Web site? The answer is the design of the site.

A Web site's *design* is the combination of the repeated graphical elements that dominate the site's look and the rules that control its feel. Some Web site designs look good and feel right. Other Web site designs, created by equally talented people, look bad and feel wrong.

What's the difference? A hundred different factors can go right or wrong in a site's design, but one factor more than any other determines the prospects for the success of a site: the Web site's navigation.

Navigation, the appropriate buckets for content, the right look for major navigational elements, and the correct mechanics for how navigation works, is the secret to successful Web site design. And graphics are the key to navigation. In this chapter, we show you some of the secrets to creating successful navigation and successful Web pages with images.

Engineers like to say that certain things are necessary, but not sufficient in order to achieve success. Along these lines, creating successful navigation is necessary, but not sufficient, to creating a successful Web site. Other elements of the design and implementation have to be carefully balanced so the site as a whole, and each and every page of the site, is a pleasure for users to interact with.

Most people who have some graphical talent, or who at least are willing to work hard at graphics, can create a successful small Web site. However, if you need a highly polished look for your small site, or if you lack the experience to tackle a big one, you may need to get outside help. To finish up this chapter, we tell you how to do that as well.

The Crucial Role of Navigation

A Web site's navigation is where the most important elements of the site's design come together. However, most people are unaware of the fact that separate roles or disciplines have to work together for a site's navigation to be right. One person can do all the work, but is unlikely to be successful if he or she doesn't realize the three different skills involved.

In fact, it's so rare for someone to understand how these pieces work together that we give you points if you know the separate elements that come together in successful navigation design:

- **Graphic design.** The look of the site's navigation greatly affects what you can do with the color scheme, text fonts, and so on, throughout the rest of the site. (At least, it should affect those things!)

  You get 0 points for knowing that graphic design is a key factor in Web navigation, because this book has "Web graphics" in the title. But you get 20 points if you understand that graphic design is not the whole ball-game in navigation (and Web site) design.

- **Information design.** The way in which the site's data is chunked into major areas and pages determines, and is determined by, the main navigation and by additional levels of navigation, if any. The overall information design for a site has a huge effect on how much information and functionality can go into a site, and on how accessible those components are.

  You get 10 points if you've treated the chunkification and organization of your Web site's content as a separate topic from its look. You get an additional 20 points if you've ever heard of information design, or information architecture, or an information architect. You get 100 points and win the game if you've actually been an information architect.

- **Interaction design.** The specifics of how the navigation area works in concert with the user's mouse movements and mouse clicks is called interaction design. Interaction designers not only work on Web sites, but also work on things like digital cameras and traffic signals. (If you've ever erased a picture from your digital camera on accident, that's an interaction design problem. You might even say that if you've ever been in a traffic accident at an intersection, that's an interaction design problem too.)

You get 10 points if you've thought seriously about how the user interacts with navigation. You get an additional 20 points if you've ever heard of interaction design, and get 100 points and win the game if you've been an interaction designer.

✔ **Scoring.** Most people just want to dump the whole problem of creating a site's navigation on a graphic designer, without any thought that there might be more than just graphics involved. So any score above 0 on this little test puts you ahead of the pack. A score up to 50 shows you know your way around the block when it comes to navigation design and Web site design. Any score over that puts you in the stratosphere in terms of understanding how Web sites are put together. (And now that you've read this section, you're in the stratosphere!)

Only the look of a site's navigation is purely a graphical concern. The contents of the navigational elements and the number of major elements and subelements are the province of information design. And the way the different pieces work together is a job for an interaction designer. As often as not, as a competent graphics person, you'll be called on to put the pieces together by yourself.

Catching the hot potato

It's completely typical for all of these tasks to get tossed in the lap of a person who's qualified to be a graphics designer for print, though not yet for the Web, or even just someone with an artistic bent. Such a person can usually find out enough about Web graphics, using resources like this book, to do a decent job. But it's a lot to ask for someone to also handle information design and interaction design tasks.

If you find yourself in the deep end of the pool on this issue, you can do three key things:

✔ **Keep the initial site simple.** Don't try to implement a multiple-level site design — a site that has several subpages within the major categories of content — if you've never designed a site before. Size the project so that you can be successful with an initial, single-level site with 6 to 8 major elements.

✔ **Borrow shamelessly.** A few key elements are in almost every site of a given kind or type; include those in your site. For example, for a business site, Home, About Us, Products and Services, and Contact Us are typical key categories. Start with this list, add a category or two if needed for your specific topic, and you've got your categories list. Don't extend it with nice-to-have categories on the first go-around.

  ✔ **Get help.** Use printed resources, such as this book, and online resources (see Chapter 16 for some online resources to start out with) to find examples of successful sites and tips on how to create your site. Ask people who've done it how they did it — you can get advice in person and online as well.

Many people are afraid to not get everything they want in an initial site design — or to tell the people paying the bills that they're asking for too much. However, you may be surprised to find that many people know of unsuccessful Web projects, and that they might actually find it reassuring to hear that you're going to simplify the project. In any case, it's better to disappoint people a little up front with a simplified site design than a lot in the end with a site that's late, over budget, ugly, and/or hard to use.

Different types of navigation

Several different kinds of nav bars, or navigation bars, are commonly used within sites. The major types are as follows:

  ✔ **Strip of text links.** A strip of text links provide navigation. Many sites that use other types of nav bars use text strips for supplementary or special-purpose navigation. Text strips are also great for use by search engines and by "screen reader" tools used by the visually impaired.

  ✔ **Horizontal strip of table cells.** A table is used to create a horizontal strip of graphical cells, each linked to a different major area of the site, which can easily support 5–7 major categories.

  ✔ **Vertical strip of table cells.** A table is used to create a vertical strip of graphical cells, each linked to a different major area of the site, which can easily support 10–12 major categories.

  ✔ **Formatted text variant of horizontal and vertical strips.** Formatted text in table cells can be used to create horizontal or vertical strips of links that look graphical, but aren't.

  ✔ **JavaScript variant of horizontal and vertical strips.** JavaScript can be used to support mouseover effects, pop-up menus, and other variations within either a horizontal or a vertical strip.

Figure 15-1 shows the *For Dummies* site.

How to choose among all these navigation options? If you're going for a professional look on your site, you need a horizontal or vertical strip of table cells. If you have seven or fewer major categories, you probably want a horizontal strip initially — it's easier to design with. If you have more categories, you need to go with a vertical strip.

Figure 15-1:
The *For
Dummies*
site shows
how
navigation
is done.

After you choose your approach, find sites on the Web that you like that have the same basic approach. Also, find sites with functionality that you like. Use these examples to help decide what functionality you want in your site. If someone comes to you with other ideas, always ask them to show you examples of what they mean; this keeps the discussion realistic rather than pie-in-the-sky.

Then get to work on the look of your nav bar. Combine the design of the navigation's look with the design of the overall site's look. For a small site, mock up all the pages; for a larger site, mock up a few key pages and templates or example pages for the rest. Strive to accommodate all the elements you need within a predictable, consistent, attractive framework.

If you lack sufficient HTML skills to implement your designs yourself, get help. But don't lose control of the look and feel. Just as graphics people often get pushed into doing information architecture and interaction design, HTML coders often end up doing graphic design because they have their hand on the mouse, so to speak. Make sure the HTML coder you're working with implements your ideas.

How to do graphical text

To create graphical text, create your navigation bar as small images that use real text and a background that makes it obvious what cell each piece of text is in. Then export the resulting graphic as a GIF image. We don't recommend using JPEG for graphical text because it does horrible things to text, creating weird wavy effects around the edges of characters. Also, GIF almost always offers compression as good or better than JPEG for text on a relatively simple background.

That's the mechanical part, but what about the look of the whole thing? The most important choice you make in creating a navigation bar is the font and font size that you choose. (These choices are related, because some fonts are hard to read at small font sizes, limiting your choices if you're trying to cram a lot of text into a nav bar.)

Fonts have a feel to them that's hard to analyze or describe, but your choice of font in navigation can make a big difference in the look and feel of your site. Here are a few tips:

- Try to choose the color scheme and background pattern for the nav bar first; these choices affect which font looks best.

- Look at a lot of fonts — with graphical text, you can use any font you want.

- Don't use novelty fonts, unless you have a novelty site.

- Don't use a distracting font.

- For the cleanest look or for small text, use sans serif fonts.

As an alternative to graphical text, you can use styled HTML text in table cells formatted to look like a graphical nav bar. However, you lose a lot of control over the look and feel of the nav bar this way. For instance, you're limited to the fonts each user has on his or her system. We recommend going with a graphical nav bar as your first choice.

One of the quickest ways to make a site look ridiculous is to create big, slow-loading navigation. Users on modems arriving at your site have to wait and watch table cells with navigation elements and graphics in them loading one . . . then another . . . then another. Sometimes the cells even load out of order, which annoys users. Keep navigation elements small and fast-loading to avoid this major problem.

Keeping Your Pages Skinny

Your most important — and most frustrating — task as a Web designer is to keep your Web pages fast-loading. It's very difficult to constantly hold your creativity in check because of the holdups that some users have in accessing the Internet.

One thing that helps is to see keeping your Web pages small as part of the creative challenge. As a Web designer, you're responsible for the usability of the Web site, not just its appearance. Therefore, part of your job is to help keep the Web page fast-loading.

Setting a budget

One of the key tools in keeping your Web page fast-loading is to set a *budget,* or upper limit on the size of Web pages on your site. The budget includes all graphics elements plus the size of the actual HTML file that contains text and layout information for the page. We recommend limiting budget for a Web page to about 30 kilobytes.

What does this mean in terms of download time for the user? A user may have many delays in Internet access, which can vary depending on a lot of factors. Typically, having a 30K page gives the following download times:

Modem speed	*Download time for a 30K Web page*
33.6 Kbps	15–20 seconds
56 Kbps	10–15 seconds
DSL or cable modem	5 (or less) seconds

Ideally, Web pages would load in 1 second or so, but users will typically wait about 10 seconds if they're really interested. Most will lose interest beyond that time. So you can see that 30K is an upper limit for 56 Kbps users and not fully acceptable for users on slower modems. You may want to set a lower budget.

It's perfectly okay to set a different page budget from what we recommend; for most Web sites, though, it's important to set some kind of limit on Web page size. Why? Because one thing users value is consistency. If some pages load quickly, and some load slowly — and they can't predict which it will be when they click a link — users soon get frustrated. So find out what you can about your users, set a page budget, stick to it for all your frequently-used pages, and warn users before they click a link to a big page that takes a longer time to download.

There's some good and bad news that affects how quickly users see your Web page:

✔ **Good news: Navigation caching.** Your navigation graphic tends to get cached in users' Web browsers after it downloads on their first page view. This means that as long as users stay on your site, navigation is likely to reappear quickly. When they leave your site, other graphics will fill up the cache, and it's possible your navigation will need to be redownloaded at the beginning of the next visit.

✔ **Bad news: Missing** HEIGHT **and** WIDTH **attributes.** You need to specify accurate HEIGHT and WIDTH attributes in the <IMG> tag (or in the image setup options of a Web page creation program). If you don't, the page will shift in a disconcerting fashion during download.

✔ **Good news: Other caching.** Besides navigation, other components of your Web page can get cached as well, further speeding page download times on some subsequent page visits.

✔ **Bad news: Network problems.** Your estimates of your Web page's download times can vary in the real world due to all kinds of problems. The Internet is amazingly good at delivering data eventually, but not at working within set or predictable time limits.

✔ **Good news: Text is (nearly) free.** Text in a Web page downloads very quickly. Even a very long all-text Web page, in which you have to scroll down 3–4 times, is only 2K — smaller than just about any graphic. But remember the old saying, a picture is worth a thousand words — use images to make your page more informative and attractive.

Sub-budgets

So if we're recommending 30K per page, how does that break down across the different elements of a page? We recommend breaking the budget for page elements as follows:

✔ **Navigation:** 10K

✔ **Featured image(s):** 10K

✔ **Text and everything else:** 10K

Now navigation is fixed on each page, so after you come up with navigation you like, you can adjust your total budget accordingly. You can also do some testing to see how well your navigation caches when used on an actual machine. You may need to keep your home page small so users see it quickly, even after accounting for the fact that the navigation will generally be going into the cache for the first time. Other pages that aren't major entry points for the site can then be allowed to be a bit larger.

Even when viewing their own Web site over a modem, people working on a site rarely wait the full length of time for a Web page to download because they visit the site so much that its elements end up stored in the browser's cache. Clear your cache every once in a while to see what regular users are experiencing. In Internet Explorer, the command to clear the cache is Tools⇨ Internet Options. On the Internet Options dialog box, click the Delete Files button and then click OK.

You also need to take into account that lots of little files can take longer to download than a few larger files. So if your navigation is made up of lots of little GIFs, for instance, it may take users a long time to see the whole page — especially the first time they visit, before any caching can kick in.

You can put up significantly larger pages without causing long waits for your users by using tables to control the order in which navigation, text, and graphics download. Create an initial table that holds the entire contents that the user sees in the browser window before scrolling down. Keep the initial table under the 30K limit. A second table can then contain the rest of the page. This way, the user sees the initial part of the page load within a reasonable time, and can then scroll down to see more. Users who start scrolling quickly, though, may still be frustrated as they wait for the second table to appear.

Breaking the rules

Throughout this book, we've recommended that you manage the size of most pages so that they load quickly, but still use big images so that users with fast access, and patient modem users, can see high-resolution images in all their glory. You can include large images on your site in a few different ways:

- **Kick off the traces.** Just put big images wherever you feel like it, without changing anything else on the page. Fast access users get big images with little penalty; modem users just have to wait a while — maybe a long while — for some pages.

- **Warn users.** Take the kick off the traces approach, but put a warning on any link to a big page. The warning can be wordy, "expect a long wait for this page if viewed over a modem," or terse, "85K." Either way, users get some warning.

- **The Texas two-step.** Create your entire site as if it were going to be accessed over a modem, with strict page budgets and small images. Then link all the little images to bigger versions wherever you have them available. You can link the small images to big images without comment, or provide a link with wording such as "Large image (85K)."

In most cases, we recommend the Texas two-step approach. Amazon (www.amazon.com) does this with book covers; on some pages, if you click the book cover, you see a larger image of the cover. (On other pages, you get a "look inside" feature that allows you to see even larger scanned images from the cover and inside pages of the book.)

On Amazon, when a user links to the image page, he or she has to click the Back button in the browser to return to the previous pages. We think that you should add a Back link underneath the image that may be a little easier for the user to find and click. But in general, the Amazon approach, we believe, preserves usability while allowing users access to the high-resolution version of the image if they want it. In fact, we've seen this approach used enough now that we're disappointed when we see a teensy little image and can't click it to see a larger version.

Making Room for Photos

A photo gallery is a cool way to make a lot of photos available for quick scanning followed by leisurely viewing of the desired photos. From a design point of view, you can make a photo gallery in a lot of different ways. One approach is shown by the AltaVista image search page at www.altavista.com/images.

We have a few suggestions for how to create a useful photo gallery:

- ✔ **Use small, highly compressed thumbnails.** The page will have a lot of images, and users know they can get to the larger image quickly, so harsh compression is forgivable.

- ✔ **Offer really big full-size versions.** Consider offering large or even really large full-size versions of the images when the user clicks the thumbnail. When people really want to look at images, they want to see the best version of the image you've got. (But keep in mind that others can copy the image from your site.)

- ✔ **Don't make the user scroll.** Pick a target resolution, such as 800 x 600, then set the thumbnails page up so users don't have to scroll vertically, or worse, horizontally. You can probably fit nine thumbnails on a page without forcing users to scroll. If you want to offer larger thumbnails, offer only six or even four.

Photoshop makes it very easy to create a photo gallery, and doing so is a great way to begin to understand how photographic images and HTML work together.

Even if you're normally a Paint Shop Pro user, we recommend you use a trial version of Photoshop or Photoshop Elements to try the photo gallery feature. If you're sharp, you can learn some HTML so you can continue to reuse the photo gallery as a template after your trial of Photoshop or Photoshop Elements expires. (Or, what the heck, you could just buy one of the programs.)

Follow these steps to use Photoshop or Photoshop Elements to create a photo gallery:

1. **Get all the images you want into one folder.**

   Start by putting the images you want to use for your photo gallery into a separate folder. Choose good images. You don't need to compress the images, though; Photoshop will JPEG-compress them for you.

2. **Start Photoshop (or Photoshop Elements).**

3. **Choose File⇨Automate⇨Web Photo Gallery (for Photoshop) or File⇨ Create Web Photo Gallery (for Photoshop Elements).**

   The Web Photo Gallery dialog box appears.

4. **Choose a style from the Styles drop-down list.**

   For your first photo gallery, we recommend the Simple style, as shown in Figure 15-2. The Simple style gives you the most options.

5. **If you want to include your e-mail address in the gallery, enter your e-mail address in the E-mail Address text box.**

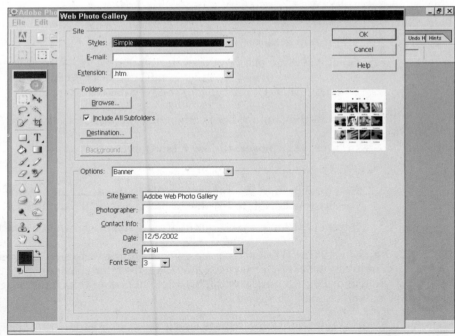

Figure 15-2.
Use
Photoshop
to create a
cool photo
gallery.

6. **Leave the Extension option set to** .htm **rather than** .html.

   This is where you specify whether the filename extension put on the HTML files generated will be .htm or .html. Every once in a while, using the .html extension may cause a problem with your Web site, and such problems can be extremely hard to identify and fix. Why take a chance? We recommend always using .htm as the extension for your HTML files.

7. **In the Folders section, click the Browse button to choose the source folder; then click the Destination button to choose (or create) a destination folder.**

   The source folder is the folder that holds the original images you want to use in the photo gallery (we suggested you create this folder in Step 1); the destination folder is any folder you care to use or create to hold the files that will make up your Web photo gallery.

8. **Use the Options drop-down list to set options.**

   This drop-down list is a bit confusing. What's going on is that you use it to access different options that affect different things about the pages and images Photoshop generates for the photo gallery. We suggest you leave these options as is at first, and then consider changing them after you generate a photo gallery or two.

9. **Click OK to generate the photo gallery.**

10. **Photoshop generates your photo gallery.**

    Several files are placed in your destination folder — thumbnail and full-sized versions of all your images, plus one or more HTML files that contain the text and formatting for the Web page(s) you create.

You can view the photo gallery with your Web browser as follows:

1. **In Internet Explorer, choose File⇨Open.**

   The Open dialog box appears.

2. **Enter the path to the** index.htm **file in the destination folder or click the Browse button to browse to the** index.htm **file; click OK.**

   Internet Explorer loads your photo gallery, as shown in Figure 15-3.

You can edit the HTML files using a text editor or Web page editor such as FrontPage 2002. When you save the HTML file after changing it, just click the Reload or Refresh button in the browser window to reload the page, which makes the changes appear.

We recommend that you spend some time experimenting with this Photoshop feature and the files that are generated. You can use the main HTML file for the gallery as a template to do all sorts of things, or just keep going back to Photoshop and creating galleries. Either way, you can do a lot with photos with this feature.

Working with a pro

You can do a lot on your own, but eventually you may need to work with a professional. There are a few things we can recommend to help.

First, learn everything you can before starting. Reading this book and doing all you can with it will help a great deal when you start working with a pro. You'll understand the language and concerns much better, leading to a more successful working relationship.

Second, ask to see each candidate's work, and don't work with that person unless you really like it. This isn't a matter of experience or objective judgment — you have to trust your gut here.

Third, check references. In some cases, what you learn will help you work better with the person. In other cases, it may cause you to avoid working with the person altogether.

Finally, keep tight control of the project. You should assign specific tasks to the consultant and, where practical, complementary tasks to yourself. That way you stay involved — and increase the odds you can figure it out enough to do it yourself next time.

With your newfound knowledge and these tips, you should be a dream client! That is, well-informed, easy to work with, and willing to share the work. You'll also be a dream project manager, able to produce great work on tight schedules and budgets.

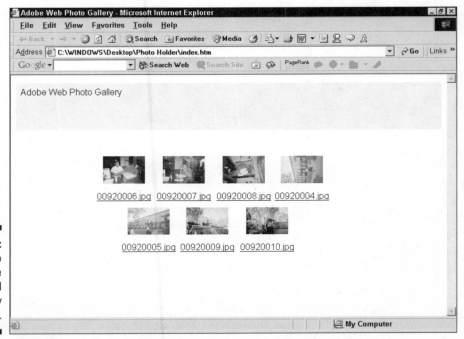

Figure 15-3:
A photo gallery page generated by Photoshop.

Part V
The Part of Tens

The 5th Wave   By Rich Tennant

"Hey- let's put scanned photos of ourselves through a ripple filter and see if we can make ourselves look weird."

In this part . . .

Top Ten lists are a great way to sum up the current state of human knowledge on almost anything, and Web graphics is no exception. Check out our Web graphics Top Ten lists and see whether you can come up with your own.

Chapter 16

Ten Cool Online Resources

*W*e've pulled together some of the online resources in this book — and a few others — to help you find cool stuff that will help you get a job done or just inspire you. We also take the chance here to go into somewhat more depth on each resource. Just point your browser to the following top graphics resources.

Adobe

The Adobe site at www.adobe.com has a wide range of resources, with the main attraction being downloads. You can download the free Acrobat reader and trial versions of two programs mentioned in this book: Adobe Photoshop and Photoshop Elements. But you can also get a whole range of other products on trial: Adobe Illustrator, the leading package for drawing and art online; Adobe Premiere, a high-end multimedia authoring program; GoLive, a top Web authoring product; Adobe Acrobat for creating and editing PDF files; and more. The Adobe site also offers technical support, user forums, online and offline training resources, and industry-specific information on how to use Adobe products.

Jasc

Jasc Software site at www.jasc.com has many rich resources. The keystone product is, of course Paint Shop Pro, available for download as a free trial version or to buy at a very reasonable price. (Jasc tosses in Animation Shop for free.) Other Jasc products featured on the site include: WebDraw, which introduces SVG, a new graphics format; Virtual Painter, designed specifically for converting photos into art with interesting effects; and Image Robot, which helps you automate repetitive authoring processes. The site includes all products for free download as a trial version and hosts product support as well.

Google

The Web's number one search engine at www.google.com is great for image searches as well as for text searches. Advanced options give you a lot of power in your searches. Also try out the Directory option to help find sites resembling the positive results of your searches — a great way to turn a single successful search result into dozens. Google is like a front door into all the photo sites on the Web. You can set preferences for searches or download and install the Google Toolbar, which gives you instant access to Web search, site search, image search, directory search, and more.

AltaVista

AltaVista, which you can reach with just a few keystrokes at av.com, is another excellent search engine. AltaVista is fair in the way it treats newer and lesser-known sites, and AltaVista's image search tends to return more results (which is a good thing sometimes and not others). AltaVista is also a pioneer in multimedia search and in international searching — not all the great graphics on the Web are just on English-language sites. Use AltaVista as a complement to Google.

Getty Images

Getty Images at www.gettyimages.com may well be the pro's first stop for photos. Getty's collection has an artistic feel and creativity that are hard to match elsewhere. Not only that, but Getty Images offers motion clips and support services, such as a clearing service. If you have some money to spend and want to do the job right, Getty Images is a great place to go.

Clipart.com

Clipart.com at www.clipart.com is like Getty Images' Bizarro World counterpart — cheesy rather than beautiful, and (luckily) cheap rather than expensive. (Clipart.com requires a small subscription fee, but you can search to see what they have before you pay the subscription.) If you need GIF images and animation fast, this is the place to go. Clipart.com has photos, too. Have fun with Clipart.com.

About.com

One of the treasures of the Web, About.com at www.about.com has answers to just about any Web authoring or graphics question you can come up with. Abounding with carefully organized directories, free newsletters, book reviews and recommendations — and, yes, a lot of ads and topic-specific marketing as well — About.com is a great place to go when you have questions about just about anything.

Useit.com

The Web's number one usability site at www.useit.com tells you more than you want to know about why so many Web pages don't work. You can find pages and pages of advice on just about any Web authoring topic, including tons of information on graphics and site design. You may only want to follow the advice up to a certain point, though — the site's author, Jakob Nielsen, is almost dead-set against using graphics for design purposes, as the site's purely functional home page shows.

Apple's QuickTime site

Apple Computer's QuickTime site at www.apple.com/quicktime is both practical and inspirational. On the practical side, you can download the free QuickTime player or the QuickTime Pro authoring tool. On the inspirational side, some of the most beautifully done multimedia on the Web, including high-quality movie trailers, uses the QuickTime format and can be found on the site. The site itself is an example of good Web design.

Photoshop Help

Okay, so it's not a Web site — but the Help files for Photoshop and Photoshop Elements are HTML-based and accessible through a browser. The Help files are also searchable and have tons of resources on graphics in general and, more specifically, Web graphics and using Photoshop to create them. Use Photoshop Help to become a graphics expert as you go along. You may also want to check out:

```
www.adobeevangelists.com/photoshop/
```

This site is created by Adobe employees who have an amazingly deep understanding of Photoshop.

Chapter 17

Ten Graphics Tips for Business Web Sites

*O*ne of the trickiest leaps to make in Web publishing is to jump from creating a personal home page to making a business site. Many of the layout and design choices that are acceptable or fun and friendly in a personal home page would be considered ugly or tacky when used in a business site.

The problem in most small business sites isn't the content — most business owners can write and organize information well enough to create a multi-page site that's useful. It's the look — graphics problems ranging from the design, to the layout, to the use of cheesy elements such as cartoonish animated graphics.

Yet creating a business site that looks good and works well is possible, even easy. Use the tips in this chapter to plan the work, then to work the plan, then to get feedback until you arrive at the promised land: an attractive, easy-to-use business site.

Keep It Simple

The more you plan to do with your business Web site, the longer it will take to do it. Most people have great ideas that might, with a lot of time and effort, become solid additions to a Web site. But what's needed first is a nice, attractive site with contact information and product descriptions. Don't plan to innovate in content or graphics until after you get your basic site up.

Consider Using a Template

Paid hosting sites, such as Network Solutions (www.netsol.com) and Bigstep (www.bigstep.com), have templates that make creating an attractive-looking site easier. So do many authoring programs. Consider using a template as a starting point to get a site up quickly, and then later creating your own custom look using what you've learned as part of an overall site upgrade.

Finish the Home Page Last

Many business Web site projects start with the layout, design and content of the home page — and, all too often, end there. Finish the home page last! It's the trickiest page to design and to do graphics for. Size up your needs for the home page at the beginning, but complete the inside pages first. Then the home page and navigation will be a snap.

Create a Simple, Attractive Navigation Bar

Here's where your graphics skills really come in — an attractive, clean, fast-loading navigation bar is what really makes the difference between a good and a bad small business site. Look at existing small business sites and see how they handle navigation. Then create a navigation bar of your own. Use colors that reflect your company logo or other company graphics you have or wish to create. Use simple foreground and background combinations with high contrast so that text is easy to read and loads quickly. You should also have a text-only version of your navigation at the bottom of your page for use by visually impaired users, search engines, and users who find themselves at the bottom of a long page and in need of quick access to navigation.

Create a Simple Design for Content Pages

If you don't use someone else's template, create a blank page design that can be used as a template for most of the pages within your site. Doing this gets your focus away from content and onto look and feel. Remember that content changes, but people will grow accustomed to and comfortable with a good design over the long term. They'll like your Web site from the beginning, through all the updates and additions you make to it over time.

Limit Fonts, Colors, and Design Elements

People commonly include three sites' worth of graphics and layout ideas in each site they create. Limit yourself — using a template for content pages and completing the home page last will help you keep things in control. Create a couple of good design elements and reuse them to create consistency, rather than proliferating cute little icons and graphics throughout your site. And keep font choices very simple — one font for body text, one for headlines, and perhaps one more (used sparingly) for emphasis.

Include Photographs

Photographs are compelling. For a business site, photos can be used to establish credibility and to make products and people real to your site visitors. Definitely include high-quality photos of any products you sell. Consider including photos of the business owner, of the staff, and of the business storefront or offices.

Be Careful with Animation and Multimedia

Animation is almost a no-no in business sites. Clever spinning buttons and animated characters look silly or unprofessional in most business sites. Multimedia can also bog down pages and create problems for users.

Yet motion can be fascinating and attractive. So use it correctly — consider creating a simple animated sequence that shows your product in use, or include a multimedia clip of the head of the company talking about what the company does. These elements can be easily skipped or avoided by those who don't want to use them, but will go far to make the site more interesting for everyone else. Putting an animation up as an introduction that users can't easily skip is a no-no.

Compare Your Site to Existing Sites

As you create a business Web site, constantly compare the look and feel to existing business sites that you like. What is it that you like about the other sites? Have you included those same elements in your own site? Ask yourself these questions as you go along; it helps you focus on making your site simple, attractive, and interesting.

Ask the Tough Questions

Ask friends and colleagues if your site has a professional appearance. People may be reluctant to tell you directly, "Your site is tacky-looking," so make sure that you ask your friendly critics specific questions. Ask them what their favorite small business site is and how yours compares to it. Or ask them to name a few things that they would change about your site if they could. Don't get upset by the feedback and keep making changes until the feedback you get is positive.

Appendix A

About the CD

The CD-ROM that comes with this book contains a wide range of software, both as trial versions and full-use versions. With the programs on the CD, you can do just about anything described in this book and keep going far beyond as well. You can even try a couple of different programs that do some of the same things and decide which one you like better before you buy the full version.

Remember: Trial versions of software will only work for a limited amount of time (usually 30 days). So when you've decided that a given piece of software does meet your needs, you need to buy a copy. Luckily, you'll be making an informed buying decision based on hands-on experience, thereby getting the most for your money. Instructions for upgrading from the trial version to the full version of the software come with each of the tryout packages included on the CD-ROM.

Buy your new software well before the expiration date of your trial software. Nothing is sadder than being in the middle of a project and having your trial software run out of time before your new, full-use software arrives. Believe us — we've been there.

Here are some of the useful things you'll find on the *Creating Web Graphics For Dummies* CD-ROM:

- ✔ A trial version of Adobe Photoshop Elements, one of the major image-editing programs described in this book

- ✔ A trial version of Jasc's Paint Shop Pro, another of the major image-editing programs described in this book

- ✔ Trial versions for the two top illustration programs, Adobe Illustrator 10 and Macromedia FreeHand 10

- ✔ A trial version of Macromedia Dreamweaver MX

- ✔ A full version of Arles Image Web Page Creator shareware from Digital Dutch, a leading tool for creating online image galleries quickly and easily

- ✔ A trial version of HyperSnap-DX screen capture software

System Requirements

Make sure that your computer meets the following system requirements (if your computer doesn't match up to most of these requirements, you may have problems using many of the programs on the CD):

- ✔ Microsoft Windows 95 or later running on a PC with a Pentium 300 or faster processor.

- ✔ A CD-ROM drive and a monitor capable of displaying at least 256 colors at 800 x 600 resolution.

- ✔ At least 64 MB of total RAM installed on your computer. For best performance, we recommend at least 128MB of RAM installed.

- ✔ Enough free hard disk space for each program that you choose to install. Most of the programs require over 100MB, and all of them together require over 1 GB.

If you need more information on the basics, check out *PCs For Dummies*, 8th Edition, by Dan Gookin, or any of the following books on Windows by Andy Rathbone: *Windows 95 For Dummies*, 2nd Edition; *Windows 98 For Dummies*; *Microsoft Windows Me Millennium Edition For Dummies*; *Windows 2000 Professional For Dummies*; or *Windows XP For Dummies* (all published by Wiley Publishing, Inc.).

Using the CD with Microsoft Windows

To install the items from the CD to your hard drive, follow these steps:

1. **Insert the CD into your computer's CD-ROM drive.**

2. **Choose Start⇨Run.**

3. **In the dialog box that appears, type** D:\WILEY.EXE.setup.exe.

   Replace D with the proper drive letter if your CD-ROM drive uses a different letter. (If you don't know the letter, see how your CD-ROM drive is listed under My Computer.)

4. **Click OK.**

   A license agreement window appears.

5. **Read through the license agreement, nod your head, and then click the Accept button if you want to use the CD. After you click Accept, you'll never be bothered by the License Agreement window again.**

The CD interface Welcome screen appears. The interface is a little program that shows you what's on the CD and coordinates installing the programs and running the demos. The interface basically enables you to click a button or two to make things happen.

6. **Click anywhere on the Welcome screen to enter the interface.**

   Now you're getting to the action. This next screen lists categories for the software on the CD.

7. **To view the items within a category, just click the category's name.**

   A list of programs in the category appears.

8. **For more information about a program, click the program's name.**

   Be sure to read the information that appears. Sometimes a program has its own system requirements or requires you to do a few tricks on your computer before you can install or run the program. This screen tells you what you might need to do, if necessary.

9. **If you don't want to install the program, click the Back button to return to the previous screen.**

   You can always return to the previous screen by clicking the Back button. This feature allows you to browse the different categories and products and decide what you want to install.

10. **To install a program, click the appropriate Install button.**

    The CD interface drops to the background while the CD installs the program you chose.

11. **To install other items, repeat Steps 7 through 10.**

12. **When you've finished installing programs, click the Quit button to close the interface.**

    You can eject the CD now. Carefully place it back in the plastic jacket of the book for safekeeping.

Using the CD with Mac OS

To install items from the CD to your hard drive, follow these steps:

1. **Insert the CD into your computer's CD-ROM drive.**

   In a moment, an icon representing the CD you just inserted appears on your Mac desktop. Chances are, the icon looks like a CD-ROM.

2. **Double-click the CD icon to show the CD's contents.**

3. **Double-click Start.htm to open your browser and display the license agreement.**

   If your browser doesn't open automatically, open it as you normally would by choosing File⇨Open File (in Internet Explorer) or File⇨Open⇨Location in Netscape (in Netscape Navigator) and select *Start.htm* The license agreement appears.

4. **Read through the license agreement, nod your head, and click the Accept button if you want to use the CD.**

   After you click Accept, you're taken to the Main menu. This is where you can browse through the contents of the CD.

5. **To navigate within the interface, click any topic of interest and you're taken you to an explanation of the files on the CD and how to use or install them.**

6. **To install software from the CD, simply click the software name.**

What You'll Find

This book's CD-ROM contains a variety of Windows and Mac programs and demos that you will find useful while creating Web graphics and designing Web pages. The programs on the CD are either free, try before you buy, or shareware versions.

While all the programs on the CD-ROM are free in their current form, some require you to pay a fee to get a fully functional version by registering the program. Other programs are functional and ready to go as is, with no payment required.

Shareware programs are fully-functional, free trial versions of copyrighted programs. If you like particular programs, register with their authors for a nominal fee and receive licenses, enhanced versions, and technical support.

Trial programs are time-limited versions of major software packages that are available in their fully released version only for a price, often hundreds of dollars. With a trial version, you can use the software free for the period of time specified by the software maker. At the end of the trial period, you can upgrade to the full version of the software for a price, or simply stop using the trial program.

Software developers assume a certain amount of trust in making shareware or trial versions of their programs available. With shareware, the developers assume that most people who use the program regularly will register the software and pay for it, thus supporting continued development of the software. With trial versions of programs, the developers assume that you'll upgrade and pay for the software if you like it. The developers also assume that you won't resort to tricks or cheats to try to get the trial version to run forever.

We, the authors, request that you honor these reasonable expectations.

The following sections give a summary of the software on this CD arranged by category. The CD interface helps you install software easily. (If you have no idea what we're talking about when we say "CD interface," flip back a page or two to find the section, "Using the CD with Microsoft Windows.")

Web graphics software

Adobe Photoshop Elements, trial version from Adobe Systems, Inc.

Adobe Photoshop Elements is amazing, award-winning software — an easier-to-use, lower-priced version of the industry-standard Adobe Photoshop graphics editing program. It might be described as following the 80/20 rule — roughly 80 percent of the features of Photoshop for roughly 20 percent of the price. Like full Photoshop, Adobe Photoshop Elements includes ImageReady, a built-in set of powerful and easy-to-use tools for creating Web versions of graphics files. Adobe Photoshop Elements is described in detail in examples throughout this book.

Paint Shop Pro, trial version from Jasc Software, Inc. (PC Only)

Paint Shop Pro is a powerful and easy-to-use image viewing, editing, and conversion program, which also happens to include many sophisticated drawing and painting tools. The evaluation version will give you an idea of its power. Paint Shop Pro contains features normally found in much more expensive programs — it's a great value for your money. The Paint Shop Pro Web site can be found at `www.jasc.com/psp.html`.

Illustration programs

Adobe Illustrator 10, trial version from Adobe Systems, Inc.
Macromedia FreeHand 10, trial version from Macromedia, Inc.

While Web graphics tools are good for making a Web-ready graphic, how do you let your mind roam free so you can create great graphics in the first place? For millions of pros and amateurs alike, the answer is by using on of these two industry-leading illustration programs, Adobe Illustrator 10 and Macromedia FreeHand 10. The programs are full-featured, yet each is distinctive in its approach to helping you do the job. That being so, the best way to choose between them is to try them both before deciding which one you want to buy. Luckily, with these trial versions, you can do just that.

Web page design programs

Macromedia Dreamweaver MX, trial version from Macromedia, Inc.

Web page design is a tricky business — it gives your imagination room to soar, yet you can find yourself constrained by the limitations of HTML and the wide range of computer setups your page needs to work on. It takes a truly top-notch Web page design tool to help you do your best work. Dreamweaver is one of the best tools out there. With the trial version on the CD, you can try it and see if you like it before buying.

Arles Image Web Page Creator, trial version from Digital Dutch, Inc.

Arles Image Web Page Creator is not for general-purpose Web page authoring. Instead, it's a special-purpose tool for creating image galleries. With Arles, you can easily create high-quality thumbnail versions of graphics files and build Web pages with image galleries. Dozens of options are available. You have to try Arles to believe it, and with the trial version on the CD you can easily do so.

Web graphics utilities

Hypersnap-DX, trial version, from Hyperionics Technology, LLC (PC Only)

Microsoft Windows has screen-capture capabilities built into it — just press the PrtScrn (Print Screen) key, and the current screen image is copied to the clipboard. Why bother with a utility to do the same thing? Well, when that utility captures full Web pages and program windows (beyond the boundaries of your screen), grabs hard-to-capture graphics images and animations, and more, it might be worth a try. Use the trial version to give Hypersnap a shot.

If You've Got Problems (Of the CD Kind)

We tried our best to compile programs that work on most Windows computers with the minimum system requirements. Alas, your computer may differ, and some programs may not work properly for some reason.

The two likeliest problems are that you don't have enough memory (RAM) for the programs you want to use, or you have other programs running that are affecting installation or running of a program. If you get error messages like `Not enough memory` or `Setup cannot continue`, try one or more of these methods and then try using the software again:

- ✔ **Turn off any antivirus software that you have on your computer.** Installers sometimes mimic virus activity and may make your computer incorrectly believe that it is being infected by a virus.

- ✔ **Close all running programs.** The more programs you're running, the less memory is available to other programs. Installers also typically update files and programs; if you keep other programs running, installation may not work properly.

- ✔ **In Windows, close the CD interface and run demos or installations directly from Windows Explorer.** The interface itself can tie up system memory, or even conflict with certain kinds of interactive demos. Use Windows Explorer to browse the files on the CD and launch installers or demos.

- ✔ **Have your local computer store add more RAM to your computer.** This is, admittedly, a drastic and somewhat expensive step. However, if you have a Windows 95/98/ME/NT/2000/XP PC, adding more memory can really help the speed of your computer and enable more programs to run at the same time.

If you still have trouble installing the items from the CD, please call the Wiley Publishing Customer Care phone number: 800-762-2974 (outside the U.S.: 317-572-3994).

Appendix B

Glossary

● ●

*T*his glossary defines important terms used in this book. If you can use these terms effectively, you will be able to have a useful conversation about Web graphics with just about anyone involved in the area. To find specific page numbers where these terms are used in the book, check the Index.

56 Kbps (Kilobits per second) modem: (Also commonly called a 56K modem.) The name of a faster standard transfer rate for Internet access that is now used by most new dial-up modems. 56 Kbps is nearly twice as fast as the previous standards, 28.8 Kbps and 33.6 Kbps. However, online access speeds are actually limited by U.S. government regulation to a top speed of about 53 Kbps, and your 56 Kbps modem may not even achieve that speed reliably, depending on the quality of the connection you get when you dial in.

Adobe Photoshop, Adobe Photoshop Elements: Adobe Photoshop is a computer program that's considered the standard tool for image manipulation on computers and for Web pages. Photoshop is available for PCs running Windows, Macintosh computers, and a wide variety of other computers. Photoshop Elements is a less expensive and less fully-featured version of Photoshop. Both products are available for PCs running Windows and Macintosh computers.

`ALT` **text:** Text that's displayed as an alternative to graphics for users who's browsers aren't set to display graphics. You assign `ALT` text to an image by using the `ALT` attribute within the `<IMG>` HTML tag.

animated GIF: A GIF graphic that includes several slightly different images in sequence. Browsers that support animated GIFs display the graphics one at a time to create an animation within a Web page.

animation: Displaying a series of still images, each of which varies slightly from one to another, in rapid succession so as to create the illusion of motion.

attribute: In HTML, an attribute is a set of characters after the first set within an HTML tag. The attribute modifies the tag's purpose or allows values to be set for the tag. For example, in the tag `<IMG SRC="budpic.jpg">`, the attribute is `SRC`, short for *source*. ***See also*** tag.

background image: An image that's displayed in the background of a Web page. Optionally, the image may be tiled, or repeated, to fill the entire background area.

backlighting: The display of an image by transmitting light through the image to the viewer, as occurs on computer monitors and TV screens.

bitmap: A graphic made up of a series of colored dots corresponding to pixels on the screen.

broadband: A newly popular term for any kind of fast Internet access, whether by cable modem, DSL, or other connection significantly faster than standard dial-up modem speeds.

browser: A program used to look at World Wide Web documents. Mosaic was the first popular browser, and Netscape Navigator and Microsoft Internet Explorer are the current market leaders.

caching: The sound a cash register makes when it rings up a purchase — whoops, sorry, that's "ka-*ching*"! Caching (pronounced the same as the word *cashing*) is the practice of storing a copy of a file so it can be available for rapid display without the need to obtain it from its original source again.

Cascading Style Sheets (CSS): A standard within HTML that allows Web designers to control the layout and formatting of a Web page in detail. Unfortunately, CSS is not yet fully standardized among the commonly used versions of Web browsers.

clickable image map: A graphic that includes areas called *hot spots,* which are hyperlinks that when clicked, take you to different Web pages or locations within a Web page. Many large Web sites use clickable image maps on their home pages to entice the user to move farther into the site.

color depth: The range of colors that a device is capable of displaying. Color depth may be expressed as a number of colors or as the number of bits of information used to store the colors — an 8-bit color depth, for instance, is equivalent to a color depth of 256 colors. A 16-bit color depth is equivalent to over 65,000 colors, and a 24-bit or 32-bit color depth is equivalent to millions of colors.

compression: The process of applying a set of rules to data so that it can be stored in less space than had previously been required.

decompression: The process of applying a set of rules to data so it can be converted from its compressed format back into its original form or into a representation similar to its original form.

dithering: Being indecisive — oops, that's a different definition for the same word. In computer graphics, dithering is simulating a color that's not available by displaying a pattern of two different colors that, when viewed together, simulate the missing color. Dithering is used when a monitor with low color depth is used to display an image with higher color depth.

dots per inch (dpi): A measurement of resolution.

download: To download something is to transfer it from another computer to your own, usually over the Internet. The term download is also used to describe a file that has been downloaded.

downsizing: Reducing the size of a photograph or other image, usually by removing data from the image such that only the data needed to display the image at the new size remains.

element: In HTML, an element is the first character or set of characters within a tag that specifies the tag's purpose. For example. in the tag `<IMG SRC="budpic.jpg">`, the element is `IMG`, short for *image*.

font: A font is a set of designs for the letters of the alphabet and, optionally, punctuation elements, that conveys a unified look for the entire set.

frames: Frames are a kind of Web page element supported by several HTML tags that allow a single Web page to contain data from multiple HTML documents. Optionally, users can resize frames and scroll frames independently within the browser window.

freeware: Software that can be used for free, without payment, though often with a license that contains some restrictions on its use. *See* shareware.

GIF (Graphic Interchange Format): Can be pronounced *jiff* or (our preference) *giff*. A format for encoding images, including computer-generated art and photographs, for transfer among machines. GIF format is the most popular means for storing images for transfer over the Internet and is supported by all graphical Web browsers. An image stored in GIF format is often referred to as "a GIF." *See* transparent GIF.

GIF animation: Taking advantage of a feature in the GIF specification that allows for simple storage and display of images in sequence in order to create an animation. *See* animated GIF.

graphics: A representation of an object on a two-dimensional surface, such as a computer screen.

hexadecimal: What the witch did to her accountant so that her tax bill would be more favorable. More commonly, a way of counting that uses 16 digits, 0–9 plus A–F, instead of the 10 digits that common decimal numbering uses. Hexadecimal numbers are often used to describe values stored inside a computer.

In hexadecimal numbering, 0–9 have their normal values, but A represents 10, B represents 11, and so on through F, which represents 15. Place values are also different; each successive place represents the next greater power of 16. For example, 2F in hexadecimal translates to 47 in decimal; the 2 represents two 16s, and the F represents fifteen 1s.

hot spots: *See* clickable image map.

hyperlink: A connection between two documents on the Web, usually specified by an anchor in an HTML document. The term *hyperlink* is commonly shortened to *link*.

HyperText Markup Language (HTML): The language used to annotate or mark up text documents so that they can be formatted appropriately and linked to other documents for use on the World Wide Web. HTML 4.0 is the most widely accepted version of the standard. HTML 4.0 is supported by all currently available Web browsers.

image map: *See* clickable image map.

interlacing (also referred to as interleaving): Interlacing is the separation of an image file into alternating bands of data so that a partially complete version of the image can be displayed quickly, followed by a more and more complete version until all the data for the image is downloaded.

Internet: The hardware and software that together support the interconnection of most existing computer networks, allowing a computer anywhere in the world to communicate with any other computer that's also connected to the Internet. The Internet supports a variety of services, including the World Wide Web.

Internet service provider (ISP): An Internet service provider offers connections to the Internet and support for Internet services, such as the World Wide Web.

JPEG (Joint Photographic Experts Group): A format for storing highly compressed images. JPEG images are directly supported by all widely available browsers. JPEG is the best format for most photographs when used on the Web.

link: *See* hyperlink.

lossless compression: Data compression in which no data is lost. Compressing data for storage in GIF format is an example of lossless compression.

lossy compression: Data compression in which some data is lost. Compressing data for storage in JPEG format is an example of lossy compression.

Microsoft Paint: A simple graphics program that is included with all versions of Microsoft Windows beginning with Windows 95. Paint sometimes includes the ability to open and save GIF and JPEG files.

modem: Modem is short for *mo*dulator/*dem*odulator and is a device for transmitting data over phone lines. The modem converts digital information into waveforms for transmission over the phone line (modulating the data), and receives waveforms from a phone line and converts them into digital information (demodulating the data).

multimedia: Literally means *many media,* and in this sense, a Web page with graphics is multimedia. However, multimedia is usually understood to mean either more than two types of media or, alternatively, time-based media such as animation, sound, or video, and space-based media such as 3-D and virtual reality. On the Web, multimedia is also used to mean any extension of the Web beyond the basics of text, hyperlinks, GIF graphics, and JPEG graphics.

multi-synch monitor: A computer monitor that can synchronize with data being transmitted at two or more different speeds to display data in the resolution corresponding to that transmission speed.

navigation: A consistently presented set of hypertext links that allows users to easily move from one part of a Web site to another.

Paint Shop Pro: Paint Shop Pro is a computer program from Jasc Software that's very popular for image manipulation on computers and for Web pages. Paint Shop Pro is only available for PCs running Windows.

Photoshop: *See* Adobe Photoshop.

pixelation: The introduction into an image of jagged or crooked elements in place of straight lines and smooth curves that frequently occurs when an image is displayed on a low-resolution device or when it loses data after being compressed and decompressed through a lossy compression process.

QuickTime: A multiplatform standard from Apple Computer, Inc. for multimedia. *See also* multimedia.

resolution: The title of a famous Beatles song that began, "You say you want a resolution . . ." — oops, that was revolution. Resolution is a measurement of the ability of a display medium to convey detail. Resolution is usually measured in dots per inch, or dpi. It can also be expressed as pixels per inch, or as overall resolution of a screen, with the width given first — 800 x 600 and 1024 x 768 are common screen resolutions.

response time: The amount of time it takes for a system to respond to a request, or for a person to react to a stimulus.

scanner, scanning: Scanning is applying a bright light to an object one line of pixels at a time and storing the reflected light from each line of pixels to create an image. A scanner is a device that scans objects.

screen resolution: A measurement of the ability of a computer monitor, or screen, to convey detail. *See* resolution.

shareware: Software that can be used for free for a limited period of time, after which the user is requested (though usually not forced) to pay a fee for continued use. *See* freeware.

sharpening: Applying a computer algorithm to an image that enhances the differences between some adjacent pixels in order to increase the contrast between various objects and background areas in the image.

shrink-wrapped software: No, this is not software developed and packaged by psychiatrists. Actually, shrink-wrapped software is just software that is sold as a product and packaged in a box, with the user paying up-front before taking possession of the software. *See also* freeware; shareware.

standard: An agreed-upon way to do something, such as building a computer system (for example, the IBM-compatible standard) or exchanging data (for example, the ASCII standard). Many different standards exist, ranging from those created by a single manufacturer for its own purposes (the DOS standard) to those created by internationally recognized standards bodies such as ISO (the International Standards Organization). In other words, in computing, the definition of standard is not very standard.

table: Tables are a part of HTML supported by a group of HTML tags that allow data to be organized into columns and rows. Tables are also used to organize some or all of the elements on a Web page, such as creating columns for text to flow in and specifying areas in which a graphic can be placed relative to a story or a caption.

tag: An HTML element that contains information besides the actual document content, such as formatting information or an anchor. For example, the opening tag <B> applies bold to the characters that follow it, and the closing tag </B> ends bolding. So to make a word or phrase appear in bold, surround it with the <B> and </B> tags.

thumbnail: A small graphical image that serves as a preview of a larger image.

tiled background image: *See* background image.

transparent GIF: A file stored in Graphic Interchange Format and modified so that the area around the objects of interest is assigned the color transparent. This capability makes the rectangular frame around the objects seem to disappear so that the graphic appears to float over the page on which it appears.

Web: *See* World Wide Web.

Web authoring: Creating documents for use on the World Wide Web. Web authoring includes creating text documents with HTML tags, as well as creating or obtaining suitable graphics and, in many cases, multimedia files.

Web browser: *See* browser.

Web client: A computer that connects to the World Wide Web and downloads Web pages and other data from it.

Web page: A text document with HTML tags to specify formatting and links from the document to other documents and to graphics and multimedia files.

Web publishing: The entire process of creating and maintaining a Web site, from creating text documents with HTML tags and creating or obtaining the graphics, to putting the documents on a server, to revising the documents over time.

Web safe color palette: A set of 216 colors that will be displayed the same on any Macintosh or PC computer monitor, even if the monitor can only support a minimum number of colors — 256 colors is the minimum specification for standard Web browsers — or is connected to a display subsystem that can only support a minimum number of colors.

Web server: A computer that connects to the World Wide Web and hosts HTML-tagged text documents, graphics, and multimedia files to be downloaded by Web clients.

Web site: One or more linked Web pages accessed through a home page. The URL of the home page is made available to users on other Web sites, and often through other advertising and marketing means as well.

World Wide Web (also known as the Web): An Internet service that provides files from servers linked by HyperText Transfer Protocol. The Web specification allows formatted text and graphics to be viewed directly by a Web browser and allows other kinds of files to be opened separately by helper applications specified in the Web browser's setup. The Web is the most popular Internet service, partly because it can also be used to access other Internet services, such as newsgroups and FTP.

ZIP disk: A removable storage medium that holds many megabytes of data and that can be read or written to by a ZIP drive. ZIP drives are commonly used by graphics professionals because of their high capacity.

ZIP, ZIP file: ZIP is the most commonly used compression standard for computer files, and a ZIP file is a single file that contains the contents of one or more files in a compressed format.

Index

• *P* •

• U •

Wiley Publishing, Inc.
End-User License Agreement

READ THIS. You should carefully read these terms and conditions before opening the software packet(s) included with this book "Book". This is a license agreement "Agreement" between you and Wiley Publishing, Inc. "WPI". By opening the accompanying software packet(s), you acknowledge that you have read and accept the following terms and conditions. If you do not agree and do not want to be bound by such terms and conditions, promptly return the Book and the unopened software packet(s) to the place you obtained them for a full refund.

1. **License Grant.** WPI grants to you (either an individual or entity) a nonexclusive license to use one copy of the enclosed software program(s) (collectively, the "Software," solely for your own personal or business purposes on a single computer (whether a standard computer or a workstation component of a multi-user network). The Software is in use on a computer when it is loaded into temporary memory (RAM) or installed into permanent memory (hard disk, CD-ROM, or other storage device). WPI reserves all rights not expressly granted herein.

2. **Ownership.** WPI is the owner of all right, title, and interest, including copyright, in and to the compilation of the Software recorded on the disk(s) or CD-ROM "Software Media". Copyright to the individual programs recorded on the Software Media is owned by the author or other authorized copyright owner of each program. Ownership of the Software and all proprietary rights relating thereto remain with WPI and its licensers.

3. **Restrictions on Use and Transfer.**

(a) You may only (i) make one copy of the Software for backup or archival purposes, or (ii) transfer the Software to a single hard disk, provided that you keep the original for backup or archival purposes. You may not (i) rent or lease the Software, (ii) copy or reproduce the Software through a LAN or other network system or through any computer subscriber system or bulletin-board system, or (iii) modify, adapt, or create derivative works based on the Software.

(b) You may not reverse engineer, decompile, or disassemble the Software. You may transfer the Software and user documentation on a permanent basis, provided that the transferee agrees to accept the terms and conditions of this Agreement and you retain no copies. If the Software is an update or has been updated, any transfer must include the most recent update and all prior versions.

4. **Restrictions on Use of Individual Programs.** You must follow the individual requirements and restrictions detailed for each individual program in the About the CD-ROM appendix of this Book. These limitations are also contained in the individual license agreements recorded on the Software Media. These limitations may include a requirement that after using the program for a specified period of time, the user must pay a registration fee or discontinue use. By opening the Software packet(s), you will be agreeing to abide by the licenses and restrictions for these individual programs that are detailed in the About the CD-ROM appendix and on the Software Media. None of the material on this Software Media or listed in this Book may ever be redistributed, in original or modified form, for commercial purposes.

5. **Limited Warranty.**

(a) WPI warrants that the Software and Software Media are free from defects in materials and workmanship under normal use for a period of sixty (60) days from the date of purchase of this Book. If WPI receives notification within the warranty period of defects in materials or workmanship, WPI will replace the defective Software Media.

(b) WPI AND THE AUTHOR OF THE BOOK DISCLAIM ALL OTHER WARRANTIES, EXPRESS OR IMPLIED, INCLUDING WITHOUT LIMITATION IMPLIED WARRANTIES OF MERCHANTABILITY AND FITNESS FOR A PARTICULAR PURPOSE, WITH RESPECT TO THE SOFTWARE, THE PROGRAMS, THE SOURCE CODE CONTAINED THEREIN, AND/OR THE TECHNIQUES DESCRIBED IN THIS BOOK. WPI DOES NOT WARRANT THAT THE FUNCTIONS CONTAINED IN THE SOFTWARE WILL MEET YOUR REQUIREMENTS OR THAT THE OPERATION OF THE SOFTWARE WILL BE ERROR FREE.

(c) This limited warranty gives you specific legal rights, and you may have other rights that vary from jurisdiction to jurisdiction.

6. **Remedies.**

(a) WPI's entire liability and your exclusive remedy for defects in materials and workmanship shall be limited to replacement of the Software Media, which may be returned to WPI with a copy of your receipt at the following address: Software Media Fulfillment Department, Attn.: Creating Web Graphics For Dummies, Wiley Publishing, Inc., 10475 Crosspoint Blvd., Indianapolis, IN 46256, or call 1-800-762-2974. Please allow four to six weeks for delivery. This Limited Warranty is void if failure of the Software Media has resulted from accident, abuse, or misapplication. Any replacement Software Media will be warranted for the remainder of the original warranty period or thirty (30) days, whichever is longer.

(b) In no event shall WPI or the author be liable for any damages whatsoever (including without limitation damages for loss of business profits, business interruption, loss of business information, or any other pecuniary loss) arising from the use of or inability to use the Book or the Software, even if WPI has been advised of the possibility of such damages.

(c) Because some jurisdictions do not allow the exclusion or limitation of liability for consequential or incidental damages, the above limitation or exclusion may not apply to you.

7. **U.S. Government Restricted Rights.** Use, duplication, or disclosure of the Software for or on behalf of the United States of America, its agencies and/or instrumentalities "U.S. Government" is subject to restrictions as stated in paragraph (c)(1)(ii) of the Rights in Technical Data and Computer Software clause of DFARS 252.227-7013, or subparagraphs (c)(1) and (2) of the Commercial Computer Software - Restricted Rights clause at FAR 52.227-19, and in similar clauses in the NASA FAR supplement, as applicable.

8. **General.** This Agreement constitutes the entire understanding of the parties and revokes and supersedes all prior agreements, oral or written, between them and may not be modified or amended except in a writing signed by both parties hereto that specifically refers to this Agreement. This Agreement shall take precedence over any other documents that may be in conflict herewith. If any one or more provisions contained in this Agreement are held by any court or tribunal to be invalid, illegal, or otherwise unenforceable, each and every other provision shall remain in full force and effect.

FOR DUMMIES®

The easy way to get more done and have more fun

PERSONAL FINANCE

Personal Finance For Dummies
0-7645-5231-7

Investing For Dummies
0-7645-2431-3

Home Buying For Dummies
0-7645-5331-3

Also available:

Estate Planning For Dummies (0-7645-5501-4)

401(k)s For Dummies (0-7645-5468-9)

Frugal Living For Dummies (0-7645-5403-4)

Microsoft Money "X" For Dummies (0-7645-1689-2)

Mutual Funds For Dummies (0-7645-5329-1)

Personal Bankruptcy For Dummies (0-7645-5498-0)

Quicken "X" For Dummies (0-7645-1666-3)

Stock Investing For Dummies (0-7645-5411-5)

Taxes For Dummies 2003 (0-7645-5475-1)

BUSINESS & CAREERS

Accounting For Dummies
0-7645-5314-3

Grant Writing For Dummies
0-7645-5307-0

Resumes For Dummies
0-7645-5471-9

Also available:

Business Plans Kit For Dummies (0-7645-5365-8)

Consulting For Dummies (0-7645-5034-9)

Cool Careers For Dummies (0-7645-5345-3)

Human Resources Kit For Dummies (0-7645-5131-0)

Managing For Dummies (1-5688-4858-7)

QuickBooks All-in-One Desk Reference For Dummies (0-7645-1963-8)

Selling For Dummies (0-7645-5363-1)

Small Business Kit For Dummies (0-7645-5093-4)

Starting an eBay Business For Dummies (0-7645-1547-0)

HEALTH, SPORTS & FITNESS

Fitness For Dummies
0-7645-5167-1

Golf For Dummies
0-7645-5146-9

Diabetes For Dummies
0-7645-5154-X

Also available:

Controlling Cholesterol For Dummies (0-7645-5440-9)

Dieting For Dummies (0-7645-5126-4)

High Blood Pressure For Dummies (0-7645-5424-7)

Martial Arts For Dummies (0-7645-5358-5)

Menopause For Dummies (0-7645-5458-1)

Nutrition For Dummies (0-7645-5180-9)

Power Yoga For Dummies (0-7645-5342-9)

Thyroid For Dummies (0-7645-5385-2)

Weight Training For Dummies (0-7645-5168-X)

Yoga For Dummies (0-7645-5117-5)

Available wherever books are sold.
Go to www.dummies.com or call 1-877-762-2974 to order direct.

FOR DUMMIES®

A world of resources to help you grow

HOME, GARDEN & HOBBIES

0-7645-5295-3   **0-7645-5130-2**   **0-7645-5106-X**

Also available:

Auto Repair For Dummies
(0-7645-5089-6)

Chess For Dummies
(0-7645-5003-9)

Home Maintenance For Dummies
(0-7645-5215-5)

Organizing For Dummies
(0-7645-5300-3)

Piano For Dummies
(0-7645-5105-1)

Poker For Dummies
(0-7645-5232-5)

Quilting For Dummies
(0-7645-5118-3)

Rock Guitar For Dummies
(0-7645-5356-9)

Roses For Dummies
(0-7645-5202-3)

Sewing For Dummies
(0-7645-5137-X)

FOOD & WINE

0-7645-5250-3   **0-7645-5390-9**   **0-7645-5114-0**

Also available:

Bartending For Dummies
(0-7645-5051-9)

Chinese Cooking For Dummies
(0-7645-5247-3)

Christmas Cooking For Dummies
(0-7645-5407-7)

Diabetes Cookbook For Dummies
(0-7645-5230-9)

Grilling For Dummies
(0-7645-5076-4)

Low-Fat Cooking For Dummies
(0-7645-5035-7)

Slow Cookers For Dummies
(0-7645-5240-6)

TRAVEL

0-7645-5453-0   **0-7645-5438-7**   **0-7645-5448-4**

Also available:

America's National Parks For Dummies
(0-7645-6204-5)

Caribbean For Dummies
(0-7645-5445-X)

Cruise Vacations For Dummies 2003
(0-7645-5459-X)

Europe For Dummies
(0-7645-5456-5)

Ireland For Dummies
(0-7645-6199-5)

France For Dummies
(0-7645-6292-4)

London For Dummies
(0-7645-5416-6)

Mexico's Beach Resorts For Dummies
(0-7645-6262-2)

Paris For Dummies
(0-7645-5494-8)

RV Vacations For Dummies
(0-7645-5443-3)

Walt Disney World & Orlando For Dummies
(0-7645-5444-1)

Available wherever books are sold. Go to www.dummies.com or call 1-877-762-2974 to order direct.

FOR DUMMIES®

Plain-English solutions for everyday challenges

COMPUTER BASICS

0-7645-0838-5

0-7645-1663-9

0-7645-1548-9

Also available:

PCs All-in-One Desk Reference For Dummies (0-7645-0791-5)

Pocket PC For Dummies (0-7645-1640-X)

Treo and Visor For Dummies (0-7645-1673-6)

Troubleshooting Your PC For Dummies (0-7645-1669-8)

Upgrading & Fixing PCs For Dummies (0-7645-1665-5)

Windows XP For Dummies (0-7645-0893-8)

Windows XP For Dummies Quick Reference (0-7645-0897-0)

BUSINESS SOFTWARE

0-7645-0822-9

0-7645-0839-3

0-7645-0819-9

Also available:

Excel Data Analysis For Dummies (0-7645-1661-2)

Excel 2002 All-in-One Desk Reference For Dummies (0-7645-1794-5)

Excel 2002 For Dummies Quick Reference (0-7645-0829-6)

GoldMine "X" For Dummies (0-7645-0845-8)

Microsoft CRM For Dummies (0-7645-1698-1)

Microsoft Project 2002 For Dummies (0-7645-1628-0)

Office XP For Dummies (0-7645-0830-X)

Outlook 2002 For Dummies (0-7645-0828-8)

Get smart! Visit www.dummies.com

- **Find listings of even more *For Dummies* titles**
- **Browse online articles**
- **Sign up for Dummies eTips™**
- **Check out *For Dummies* fitness videos and other products**
- **Order from our online bookstore**

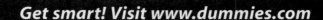
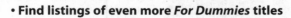

Available wherever books are sold. Go to www.dummies.com or call 1-877-762-2974 to order direct.

FOR DUMMIES

Helping you expand your horizons and realize your potential

INTERNET

0-7645-0894-6

0-7645-1659-0

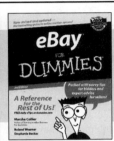

0-7645-1642-6

Also available:

America Online 7.0 For Dummies
(0-7645-1624-8)

Genealogy Online For Dummies
(0-7645-0807-5)

The Internet All-in-One Desk Reference For Dummies
(0-7645-1659-0)

Internet Explorer 6 For Dummies
(0-7645-1344-3)

The Internet For Dummies Quick Reference
(0-7645-1645-0)

Internet Privacy For Dummies
(0-7645-0846-6)

Researching Online For Dummies
(0-7645-0546-7)

Starting an Online Business For Dummies
(0-7645-1655-8)

DIGITAL MEDIA

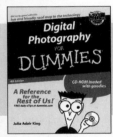

0-7645-1664-7

0-7645-1675-2

0-7645-0806-7

Also available:

CD and DVD Recording For Dummies
(0-7645-1627-2)

Digital Photography All-in-One Desk Reference For Dummies
(0-7645-1800-3)

Digital Photography For Dummies Quick Reference
(0-7645-0750-8)

Home Recording for Musicians For Dummies
(0-7645-1634-5)

MP3 For Dummies
(0-7645-0858-X)

Paint Shop Pro "X" For Dummies
(0-7645-2440-2)

Photo Retouching & Restoration For Dummies
(0-7645-1662-0)

Scanners For Dummies
(0-7645-0783-4)

GRAPHICS

0-7645-0817-2

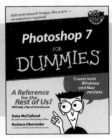

0-7645-1651-5

0-7645-0895-4

Also available:

Adobe Acrobat 5 PDF For Dummies
(0-7645-1652-3)

Fireworks 4 For Dummies
(0-7645-0804-0)

Illustrator 10 For Dummies
(0-7645-3636-2)

QuarkXPress 5 For Dummies
(0-7645-0643-9)

Visio 2000 For Dummies
(0-7645-0635-8)

Available wherever books are sold. Go to www.dummies.com or call 1-877-762-2974 to order direct.

FOR DUMMIES®

The advice and explanations you need to succeed

SELF-HELP, SPIRITUALITY & RELIGION

0-7645-5302-X

0-7645-5418-2

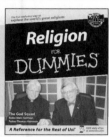
0-7645-5264-3

Also available:

The Bible For Dummies
(0-7645-5296-1)

Buddhism For Dummies
(0-7645-5359-3)

Christian Prayer For Dummies
(0-7645-5500-6)

Dating For Dummies
(0-7645-5072-1)

Judaism For Dummies
(0-7645-5299-6)

Potty Training For Dummies
(0-7645-5417-4)

Pregnancy For Dummies
(0-7645-5074-8)

Rekindling Romance For Dummies
(0-7645-5303-8)

Spirituality For Dummies
(0-7645-5298-8)

Weddings For Dummies
(0-7645-5055-1)

PETS

0-7645-5255-4

0-7645-5286-4

0-7645-5275-9

Also available:

Labrador Retrievers For Dummies
(0-7645-5281-3)

Aquariums For Dummies
(0-7645-5156-6)

Birds For Dummies
(0-7645-5139-6)

Dogs For Dummies
(0-7645-5274-0)

Ferrets For Dummies
(0-7645-5259-7)

German Shepherds For Dummies
(0-7645-5280-5)

Golden Retrievers For Dummies
(0-7645-5267-8)

Horses For Dummies
(0-7645-5138-8)

Jack Russell Terriers For Dummies
(0-7645-5268-6)

Puppies Raising & Training Diary For Dummies
(0-7645-0876-8)

EDUCATION & TEST PREPARATION

0-7645-5194-9

0-7645-5325-9

0-7645-5210-4

Also available:

Chemistry For Dummies
(0-7645-5430-1)

English Grammar For Dummies
(0-7645-5322-4)

French For Dummies
(0-7645-5193-0)

The GMAT For Dummies
(0-7645-5251-1)

Inglés Para Dummies
(0-7645-5427-1)

Italian For Dummies
(0-7645-5196-5)

Research Papers For Dummies
(0-7645-5426-3)

The SAT I For Dummies
(0-7645-5472-7)

U.S. History For Dummies
(0-7645-5249-X)

World History For Dummies
(0-7645-5242-2)

Available wherever books are sold. Go to www.dummies.com or call 1-877-762-2974 to order direct.

FOR DUMMIES®

We take the mystery out of complicated subjects

WEB DEVELOPMENT

Creating Web Pages FOR DUMMIES

0-7645-1643-4

HTML 4 FOR DUMMIES

0-7645-0723-0

Dreamweaver MX FOR DUMMIES

0-7645-1630-2

Also available:

ASP.NET For Dummies
(0-7645-0866-0)
Building a Web Site For
Dummies
(0-7645-0720-6)
ColdFusion "MX" for Dummies
(0-7645-1672-8)
Creating Web Pages
All-in-One Desk Reference
For Dummies
(0-7645-1542-X)

FrontPage 2002 For Dummies
(0-7645-0821-0)
HTML 4 For Dummies Quick
Reference
(0-7645-0721-4)
Macromedia Studio "MX"
All-in-One Desk Reference
For Dummies
(0-7645-1799-6)
Web Design For Dummies
(0-7645-0823-7)

PROGRAMMING & DATABASES

C++ FOR DUMMIES

0-7645-0746-X

XML FOR DUMMIES

0-7645-1657-4

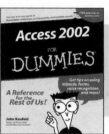

Access 2002 FOR DUMMIES

0-7645-0818-0

Also available:

Beginning Programming For
Dummies
(0-7645-0835-0)
Crystal Reports "X"
For Dummies
(0-7645-1641-8)
Java & XML For Dummies
(0-7645-1658-2)
Java 2 For Dummies
(0-7645-0765-6)
JavaScript For Dummies
(0-7645-0633-1)
Oracle9*i* For Dummies
(0-7645-0880-6)

Perl For Dummies
(0-7645-0776-1)
PHP and MySQL For
Dummies
(0-7645-1650-7)
SQL For Dummies
(0-7645-0737-0)
VisualBasic .NET For
Dummies
(0-7645-0867-9)
Visual Studio .NET All-in-One
Desk Reference For Dummies
(0-7645-1626-4)

LINUX, NETWORKING & CERTIFICATION

Red Hat Linux 7.3 FOR DUMMIES

0-7645-1545-4

Networking FOR DUMMIES

0-7645-0772-9

A+ Certification FOR DUMMIES

0-7645-0812-1

Also available:

CCNP All-in-One Certification
For Dummies
(0-7645-1648-5)
Cisco Networking For
Dummies
(0-7645-1668-X)
CISSP For Dummies
(0-7645-1670-1)
CIW Foundations For
Dummies with CD-ROM
(0-7645-1635-3)

Firewalls For Dummies
(0-7645-0884-9)
Home Networking For
Dummies
(0-7645-0857-1)
Red Hat Linux All-in-One
Desk Reference For Dummies
(0-7645-2442-9)
TCP/IP For Dummies
(0-7645-1760-0)
UNIX For Dummies
(0-7645-0419-3)

Available wherever books are sold.
Go to www.dummies.com or call 1-877-762-2974 to order direct.

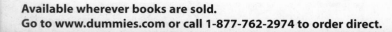

WILEY